The Bank of Virginia: A History

Thomas C. Boushall, founder of The Bank of Virginia

The Bank of Virginia

A History

John H. Wessells, Jr.

Foreword by
Virginius Dabney

The University Press of Virginia
Charlottesville

THE UNIVERSITY PRESS OF VIRGINIA
Copyright © 1973 by the Rector and Visitors
of the University of Virginia

First published 1973

ISBN: 0–8139–0524–9
Library of Congress Catalog Card Number: 73–78208
Printed in the United States of America

Foreword

THE BANK OF VIRGINIA, which recently took the name Bank of Virginia-Central, began operations in Richmond half a century ago on a shoestring of $85,000 available in cash, and it has burgeoned with its branches and affiliates into one of the largest banks in the state, with a record of pioneering in the banking field unequaled by any of its competitors. Today it is the flagship bank of the Bank of Virginia Company, formerly Virginia Commonwealth Bankshares, Inc., which, fifty years after the bank's founding in 1922, has more than a billion dollars in assets.

The Bank of Virginia has a truly impressive list of firsts to its credit, a list difficult to match in the banking field. It has broken new ground in services to the individual and to the general public as well as to the banking world in its effective advocacy of branch banking. Beginning as The Morris Plan Bank of Richmond, a small, so-called remedial loan society as the conventional-minded bankers of the 1920s saw it, this institution made history in various directions by its innovative procedures and practices.

As early as 1923 it began offering credit life insurance on loans —a first for the entire South. Three years later it advertised home improvement loans, thus antedating the Federal Housing Administration Title I home improvement plan of the ensuing decade. It was the first bank in Virginia to render this service. As early as 1928 the bank was the first in Virginia since the Civil War to offer services statewide. By then it had offices in Richmond, Petersburg, Newport News, Roanoke, and Norfolk.

Changing its name to The Morris Plan Bank of Virginia, it opened its new headquarters building at Eighth and Main streets in June 1932 during the depth of the Great Depression, thus moving counter to nearly every other business institution in the United States. At the same time it pioneered by "manufacturing its own weather," i.e., installing air conditioning—the first office building in Virginia to make this breakthrough. The first FHA loan in the state was made in 1934 by The Morris Plan Bank of

Virginia. In 1935 over-the-counter automobile loans were introduced to the area. Under this plan, a new car served as collateral
requiring no endorsement. Popular checking was another innovation at the bank. It was offered there in 1936 for the first time
in the South and permitted the customer to purchase twenty
checks for a dollar.

The Morris Plan Bank was the first bank in this area to offer
group life insurance coverage for the staff. It was likewise the first
bank in Virginia to provide a pension plan for its officers and
employees. Steadily developing benefits for its personnel, the bank
has been among the very first to include group hospitalization,
major medical care, and long-term disability coverage. By 1941
the bank was handling more accounts of all types than any other
bank in the state. The following year it decided to enter the field
of commercial banking on a full-time, full-fledged basis and in
1945 changed its name to The Bank of Virginia.

The bank's rapid expansion and growth gave concern to competitive institutions. The Virginia Bankers Association accordingly obtained an amendment to the banking law by the General
Assembly in 1948, which forbade banks to open additional
branches in cities of fifty thousand and more outside the head
office city. This thwarted certain plans of The Bank of Virginia,
but the law rose later to plague other banks of the Commonwealth.
Yet The Bank of Virginia continued to grow and in 1949 made
its millionth loan. Entry into the credit card field was the bank's
notable advance of 1953. It became one of the very first banks
in the country to offer a charge card service when it launched
Merchants Bank Credit Service in Norfolk. Charge Plan, as it
was later called, continued to flourish and in 1968 converted to
Master Charge, the present widely accepted nationwide all-
purpose card.

In the public mind and in actual fact, the original Bank of
Virginia is the lengthened shadow of one man, Thomas C. Boushall. It was Boushall who built the bank up from almost nothing
and who successfully countered the old-line bankers of his time
with imaginative innovations in consumer banking, branch banking, and other fields. Many of his ideas have been adopted by
those who once opposed them so fervently. It would be a serious
distortion, however, to attribute all the progress of The Bank of
Virginia to Boushall. He would be the first to emphasize this
point. He retired as the bank's president and chief executive

officer in 1959. While remaining chairman of the board, he placed full authority in the hands of Herbert C. Moseley, his successor as president and chief executive officer. Boushall relinquished the board chairmanship in 1966 and became honorary board chairman. The astonishing development of the bank and its branches and affiliates in the past dozen years has taken place under the leadership of Moseley, with the able assistance throughout of Frederick Deane, Jr., and, more recently, of William T. Gordon.

In the early 1920s, when The Bank of Virginia was called The Morris Plan Bank of Richmond, it was a part of the Morris Plan system, originated by Arthur J. Morris. A forward-looking North Carolinian and graduate of the University of Virginia, Morris had gone north, after establishing in Norfolk his concept of making bank credit available to the "little man." At that time, banks throughout the United States were not lending money to persons of modest income.

Arthur Morris had established the Industrial Finance Corporation, successor to the Fidelity Corporation of America, the first bank holding company, which in time had an interest in 110 banks and companies in thirty-seven states. Tom Boushall, the twenty-seven-year-old fledgling banker, also a North Carolinian, was just back from service overseas in Dr. Stuart McGuire's Base Hospital No. 45, and two years in Brussels as submanager of The National City Bank of New York's new branch there. He read that Morris was interested in "banking organized down to the needs of the people" and went to New York to see Morris. Boushall asked Morris to let him open a bank in Richmond that would seek to meet the needs of the average citizen for banking services. He suggested that this new bank, plus two others in Virginia, together with eleven small, separate units already in North Carolina and one each in South Carolina, West Virginia, Maryland, and the District of Columbia, could be the nucleus for a regional banking system. Morris, who was at first skeptical, finally agreed to let Boushall try. Although the regional banking system concept was only partially successful, the Richmond bank prospered and the details of its operation—its ups and downs, the numerous head-on clashes between Boushall and Morris over the years, during which Boushall offered his resignation a dozen times only to have it refused—are recounted in the pages that follow.

Those who are today acquainted with chuckling, jovial Tom

Boushall have difficulty envisioning his bluntly challenging the ideas of his boss, impertinently facing him down, or otherwise demonstrating his own unwillingness to compromise principles that he deemed important. On some of these occasions, Morris was highly indignant, on others he appeared somewhat stunned over the manner in which young Boushall was talking back to him, but he had the good sense to take it in stride. Despite his frequent run-ins with Tom Boushall, the latter retained his respect and admiration. In fact it appears that Boushall's willingness to express his opinions with complete candor and without fear of any possible consequences was a principle reason why Morris valued his advice so highly. Morris has publicly acknowledged his great debt to Boushall on many occasions. Consider his words at the fiftieth anniversary dinner of the Consumer Bankers Association, which took place on October 30, 1970. Morris drew a sharp distinction in his address between his own role in originating certain concepts in consumer banking and that of Boushall in developing and enlarging them. "Had it not been for the authentic development by an experienced student and master of banking, Thomas C. Boushall," Morris declared, "my creation of consumer credit, its national and international importance to the banking fraternity of this great country and elsewhere, would have been impossible and uncreative."

Mr. Boushall's innovations in banking are extraordinary, but hardly more so than the fact that during the years when he managed to put many of them into effect his health was so bad that his life was in jeopardy. Afflicted with tuberculosis, he underwent numerous major operations, some of which were so gruesome that more than one orderly at Walter Reed Hospital in Washington, D.C., fainted while watching the surgeon sawing out the youthful banker's ribs and probing around his heart and lungs. Boushall was told that his chance of recovery from the most serious of these operations was one in twenty. He recovered through sheer determination and fortitude, and it took him about a decade. From 1923 to 1932 he was in and out of bed at irregular intervals. His devoted wife Marie, a former registered nurse, was a great source of strength to him throughout this ordeal. Boushall has only one lung today, and the ribs on his left side are gone. His heart beats under the skin. Although he cannot walk up the hill from his office at Eighth and Main to St. Paul's Episcopal Church—in which he has been a leader for decades—without stopping several times for breath, his health at age seventy-eight is extraordinarily good. His only form of exercise is an occasional swim, but except for a touch of bronchial pneumonia in Florence, Italy, in 1959, he has not been sick in bed for a single day since 1932. His mind, furthermore, is active and clear and as alert as ever to spot new trends in banking, economics, education, or other fields.

Thomas C. Boushall, as we have noted, is a North Carolinian. Legend has it that Tar Heels find considerable opposition in conservative Richmond. They are supposedly received in the former capital of the Confederacy with something less than enthusiasm. The falsity of this notion is shown in Boushall's career. Nobody could have been more cordially welcomed in Richmond, nor could anyone have entered more wholeheartedly into the life of the city and state. Countless awards, citations, and accolades have come to him. They are in recognition of his enormous contributions to community well-being in such fields as health care, social service, race relations, and education. His awards as a banker are comparable in number and importance.

As far back as 1935, Boushall headed a group hospital movement in Richmond that ultimately developed into Blue Cross and Blue Shield. He was chairman in 1939 of the Richmond Committee on Organizing Social Forces and in 1940 was president of the Richmond Community Council. Arthur A. Guild, director of the Richmond Community Fund, termed him "one of the foremost lay leaders in the United States in the field of social planning and organizing, and certainly unsurpassed in this field in the South." To education he has rendered a service national in scope, in addition to his activities on both the City School Board and the State Board of Education and as chairman of the Sweet Briar College board of trustees. His opportunity for national service came with his chairmanship of the Committee on Education of the United States Chamber of Commerce. It was under his inspirational leadership that the chamber arranged for the report "Education—An Investment in People," in which it was demonstrated that there is a direct relationship between the educational level of any community or state and its economic status. Boushall urged the adoption of an employee use tax of from five to fifty dollars on each employee, to be paid by the employer for the benefit of education. He contended that business itself would be a major beneficiary of such a plan. While this specific proposal was not widely followed, the publicizing of the concept that it is in the best interests of business to pay higher taxes for education was of great value. Boushall performed a further signal service to education and other causes in 1966 when he proposed that Virginia abandon its pay-as-you-go policy to permit the issuance of general obligation bonds. This was the beginning of the end for Virginia's stubborn unwillingness to permit the issuance of such bonds and was of vast importance to the progress of the state.

Throughout the entire period from the 1930s to date, Boushall has been almost incredibly active in public service, despite his equally arduous involvement in banking. In 1972 the *Richmond News Leader* termed him "Virginia's preeminent public servant." A civic, cultural, or religious organization that is having difficulty in making ends meet or in achieving its goals in other directons often goes to the ever-willing Tom Boushall for help, and he frequently concludes by agreeing to work temporarily with the agency—a circumstance that has occurred too many times to bear specific recounting here. A man in his position, with his obviously great financial ability, probably could have been a millionaire several times over if he had put his mind to it. He preferred, however, to devote his spare time and surplus energy to building up the community and state in ways that must have given him great inner satisfaction, but which were not at all financially remunerative. Today he is in comfortable circumstances, but is by no means wealthy.

Boushall has generally voted Democratic in state and Republican in national affairs, and he has been consulted frequently by Virginia governors of both parties. His great frankness in discussing public questions with them and their awareness of his complete integrity have caused them to rely on his counsel.

As a banker, Boushall is the exact opposite of the legendary cold-eyed, unapproachable guardian of the moneybags. Indeed most present-day bankers are far from resembling their frosty precursors of an earlier era, but no one is less in that tradition than Tom Boushall. In addition to his approachability, his sense of humor is obvious and contagious, and he is always ready with a good story for every occasion. His photographs fail to do him justice, for they are too stern and lack the twinkle that is so important an element of his personality. The Boushall handwriting is a subject of amused comment around the bank. Those who encounter this almost undecipherable mode of communication for the first time wonder if, by mistake, they have perhaps gotten hold of a scrap of Sanskrit. Tom Boushall's secretaries have to be able to cope with his inscrutable calligraphy, and his frequent handwritten notes to associates in the building are usually transcribed on a typewriter before being transmitted. For many years Boushall has been almost completely bald, a fact about which he is fond of joking. His hair was once red, but over a long period it has been largely nonexistent. When a friend remarked on one occasion to his red-haired daughter, Frances (Mrs. Granville G. Valentine, Jr.), that she had evidently gotten her father's hair, she remarked laughingly, "Somebody certainly got it."

Herbert C. Moseley, who succeeded Thomas C. Boushall as president and chief executive officer of The Bank of Virginia, and who later became chairman of the board and chief executive officer of that institution and of Virginia Commonwealth Bankshares, also has red hair, now graying. Being younger and less inclined to baldness, his hair is considerably more visible than Boushall's, although not as ruddy as it was in earlier days. He was born on a farm in Campbell County, Virginia, into a family prominent before the Civil War, but which, like so many others, was impoverished by that conflict. Moseley's father raised tobacco, and his income was not large, but the farm furnished plenty of food and the family was comfortable. Moseley, Sr., always kept a good riding horse and was an excellent tournament rider. He participated successfully in many of the tournaments of that era. Young Herbert sought to emulate his father as a horseman. He confesses that he was never able to hook one of the small rings in the tournaments, only the large ones.

Herbert attended the public school at the small town of Gladys. While in high school, he had the misfortune of having a horse fall on him while riding. Luckily the youth landed in soft sand between two stumps, but his shoulder was seriously injured. Osteomyelitis developed to an almost fatal extent, and he was completely unconscious for about thirty days. He barely survived, and when well enough, had to have an operation on his shoulder. He did not completely recover for three years. For the first year his arm was supported by a specially designed brace and for two more years was carried in a sling. He missed one entire school session. Today one of his shoulders is slightly lower than the other, but otherwise Herbert Moseley shows no signs of this almost lethal illness from which few recover. The hospitals, doctors, and nurses were so expensive during his convalescence that the money his father had carefully saved to send him to Lynchburg College was exhausted, and Herbert had to forego a college education. But he showed the same application and determination at that stage of his career that he has shown ever since. He worked hard and took advantage of every opportunity for advancement. Today, in his sixties, he rises regularly at 5:30 A.M., is at the bank at 7:00 or 7:30, and puts in as long hours as anybody in the organization.

In 1927 when Herbert Moseley had graduated from Gladys High School and had recovered sufficiently from his illness, he got a job in the Campbell County Bank at Rustburg. After work he traveled to Lynchburg and took evening courses given there by the American Institute of Banking. As the bank's "low man on the totem pole," with the title of assistant cashier (there was only one other man on the staff), Moseley swept the floor, hauled drinking water, dusted the counter, and posted the books. He remained with the bank for seven years. In 1933 almost at the depth of the Depression, and only a few months after President Roosevelt's bank holiday, he married Miss Ellen Thompson of nearby Pittsylvania County. "I wouldn't have the nerve to do that now," he said recently. "Times were certainly tight." Another eventful episode of those years was the bank holdup during which Moseley and his superior were shoved into a vault and the robber made off with eight thousand dollars—every cent of cash the bank possessed.

Moseley left the bank in 1935 to take a position as an assistant examiner with the State Banking Department and kept it for nearly three years. His objective, as he recalls, was to "learn more about banking." At the end of that period, he accepted the managership of the branch that had been established at Brookneal by his former employer, the Campbell County Bank. He remained there for seven years. He was in Richmond one day in September 1944, on business, and a friend suggested that he call on Thomas C. Boushall. "After five minutes, I knew that if he wanted me to work for him, I'd accept," Moseley said later. Boushall offered him the post of assistant vice-president and cashier, and manager of The Bank of Virginia's Petersburg branch. Moseley went to work in Petersburg the following January. He did such a splendid job, according to Boushall, that when a vacancy arose in the managership of the Roanoke branch, he was transferred there. Again, he was exceptionally successful in building a place for the bank in the community, and promoting its prosperity in various ways. And so Herbert Moseley was brought to Richmond in 1953 as vice-president of The Bank of Virginia and coordinator of branches. Six years later, in 1959, he was named president and chief executive officer of the bank as successor to Thomas C. Boushall.

In 1962 Virginia Commonwealth Bankshares was organized under the leadership of Moseley and Deane, and Moseley became its president and chief executive officer January 1, 1963, with Deane as executive vice-president. The character of the leadership furnished by Moseley is seen in the fact that when The Bank of Virginia celebrated its first half century in 1972, the banking complex developed around it had grown into an institution with assets in excess of a billion dollars, ranking fourth among Virginia banking organizations. Affable and approachable, the six-foot two-inch Moseley is impressive in appearance, effective as an executive, and is a man who keeps in touch with every phase of his banking operation. However, he is careful to delegate authority and holds each officer responsible for his particular area of activity. Having grown up in rural Virginia, Moseley has a special rapport with the officers and staff of the smaller branches of the bank, but he is equally at home when calling on the head of the biggest financial institution in New York or Los Angeles. Active in community, business, civic, and religious affairs, he is a leader in numerous areas, and he holds important assignments in the state and national banking community. Having taken the course in advanced management at Harvard in 1953, he is a member of the Harvard Club of Richmond, as well as several other clubs, both business and social.

Moseley's office is on the sixth floor of the imposing new Virginia Commonwealth Bankshares building, while Boushall remains on the second floor of The Bank of Virginia headquarters building, thus emphasizing his separateness from the affairs of the bank as well as from those of Virginia Commonwealth Bankshares, which recently changed its name to Bank of Virginia Company. The executive offices of the latter are all on the sixth floor of the new building. William T. Gordon, chosen president of The Bank of Virginia in 1969 and its president and chief executive officer in 1971, has his office in the bank headquarters building where Herbert Moseley previously presided. Moseley's new quarters are attractively furnished with antiques. Frederick Deane, Jr., the other top executive, occupies an office on the same floor with handsome ultramodern decor.

In contrast to the struggling bank that Tom Boushall launched in 1922, these two men direct an organization with worldwide connections. Deane is frequently in Canada attending to the affairs of the bank's affiliates there. The president and chief executive officer of Bank of Virginia International does business in places as distant as Borneo. The Bank of Nassau, Ltd., in the Bahamas is an affiliate of Bank of Virginia International, as is the Cayman Banking Corp., Ltd., of Grand Cayman, British West Indies, now Bank of Virginia (Grand Cayman), Ltd. Both Moseley and Deane travel thousands of miles annually in Virginia by chauffeur-driven car. This is not only relatively relaxing; it enables them to work on current problems while moving from place to place. They also do a good deal of traveling by plane around the United States and abroad.

Frederick Deane, Jr., is a Mayflower descendant, but this has been no more of a liability to him in Richmond than Tom Boushall's North Carolina background was. On the contrary, he has been most hospitably received in Virginia. By a strange coincidence, both Deane and Boushall married into aristocratic Charleston, South Carolina, families. Mrs. Deane is the former Dorothy Legge, while Mrs. Boushall was Marie Lebby. Handsome, six-foot four-inch Rick Deane, a native of Boston's Back Bay, attended Milton Academy in Massachusetts and then went on to Harvard as a member of an old New England family should. Both in prep school and in college he was an able student, as well as a leader in other respects. At Milton Academy he was valedictorian of his class. At Harvard he belonged to Hasty Pudding and the Delphic Club, irreverently known as "Gas House." He was also a member of the Student Council of the college and was active in other student affairs. But Deane's education was interrupted by service in World War II. He enlisted in the army in 1944 after a summer course at Harvard, following his graduation from Milton Academy, and rose from private to first lieutenant. He returned to Harvard upon his discharge from the army in 1946. Before finishing the undergraduate course, he was allowed to enroll in the Graduate School of Business Administration, and he earned his M.A. without the benefit of a B.A. degree. In the middle of his final examination, he was suddenly notified that he was being called up as a reserve officer in the Korean War. Deane was married at the time and had one child, and this call up was disturbing. Despite his state of mind, he did well enough on the examination to get his master's in business administration "with distinction."

Deane served with the Central Intelligence Agency during the Korean War and rose rapidly, becoming assistant to a deputy director. In that post he was privy to the major decisions made by the CIA during that conflict, including plans for cloak-and-dagger operations. It was, he says, a fascinating assignment—so much so that he was tempted to remain with the agency. The CIA, he feels, performs a highly useful function, but is in the unfortunate position of not being able to defend itself from criticism, owing to the secrecy that must surround it. Deane finally decided to go into business. On a trip to Richmond, he was brought into contact with Thomas C. Boushall. The latter had him in for a talk. That did it. Deane, like Herbert Moseley, knew when he met Tom Boushall that if Boushall made him an offer, he would accept. The offer was soon forthcoming, and he went to work as Boushall's assistant in 1953. In 1965 at thirty-nine, he became president and chief administrative officer of Virginia Commonwealth Bankshares. Two years later he was named president of The Bank of Virginia, and he assumed the title of vice-chairman of the board in 1969.

Like Tom Boushall and Herbert Moseley, Rick Deane had a major illness that threatened to end his career, and like Boushall and Moseley he successfully overcame it, with no serious after-effects. A blood clot, which began in his leg and moved up to his heart, almost proved fatal and necessitated an eight-hour operation in 1965. At one point there was grave doubt whether he would survive, but he did, and he was one of only seven patients in the world who, at that time, had survived that particular operation. Today he is as strong and rugged as ever. Deane is active in civic, cultural, educational, and religious affairs and, like Boushall and Moseley, serves on various important boards. Like them again he is also active in banking circles.

William T. Gordon, who became president and chief executive officer of The Bank of Virginia in 1971, after serving as president and chief administrative officer since 1969, is a native Richmonder. His father was in banking for only a short time, but his brother, Robert L. Gordon, Jr., is chairman of the board and chief executive officer of the First and Merchants National Bank of Richmond. Thus two brothers serve as chief executive officers of large rival banks in the same city, a circumstance believed to be without a parallel in this country. Bill Gordon was a three-letter man at Episcopal High School and captain of the baseball team. He attended the University of Virginia and joined the staff of The Bank of Virginia in 1936 as a bookkeeper. He rose steadily thereafter. He is an active churchman, a former senior warden, past president of the Virginia College Fund, and a leader in Red Cross and other civic activities. Gordon was a naval officer in World War II, and served on the aircraft carrier *Wasp* in some of the most violent actions against the Japanese. The *Wasp* was severely hit off Okinawa at the same time that the *Franklin* was almost sunk, and the *Wasp*'s guns shot down the last Japanese kamikaze of the war.

Under the leadership of Boushall, Moseley, Deane, and Gordon, The Bank of Virginia, founded half a century ago on a shoestring, has burgeoned into the great institution that we have today. Courage, imagination, and the ability to outguess the opposition are the ingredients that have brought about these remarkable results. Thomas C. Boushall, of course, did it all for decades, and won the respect of his rivals, who ended by admitting that he was right in his pioneering. Herbert Moseley, Frederick Deane, and William Gordon have built firmly and imaginatively on the foundations he laid so well.

We have here one of the most exciting stories in the history of American banking. Businessmen are sometimes considered ultra-conservative and incapable of advancing or accepting new ideas. The history of The Bank of Virginia's first fifty years that follows should refute any such notion as far as this particular group of businessmen is concerned. They have repeatedly broken new ground, and their creative concepts have been accepted by their colleagues and the law-making and regulatory bodies of the commonwealth and the nation. The notable results are there for all to see.

VIRGINIUS DABNEY

Contents

The Bank of Virginia: A History

CHAPTER I

In the Beginning

ONE MORNING, just after the turn of the century, a young railroad worker, dressed in his Sunday best, walked hesitantly into the offices of the prosperous downtown law firm of Morris, Garnett, and Cotton in Norfolk, Virginia. To A. J. Morris, the firm's young founder, he told a familiar story. His wife needed an operation. Although he had a steady job, the banks would not lend him the necessary five hundred dollars on terms he could afford.

"Mr. Morris," he said, "I don't want my wife to go to the hospital as a charity case. I don't want to put my family at the mercy of the loan sharks. You are counsel for the Bank of Norfolk. Will you try to get them to give me a loan?"

Impressed with the man's sincerity, Morris promised to see what he could do. At the next bank board meeting he raised the question, but the board was reticent. Banks were for business. They would lend to small businessmen or finance industrial empires, but instalment loans for the working man were beyond the pale. Morris persisted. Finally the board agreed to the loan, but only if Morris himself countersigned the note. From this beginning in human need was born the Morris Plan, the first nationally organized attempt to meet America's rising demand for consumer credit.

At twenty-eight Morris was a successful and relatively wealthy attorney with a blue-ribbon list of clients, including International Harvester and the Equitable Life Assurance Society of New York, in addition to the bank connection. But the absence of credit for wage earners and small-salaried people continued to bother him. Although he had attended the University of Virginia and graduated from its law school at twenty-one, banking was in his blood. His father had opened a chain of commissary stores in rural North Carolina, extending credit to farmers on their crops and helping to organize rural banks in the credit-starved countryside of the post-Civil War South.

Young Morris's own concern was reenforced during the three

years after he had countersigned the young railroad worker's note. The word soon spread and by 1910 he had been comaker on more than forty thousand dollars' worth of paper, virtually every cent of it faithfully repaid. But commercial banks were still not suited to the need that Morris could envision stretching far beyond the city of Norfolk. A bank tailored to that need would be able to render better service and, it was hoped, would make money at the same time. Accordingly, on April 5, 1910, the Norfolk Fidelity Savings and Trust Company opened in offices adjacent to Morris's own in the Seaboard Bank Building.

By banking standards it was a precarious beginning. Capital was twenty thousand dollars, with a ten-thousand-dollar surplus. Half of it was Morris's own. The other half he obtained from the bank directors on the strength of his own reputation—and the guarantee that they would not lose their investments. The first year, business surpassed even Morris's expectations. Several times the original investment had been loaned out, using lines of credit Morris established with local and New York banks. The new bank's hard-sell advertising program had come to the attention of others concerned with the absence of instalment credit at reasonable rates. From Atlanta, Georgia, Woods White, a fellow attorney who had helped a number of Pullman porters victimized by loan sharks, extended Morris an invitation. Would he come down and talk about his plan for consumer credit?

Morris did more than talk. With White's help, he organized the Atlanta Fidelity and Trust Company, a duplicate of his Norfolk bank. Among the guests White had invited to discussions with Morris was the editor of the powerful *Atlanta Constitution*. Shortly thereafter, the newspaper carried a series of editorials about "Morris' plan of banking." From all over the *Constitution*'s wide circulation area, letters began to pour into Norfolk, asking how other cities could establish consumer banks according to Morris's plan. Convinced that the demand he had tapped in Norfolk and Atlanta was equally strong elsewhere, Morris determined to meet it.

Calling on business friends, he accumulated five hundred thousand dollars in capital, including a hundred thousand of his own. With this nucleus he organized the Fidelity Corporation of America, probably the nation's first true bank holding company. On the strength of Morris's persuasive powers, banks were established in Baltimore, Washington, D.C., Portsmouth, Virginia, and in Richmond, Virginia's financial center.

Only the original Norfolk Fidelity was controlled by the holding company. In order to stretch his capital as far as possible, Morris told bankers and businessmen in the other cities his company would put up 25 percent of the capital to start a consumer lending bank or company, if they would raise the other 75 percent. As an organization fee and for the use of his know-how, the holding company would charge 10 percent of the total capital paid in. Community-minded business and financial leaders realized the need for such personal credit. Morris offered them proof that it could be provided at small risk and appreciable profit. Although it was not yet so named, the Morris Plan was off to a good start.

It was another historic merger of a man and his times. Small of bone and stature and limping from a slightly clubbed left foot, Arthur Morris had strong convictions, persuasive powers as a public speaker, and the ability to impress older men. His main thesis was that the American economy depends essentially on mass production; mass production depends on mass distribution; and mass distribution depends on mass credit. For those who supply the final ingredient, the market is unlimited, bound to grow as the country does, and offers an almost certain return on funds invested. Although many early Morris Plan backers may have seen only a safe solution to a community problem, Morris himself sensed the financial implications of a great incoming tide—the rise of the little man and his needs.

The century had just turned, and the Industrial Revolution was gathering momentum in America. The empty spaces of the nation were filling up. Small towns, sprinkled along the rails, were feeling the first faint stirrings of the coming exodus from the farm, and cities were beginning to emerge. By 1910 fifty metropolitan areas contained one-fifth of the population. The Progressives, who had fought the railroads and big business to a standstill from their home base in Wisconsin, were leading a revolt against Taft in the White House. As president of the leftist International Workers of the World, the Fabian Socialist Eugene Debs was planting the seeds of industrial unionism. On another front the developing electric utilities and burgeoning cities nurtured the beginnings of the home appliance industry, adding more pressure for consumer credit. In 1909 Henry Ford decided to concentrate on a single low-cost utility car and began raising industrial wages and perfecting the assembly line, establishing Detroit as the center of the nation's automotive industry. Soon thereafter, truck lines began to appear, most of them financed by bank credit. New steel, glass, rubber, and oil empires were founded on the automobile. With its dependence on mass consumption, the automobile industry would finally supplement established banking practice with its own customer financing and help open the way for general consumer credit.

Meanwhile in the South the bitterness of Reconstruction was coming to an end, and the handicaps it had imposed on the region were gradually being alleviated. In most of the old Confederacy, relatively conservative elements had regained political control and brought a degree of stability. Agriculture was still basic, but southern industry and commerce were growing. An emerging South, starved for both consumer goods and capital, began to attract northern business and industry.

In Virginia in 1905 the famous May Campaign, the first statewide nonpolitical citizen-sponsored drive, brought major advances in the quantity and quality of public schools. In 1907 the first demonstration farms marked the beginning of the extension service. Normal schools for white women were established at Harrisonburg in 1909, Fredericksburg in 1911, and Radford in 1912. A normal school offering other academic subjects to both male and female Negro teachers had been opened at Petersburg in 1882 and a normal school for white teachers at Farmville in 1884. The need to get children to school prompted a series of good roads conventions. In 1906 counties were authorized to issue bonds for road construction, and the State Highway Commission was created. By 1910 the General Assembly was establishing speed limits and licensing automobiles to provide more road money.

From its beginnings, banking in America had been a blend of Hamilton's Federalism and Jefferson's Republicanism. By the early 1900s, national and state banks flourished side by side, the former providing a uniform if somewhat restrictive pattern of bank legislation, the latter following a variety of state statutes and providing flexibility of credit for a developing economy. In 1900 Congress reduced the minimum capital for national banks in small towns from fifty thousand to twenty-five thousand dollars. The total number of state and national banks mushroomed from just over twelve thousand to thirty thousand by 1920. Between 1865 and 1914 the quantity of money in the United States increased about tenfold, with commercial banks supplying about 90 percent of the expansion. Bank notes declined and deposits increased, until by 1915, the latter accounted for 85 percent of the money supply. By 1914 checks, based on deposits, constituted about 90 percent of the flow of business payments. The postal savings system was established in 1910; the Federal Reserve System was born in 1913; and in 1916 the Federal Land Banks were formed.

Farm loans were restricted to small-town banks until 1914, when national banks were given authority to make such loans. But most banks were still shying away from making small loans to nondepositors. One exception was the Bank of Italy in California, where the personal magnetism of A. P. Giannini created a branch-banking system geared to personal and small business loans and high-risk paper from fruit and vegetable growers, and even the fledgling movie industry.

There were a few other harbingers of credit for the little man, most of them with European roots. They were largely credit unions or savings and loan associations modeled along French, German, Italian, or Scandinavian lines, and usually associated with craft unions. One of these was the forerunner of the Merchants and Mechanics Savings and Loan Association of Newport News, established in 1904, originally created at the request of metalcraft union members at the Newport News Shipbuilding and Dry Dock Company who had come from Germany. These early consumer credit sources served only their own areas, usually only the members of a specific organization or nationality. Morris's conception of a general public consumer lending system was unique.

By 1914 the lending banks and companies he had established in three states and the nation's capital had absorbed virtually all of Fidelity Corporation of America's capital funds. Not all of them had been spectacular successes, since they lacked Morris's personal drive and dedication. But they had proved, with astonishingly low loss ratios, that the average American would repay his honest debts. They had also helped to translate Arthur Morris's dream into reality.

Morris himself had New York banking connections. So did

Fergus Reid, a wealthy Norfolk investment banker and a Fidelity
Corporation of America director. In 1913 Morris and Reid went
to New York with the intention of raising the money to spread
Morris's plan of banking nationwide. Their visits to businessmen
culminated in a meeting at the offices of J. P. Morgan and Company. There Morris presented his plan for a much larger version
of the Fidelity Corporation. When he had finished, the assembled
bankers and businessmen agreed to provide a pool of $25 million,
with Morris putting up five hundred thousand dollars, all the
capital he could raise from his own sources. The holding company thus formed was called Industrial Finance Corporation.
Morris thought of personal loans in terms of industrial life insurance such as policies sold to wage earners by the Metropolitan
Life Insurance Company. The Morgan group felt the individual
local companies should have a uniform identification and a symbol. One of them, Willard Straight, drew a black diamond with
white letters, reading "Morris Plan," and thus completed an organized method of massive consumer loans available to a credit-
hungry America.

The holding company's original board of directors was an impressive group. There were members of the Morgan firm; officers
of the National City Bank of New York, and the Guarantee Trust
Company, which had extended Morris lines of credit in Norfolk;
J. P. Morgan's son-in-law, Herbert Satterlee, a lawyer; and General Coleman DuPont, owner of the Equitable Building on
Broadway, and later the company's president. Morris himself was
vice-president and general counsel.

Local Morris Plan companies were to be organized on the same
basis as those already in existence, with the holding company
buying only 25 percent of the capital and taking 10 percent of
the total capital raised as a condition of the franchise. First to be
organized was The Morris Plan Company of New York. During
the next few years, spent mostly in Pullman cars, Arthur Morris
established 110 Morris Plan banks and companies in more than
twenty-four states.

Expansion slowed by 1920. Most of Industrial Finance Corpo-
ration capital was then invested in minority ownership of local
Morris Plan institutions. Although they pioneered in filling a
void in the banking industry, those units organized as Morris
Plan companies were not all banks by legal or financial definition.
They were more nearly a cross between American Savings and

Loan Associations and European craft credit unions. Replying to Morris's request for a bank charter for the original Norfolk Fidelity Savings and Trust Company, Robert R. Prentis, chairman of the Virginia State Corporation Commission, set forth the dilemma of definition and at the same time said something about Arthur Morris and his mission:

Dear Arthur:

I have carefully considered your application for a charter for your hybrid and mongrel institution. Frankly, I don't know what it is. It isn't a savings bank; it isn't a state or national bank; it isn't anything I ever heard of before. Its principles seem sound, however, and its purpose is admirable. But the reason I am going to grant a charter is because I believe in you.

Morris's "mongrel" institution provided for the savings function by offering fully paid certificates of investment or instalment certificates of investment of fifty dollars, a hundred dollars, or more to be subscribed to and paid for on a weekly or monthly basis. For use in the lending function, Morris provided for subscription to a certificate of investment equal to the face amount of the loan applied for. The certificate was to be paid for on a weekly or monthly basis until subscription to the certificate was fully paid. This subscribed-for certificate was to be attached to the loan as collateral, valueless at the beginning, but equal to the face of the loan at maturity. Being then cashed, the proceeds would be used to pay off the one-year note, a usual period for such loans. Thus no payment was made on the note itself. The payments were to be instalment purchase money to build up the face of the pledged certificate. Morris's term for this class of certificate was "an instalment investment certificate hypothecated." Because the 6 percent note ran for twelve months with no payments received or applied to it, there could be no charge of usury. This then was the Morris Plan's unique mechanism for making nonusurious loans to individuals. The pattern conformed to the practice of the German urban credit unions.

Morris Plan banks and companies loaned money. But since they did not accept demand deposits, they were not true banks. Instead, Morris Plan loan banks and companies accepted savings in the form of investment certificates. They could be bought in multiples of a hundred dollars or a borrower could subscribe to an instalment investment certificate and pay for it on a weekly or monthly schedule.

Commercial banks were mostly borrower oriented. Men with some money, who wanted to make more of it by building railroads or barge lines or businesses of any kind, pooled their resources, sold stock, and started a bank. They could then borrow money as it accumulated in the form of rising demand deposits. Following the free-wheeling, free-enterprise pattern of the country itself, American banks had developed largely to finance business and, to some extent, agriculture.

Banking in the South had been built around cotton and tobacco. The Midwest had spawned a host of small banks to finance smaller farming operations.

As a consequence of their main purpose, financing business, the standard commercial bank of the early 1900s loaned only on collateral or against substantial net worth and then only to its depositors. For this reason, businessmen kept their money at a given bank, so they could borrow from it. Many city banks went so far as to require that new depositors be recommended by old depositors in order to discourage new customers from making small deposits and then demanding large loans. Loans of less than a thousand dollars were rare. Smaller commercial loans were generally ninety-day renewable notes backed by collateral. Morris's idea of loans to salaried men or wage earners, with twelve months to repay in low monthly amounts and no collateral, was considered beneath the dignity of the banking fraternity and unsound into the bargain. But Morris was sure the market for small loans existed, and experience had taught him that small borrowers were conscientious about repaying their borrowings. All he needed was a method to fit the times.

American building and loan companies and savings banks had long raised funds to lend to individuals by offering shares on passbook savings. People with small incomes could sign up for a savings certificate of fifty or a hundred dollars or more, make regular weekly or monthly payments according to the schedule of the certificate, until the face value was accumulated, and earn interest on such savings.

What Morris did was couple a similar certificate to a one-year note for the same amount, so that one year later the certificate that was pledged to the loan would be fully paid and cancel the note. In addition to this self-collateralizing of the loan by the borrower, two comakers were required. No stocks, bonds, or mortgages were required. Morris described this arrangement as credit based on character and earning power.

From the beginning he was forceful about insisting that people wisely use the credit he extended. While Morris Plan banks would lend where commercial banks would not, each prospective borrower had to convince the bank officer that his loan was for a worthwhile purpose. Although the practice was later modified, loans were not initially supposed to exceed 10 percent of the borrower's annual income. Nor was Morris's faith in character and earning power absolute. Potential borrowers were investigated and charged a fee for the work equal to 2 percent of the face amount of the loan.

While the average employed person could find a friend or a relative or a fellow worker to cosign his note, there was a degree of reluctance because of the contingency of the borrower's death. To circumvent this possibility, Morris set out to find a major insurance company that would issue a one-year term life policy for the face amount of the loan. But in visits to one insurance company after another, he found the same resistance to borrower coverage during the life of the loan that he had found at commercial banking houses to lending an individual money in the first place. Finally in 1917 he solved the problem himself by organizing the Morris Plan Insurance Society. For an additional 2 percent deducted from the face value of the loan, the borrower received a life insurance policy covering the face amount of the loan in the event of the borrower's death. Later on, the insurance coverage was reduced to payment on the unpaid balance of the loan. The rate was reduced to 1 percent. Now known as Bankers Security Life, the Morris Plan Insurance Society does an annual business in excess of $500 million.

Morris had also taken an extra precaution to protect not only the borrower and his comakers, but the lender as well. In theory, Morris Plan companies were foolproof, given their basic premise that 90 percent or more of the people were honest. By making a large number of small loans, risk was spread over a wide range, thus removing the possibility of a large borrower's going bankrupt and breaking the company.

In addition to these built-in safety factors, Morris included in the language of each savings certificate the reservation that no Morris Plan bank or company could be required to pay out in any one month more than it had taken in during the previous month. Local Morris Plan banks and companies capitalized on this feature by advertising themselves as the unbreakable banks. The safety features, however, sometimes turned out to be liabilities rather than assets. In a typical city, local bankers and businessmen listened to Morris outline his plan. They recognized its worth as an answer to community credit problems, but they often did not see it in the light of his own missionary zeal. What many visualized instead was a glorified remedial loan society with a modest return on investment, virtually no risk, and requiring no great ability or energy on the part of company management. Since Industrial Finance Corporation usually did not own a controlling interest in the local Morris Plan Company, this is exactly what many of his local units turned out to be.

Local offices were never elaborate. Marble lobbies would add too much to overhead. In addition, they were hardly reassuring to the man in overalls or open shirt, already ill at ease at his first contact with formal bank-type credit. Morris's own Norfolk Fidelity Savings and Trust Company advertised heavily and with utter disregard for the conventional dignity of commercial banking ads. With tongue in cheek one such Norfolk advertisement warned that there would be no financing of automobiles "for petting purposes." But many other Morris Plan companies were neither as aggressive nor as interesting in their promotion and advertising programs.

While he felt a need to fill a vacuum in the nation's credit structure, Morris had never intended the lending institutions bearing his name to be philanthropic. If well managed, they had an excellent profit potential. Theoretically, deducting 6 percent from the face of each loan when it was made and relending savings deposits as they came in, also at 6 percent, gave a yield of 11.2 percent. In practice, the return was better than 9 percent, whereas the average commercial loan at 6 percent, with a 20 percent compensating balance, yielded a net of 7.5 percent. Even with much higher processing costs for a large number of small loans, Morris Plan companies were potential money-makers. Riding the incoming tide of consumer credit as they did, they were a ready vehicle for further credit innovations, and the fertile mind of Arthur Morris was soon at work on still another.

From their early beginnings as an answer to personal emergencies, the companies had quickly moved into financing household appliances, indoor plumbing, central heating, and similar luxuries that were becoming necessities. Then there was the automobile, which offered the greatest potential of all. The evolution of the horseless carriage put real power behind consumer credit demands and finally broke down the resistance of the commercial banks. But first, the industry, and men like Arthur Morris, had to take the field.

From its first year, Norfolk Fidelity Savings and Trust had put consumers behind the wheel with standard Morris Plan loans. By 1915 Morris Plan companies were undoubtedly the largest underwriters of automobile loans among independent lending agencies. But an expanding automotive industry was still handicapped by a shortage of commercial credit to finance dealer inventories. In order to open a showroom and keep cars on hand, a dealer had to have either cash or credit of his own, or the manufacturer had to carry him until the cars were sold.

Detroit had been experimenting with specialized lending institutions to meet this need. Early in 1916, Morris and the Studebaker Corporation formed the Industrial Acceptance Corporation, second of its type in America, and based on the Morris plan of floor financing for dealers. When a dealer received a shipment for display on his showroom floor, he paid the manufacturer 10 percent of the factory price. Many Morris Plan companies loaned the dealer 90 percent of factory cost to help pay the manufacturer, at the usual 6 percent, taking a lien on the cars. In turn the automobile dealer sent his purchasing customers to the Morris Plan company for their individual financing of the purchase price. The dealer then paid off his loan on that car.

Automobile financing placed a further strain on Morris's faith in character as a guarantee of repayment. In the beginning Studebaker agreed to repurchase any cars not sold and the individual car purchaser was required to make a 25 to 50 percent down payment. The initial success of Industrial Acceptance Corporation brought Morris an offer to be president of what was to become General Motors Acceptance Corporation, but Studebaker would not release him from his contract.

While his consumer credit instincts were sound in pursuing automobile finance, the project led Morris to the brink of crisis. Lacking a controlling interest in most Morris Plan companies, Morris enticed them by arranging to have New York banks extend them lines of credit through the Industrial Acceptance Corporation. Local Morris Plan companies advanced floor plan loans to dealers and then in turn discounted the resulting paper through Industrial Acceptance in New York. When the panic of 1921 reverberated throughout Wall Street, the New York banks curtailed their lines of credit. Local Morris Plan companies suddenly found themselves getting their dealer notes returned from New York instead of the cash they expected. To meet these obligations and to keep the dealer's business, company management and directors had to raise more capital locally to replace the cash Industrial Acceptance Corporation had been arranging. But whenever they did find additional capital, Industrial Finance Corporation demanded a 10 percent payment on that capital under the terms of the original Morris Plan franchise agreement.

Local Morris Plan company managers were already at odds with Arthur Morris over his attempts to spur them along, dictate policy, and gain control through stock purchases. As a counterforce they organized The Morris Plan Bankers Association in 1919. Many of them had gone into dealer financing reluctantly in the first place. When their New York lines of credit were cut off, their wrath had the righteousness of their original convictions. When, in addition, another corporation headed by Arthur Morris demanded 10 percent of the replacement capital they had found it so difficult to raise, they reached the limit of their patience.

CHAPTER II

Another Young Man with a Mission

EARLY IN FEBRUARY 1921 a young North Carolinian, already an experienced bank officer, entered New York's Pennsylvania Station on his way to see about a job in a Philadelphia bank. He had already severed a promising connection with the National City Bank of New York to pursue a developing urge to create a type of banking responsive to everyday human needs and to extend that financial philosophy beyond the reach of a single bank. Like so many of his contemporaries he was a Southerner who had gone north in search of his fortune, and his dream was to make a contribution to his distressed southern homeland.

At a newsstand he picked up a copy of the *American Magazine,* in which he had read stories of successful businessmen during his college days in North Carolina. As the train pulled out he opened it. The first article was a story about Arthur Morris and the Morris Plan. In Philadelphia he sat through his job interview in a trance. When it was over he took the first train back to New York and sped to the offices of Industrial Finance Corporation at 52 William Street. The magazine article was one link in a chain of circumstances that would profoundly affect the structure and success of the Morris Plan and, more particularly, of banking practice in the Commonwealth of Virginia. But first the eager young man had to get in to see Arthur Morris. As it turned out, the founder of the Morris Plan was out of town, and the caller talked instead to T. P. Junkin, vice-president of Industrial Finance.

What Junkin saw was a tall, spare, earnest young man, impeccably dressed in the Continental fashion, his head prematurely bald, with remaining wisps of red hair not unlike Arthur Morris's own. But it was what he heard that struck a responsive chord in Junkin. His visitor was from Raleigh, North Carolina.

"Well," said Junkin, "you must know my Aunt Betty Penick."

"Of course I know Miss Betty," said his visitor.

"Anyone who knows my Aunt Betty Penick can have anything

he wants from me," said Junkin. "You will see Arthur Morris tomorrow."

Next morning there began the relationship that opened a half century of mutual, if often turbulent, friendship between two strong men, each fired with the same mission, each with his own stubborn notions of how to accomplish it—Arthur Joseph Morris and Thomas Callendine Boushall. The interview began in the usual fashion. Morris was impressed with the tailor-made clothes, the aristocratic Southern charm, and the connection with National City, which had been one of the Morris Plan backers. He was not long in finding out his caller's mission.

Industrial Finance had franchised eleven small banks in North Carolina. If Morris would turn the holding company's stock over to him, Boushall would weld those small-loan offices into a statewide consumer banking system.

It couldn't be done, Morris said. Industrial Finance owned only 25 percent of the stock in most of the eleven North Carolina companies.

Why only 25 percent? Boushall wanted to know. And why, he pressed, had Mr. Morris given his own name to his plan for consumer banking?

Morris replied that the board chose the name despite his protest.

Boushall's eyes twinkled. His face relaxed into the smile that softened the sharpness of his words. "If you have any money," he said, "I'll go down there and buy those eleven banks for you."

Already squeezed between curtailed lines of New York bank credit on the one hand and irate Morris Plan managers on the other, Morris was in no position to commission eleven bank purchases. But he wanted control of them. If Boushall could persuade North Carolina Morris Plan managers and directors to relinquish control, it would be worth the try. It took three more interviews to work out details. Boushall was to have an expense account of two hundred dollars a month to visit the North Carolina Morris Plan companies. A letter of agreement promised that if he was successful, his salary would be five thousand dollars a year, retroactive to March 1921. Boushall took the train south.

Thomas C. Boushall was the third son of Joseph Dozier and Mattie Heck Boushall, successful, well-connected residents of Raleigh. Of mixed French, English, and German backgrounds, the Boushalls were thoroughly Southern after five generations in

North Carolina. Ancestors on both sides had been Confederate officers. The surname was an anglicized form of the French name Bouchelle, brought to Maryland in the early 1700s by French Huguenots. Originally the accent had been on the second syllable, which the future president of The Bank of Virginia preferred, but North Carolina was more familiar with the local pronunciation of "Bushel."

Young Thomas had been graduated at sixteen from Raleigh's first public high school in 1910, two months after Arthur Morris opened the Norfolk Fidelity Savings and Trust.

Although his activity always belied it, his health was not robust. His parents kept him at home for a year before he entered the University of North Carolina, and in his junior year, he developed mastoiditis, often fatal in the days before penicillin. An early mastoid operation saved him, but not before a heart specialist had noted what later turned out to be early symptoms of tuberculosis.

At the university he majored in economics, won intersociety debating honors, managed the UNC football team, and carried extra classes after the bout with mastoiditis to graduate in January 1915. He was selected the following April to represent the student body at Dr. Edward Kidder Graham's inauguration as president of the university. He also played football on the freshman class team, captained by his roommate Philip Woollcott, a Raleigh boyhood friend.

Following graduation he served for a year as secretary of the university YMCA, but from his earliest years he had wanted a business career. In 1916 an uncle told him about a bank executive training course for young men at the National City Bank of New York. Armed with recommendations from the governor, a North Carolina supreme court justice, Josephus Daniels, then Secretary of the Navy, the university's president, the business manager, and the president of the American Chemical Society, he headed north. National City was accepting Southern applicants only from the University of Virginia, but young Tom Boushall impressed Ferdinand C. Schwedtman, the vice-president in charge of the program, who referred him to a bank affiliate, International Banking Corporation, which offered him a position in India. Not Tom Boushall. He had come to join National City's program. Back in Raleigh, he wired International Banking, turning down the overseas job, and then wired Schwedtman: "Have refused Mr. Green's offer. When do I report to your class?" Thus on June 16, 1916, Tom Boushall at last began his chosen business career, as usual, in his own way.

One of the training-class lecturers narrowed this goal in life. Explaining that the Bank of France discounted merchants' trade acceptances in amounts as small as twenty francs, or four dollars, William C. Redfield, Secretary of Commerce under Woodrow Wilson, summed up:

"That gentlemen, is banking organized down to the needs of the people."

Tom Boushall wrote the phrase down. He would repeat it verbatim to Arthur Morris five years later and many times thereafter in many contexts.

Meanwhile the needs of the people were shelved. On special assignment from Schwedtman, he produced a study that reorganized the bank's filing system, contradicted a committee of five bank officers on how to speed up elevator service, soundproofed the secretarial pool ceiling with cotton batting and cheesecloth, and introduced the dictaphone into the bank routine.

Then came the war. In November 1917 he enlisted as a sergeant in the gas defense section of the Medical Corps, won a commission as a first lieutenant in ninety days, and got an assignment to Base Hospital No. 45 bound for France. Once abroad destiny provided another nudge or two. The unit was commanded by Dr. Stuart McGuire, of Richmond, Virginia, and included such future associates as Major W. Lowndes Peple, Major John Garnett Nelson, Captain James Henderson Smith, and Lieutenant Carrington Williams, later a Bank of Virginia director.

Near the front, the unit was joined by a hundred nurses, among them Marie Mikell Lebby, a Charleston, South Carolina, aristocrat, with a mind and wit to match his own. They were to see much more of each other.

Orders home finally came in February 1919, but a telegram from Schwedtman in New York suggested demobilization in France. Young Boushall was directed to Brussels, there to help in establishing a new National City branch. At Toul during the rush of turning the unit over to new officers and staff, he caught a cold that developed into a severe case of influenza, from which three years later his latent case of tuberculosis was to surface.

His experiences in Brussels were broadening. There was President Wilson's reception at the home of the American ambassador, dances and teas at the Royal Belgian Golf Club and the English Lawn Tennis Club. There was work from morning until late at night at the bank, where he soon became submanager while the manager stayed on the road. There was also pursuit of "banking organized down to the needs of the people," through readings concerning the Scotch cash credit system and European peoples' banks, which had likewise fascinated Arthur Morris. But a growing frustration with the Brussels bank manager kindled a desire in Tom Boushall to return to his leisurely and gracious homeland. By August 1920 when Schwedtman arrived from New York for a visit, Boushall was ready to resign. Schwedtman, in effect, said he was a fool. Ahead lay the chance to organize National City banking to meet the needs of the Belgian people. He offered a raise in salary from five to six thousand dollars. But Tom Boushall had made another decision. He remained until January 1921 to round out two full years in Brussels and then set sail for New York where he tendered his formal resignation.

On his arrival he found banks failing all over America and his National City mentor indignant over what he viewed as gross ingratitude. But the resignation stood. After two and a half years abroad, it was time for a visit home and for a trip to Charleston to solidify a tacit understanding with Marie Lebby.

In North Carolina there was ample opportunity for a bright young man with two years' experience in Wall Street banking. The Wachovia Bank and Trust, already on its way to landmark status in North Carolina, offered him a choice of two positions in Winston-Salem. But Tom Boushall's goal was fixed elsewhere. The branch banking portion of that goal was not unique to America's highly individualistic, borrower-oriented credit system. Statewide branch banking systems, subsidized by state governments, had flourished in the antebellum South until they went under in a flood of their own worthless bank notes when the Confederacy collapsed. Spreading westward with the country, the concept had been resisted by independent-minded Midwest farmers, but on the West Coast, the Bank of Italy by 1920 had blanketed the state of California with its branches, despite the fervent opposition of other banks. Consumer credit had also gained a little ground, but only a little.

In the 1920s labor unions moved into banking to augment ethnic cooperatives and other variations of consumer credit that had taken root in patches of fertile ground around the nation.

The Russell Sage Foundation and other city-oriented consumer groups were pushing for enactment by states of the Uniform Small Loan Law, permitting realistic interest rates on small personal loans, under rigorous inspection and licensing of lenders. But they were still the exceptions. The rule, particularly in the South, was that banking was for business. Big city banks in the South were consolidating to meet the needs of burgeoning business and industry and had little time or patience for consumer loans. Small-town banks were largely one-man operations and were fiercely independent.

Before they could combine branch banking and consumer loans into a full-fledged banking operation, Thomas C. Boushall and those around him would wage many battles against heavy odds over a long period of years and would taste many bitter defeats.

His first self-imposed assignment, an attempt to gain control for Arthur Morris of Morris's North Carolina companies, was also his first setback. He found Morris Plan company management and directors ruffled over the turn of events in dealer floor plan financing and generally satisfied with their relatively independent status. He managed to buy control for Morris in the Greensboro and Winston-Salem banks and persuaded Raleigh to accept contractual control. But by June it was clear that his dream of statewide branch banking for North Carolina under the Morris Plan black diamond was premature. The contract with Morris Plan local managers was to prove valuable to him in a somewhat negative way. They let him know that Industrial Finance was in almost desperate need of cash and that local management was personally antagonistic to Arthur Morris.

Morris was essential to Boushall's own plans. In any trouble with local managers, he would have to be a Morris man. But he could afford to be independent, knowing that Morris was having troubles of his own.

During their discussions in New York, he had sensed that Morris wanted control of local companies and that he had been intrigued by the idea of a closely linked branch banking system by which he could achieve it. On the way back to New York, Boushall decided on another tack. There were Morris Plan companies throughout the Fifth Federal Reserve District. Boushall knew where they were because he had laid out a plan for Liberty Bond sales through local banks for Schwedtman at National City in the early days of World War I. Industrial Finance had no money to buy control of all these banks, even if local managers and board members were willing to sell, but it did have at least 25 percent of the stock. In some cases it already owned a controlling interest. That stock in his hands would be a start toward putting his dream back together in five states instead of one.

With pencil and graph paper, he began to formulate the idea. Morris would turn over to him all the stock he owned in Fifth Federal Reserve District Morris Plan banks and companies in exchange for stock in a new Morris Plan reserve bank in Richmond District headquarters. Morris would also provide cash to capitalize the new bank, which he would then control. From this central bank Boushall would undertake to develop and gain control of the local banks and companies in the Fifth District. It was an audacious plan. With Morris's money Boushall proposed to buy Morris's shares in Morris Plan companies in Virginia, North and South Carolina, Maryland, West Virginia, and the District of Columbia, and have enough left to create another Morris Plan bank in Richmond where one already existed.

At first Morris was not enthusiastic, but Tom Boushall would not let go. He followed Morris around golf courses, showing his charts between greens. He walked the streets of New York, talking between meetings and speaking engagements. He rode with Morris up the Hudson. He slept at Morris's apartment off Gramercy Park when Morris would no longer stay up to talk. Finally on August 1, 1921, Morris agreed. He would underwrite $375,000 in capital and surplus for the new bank. The bank in turn would buy Morris's stock in local banks in the Fifth Federal Reserve District for $280,000. This would leave $95,000 in cash to organize and operate the bank in Richmond.

But Morris was in for another shock. No sooner was the agreement signed than Tom Boushall pulled out the March letter, stipulating that his salary, retroactive to March 1, was due when the North Carolina assignment was complete. Now that a much bigger deal had been committed to paper, Boushall wanted his money. Shaking his head, Morris countered that an agreement on August 1 meant salary as of August 1. In a torrent of words Tom Boushall offered Arthur Morris the first of many resignations. Here was a breach of good faith he had never suspected from the head of such a major lending enterprise. He was finished as of that day. All plans were rescinded. Boushall was through with Arthur Morris.

Morris replied with what he thought would settle the controversy. If his vice-president and treasurer would agree that Boushall was right and he was wrong, he would go along with him. Boushall pulled out a check for the full amount due him already signed by the vice-president and treasurer. Outmaneuvered, Morris countersigned.

Behind this heated altercation had been Boushall's plan to marry Marie Lebby. He needed the back pay for a ring, a wedding trip, and housekeeping expenses. Heading south once more, he stopped in Richmond for a quick look at possible bank locations, visited his parents in Raleigh, and proceeded to Flat Rock, North Carolina, where Miss Lebby and her parents were staying. The engagement was announced and the wedding set for February 23, 1922.

On the surface 1922 was not a choice year for bank-launching. Plummeting farm prices in 1920 had produced a chain reaction that toppled or merged many city banks as well as those in small towns. But there was latent power and major change in the young nation.

In perspective the depression of 1920 and 1921 was a readjustment. America, her financial glands and industrial tissues suddenly developed by war, would embark on a binge of sheer exuberance, sparked by the automobile and sustained by the speakeasy. She would suffer the consequences in the Great Depression and emerge into maturity. In a historic parallel, The Morris Plan Bank of Richmond would likewise mature into The Bank of Virginia.

Although the country had yet to understand its significance, the war had made America a world power. From a debtor nation, she had become Europe's major creditor. Responding to the need to equip a major army and navy, the country suddenly became aware of its own fantastic productive capability. But it was not ready for Woodrow Wilson's dream of making the world safe for democracy through the League of Nations. The war had been too costly, and there was too much to do at home.

In 1920 Warren Harding had been elected on the promise of a return to normalcy. Higher tariff and strict immigration quotas reflected the mood of the business community. By 1922 industrial capital had almost doubled the $51 billion figure of 1900 as industry shifted from military hardware to consumer goods. Home ownership had doubled from the 1900 figure by 1922, and the postwar depression was vanishing before a growing demand of industry for workers and of better paid industrial employees for automobiles and appliances.

American technology began its long rise to dominance. In 1919 just sixteen years after Kitty Hawk, the airplane made its first transatlantic flight via Newfoundland and Ireland. Two years later the carrier *Langley* joined the U.S. fleet. By 1923 Henry Ford had sold his two-millionth Model T, and General Motors was emerging as his major competitor. The first commercial radio station began broadcasting in 1921, setting the stage for a communications network tying the country together via the airwaves. By 1925 overlapping frequencies had forced the creation of the Federal Communications Commission, and the first talkies were just around the corner in 1927.

A nation coming of age began to be concerned with itself. The states and the federal government reflected a popular concern for the reckless depletion of natural resources. More important and more diverse and emphatic in its expression was the concern for human resources. The Department of Labor's Children's Bureau established in 1912 was followed in 1920 by a Women's Bureau. The same year saw passage of the Nineteenth Amendment, giving women access to the ballot box. The year 1920 also witnessed the paradox of the "noble experiment," the Eighteenth Amendment, an attempt to legislate morality that produced instead big-league crime and widespread defiance of the law. Communism became the focus of a continuing battle between human and property rights. Fear of the Red Menace slowed the growth of left-leaning unionism and at the same time solidified the working man's support for the right to strike and to bargain with his employer.

Although the term had not yet been coined, the Establishment came under increasing attack from men like Sinclair Lewis, Sherwood Anderson, and H. L. Mencken. Lewis in particular had a field day ridiculing Babbitts, and Mencken chimed in by ridiculing Rotarians, Kiwanians, and what he termed the "boob-oisie." The Federal Trade Commission and the Clayton Anti-Trust Act, established earlier, began to make themselves felt. But the reformers and the intellectuals were still ahead of their time. The business of the United States, as Calvin Coolidge was to put it, was business.

Most of the commercial banks were preoccupied with meeting

an insatiable demand for credit. More than three-fourths of the country's bank credit was tied up in economic expansion from the top. In the early 1920s, commercial banks held only about 6 percent of the nation's home mortgages. Industrial Acceptance Corporation, GMAC, and others were largely meeting the credit needs of the automotive industry, but credit for the workingman and his family to purchase their homes and household appliances was yet to come in sufficient volume.

Farmers, still suffering from the recession of 1921, were still largely dependent for credit on the country merchant and such rural banks as still survived. Bank failures and foreclosures during the economic slowdown had reenforced the traditional suspicion of banks on the part of men of the soil.

In Richmond a mixture of northern and home-grown business and industry was setting a new and encouraging economic tone. Broad Street dominated retail trade for miles around. Valentine Meat Juice Company and C. F. Sauer's were flourishing. The Mutual Assurance Society of Virginia, established in 1794 and the second oldest insurance company in America, was growing slowly but steadily.

Chemical industries began to build on the James River below the city. Hopewell rejoiced at the coming of its first rayon plant. Cigarettes, the universal symbol of the age, had grown to about 19 percent of tobacco consumption, booming Virginia flue-cured and Burley leaf and Richmond's cigarette factories.

Following the pattern and the demands of industry, small banks were merging into larger ones. First National's impressive building on the southwest corner of Ninth and Main had stamped that intersection as financial headquarters for the Commonwealth in 1911, and by 1925 it would become First and Merchants National Bank, the state's largest, to be challenged the following year by consolidated State-Planters Bank and Trust Company.

Virginia bankers were still true to the state's long history of financial conservatism. Unlike some of her sister states of the South, Virginia had not repudiated her Civil War debt, and had readjusted that debt only after a long series of major political battles. None of her thirty-six national banks and only about half a dozen state banks and trust companies had failed in the crash of 1893, when 153 banks had gone under in the South and West alone. But conservative commercial banking philosophy was now impeding the credit desperately needed on the farm and increas-

ingly demanded by the average city dweller. Commercial bankers
seemed oblivious of this. When young Tom Boushall stepped off
the train in downtown Richmond in August 1921, he saw from
the station platform a billboard typical of the self-satisfaction in
the capital of the Old Dominion: "Banking Centuries Old Today
Stands Complete." Many times in the years to come, he and his
associates were to recall that sign.

CHAPTER III

A Shoestring Stretches

TOM BOUSHALL'S FIRST STOP was at Fidelity Loan and Savings Company, which held the Morris Plan franchise and its black diamond trade name. With customary frankness he told Littleton Fitzgerald, the cashier, that he represented Arthur Morris and wanted to buy the bank. Fidelity's stated capital was $150,000. Boushall asked to see the statement and the last audit.

"You've been frank with me," said Fitzgerald, "I'll be frank with you. The true book value is five thousand dollars." He explained that Fidelity had been lending money to company directors based on the dubious collateral of liens on used cars stored in warehouses.

Oliver J. Sands, president of the American National Bank, controlled the directors. Wasting no time, Boushall went to see Sands. Anxious to unload Fidelity, Sands agreed to forward all the stock to New York in exchange for a draft. Then came the shocker. As a price, Sands had in mind Fidelity's last statement and suggested $150,000.

"No," Boushall told him. "Five thousand dollars."

Indignant at the young upstart who knew more than he should about Fidelity Loan and Savings Company, Sands flatly refused. But on the way down to American National, Boushall had been thinking. Fidelity's background and reputation would be a handicap. Its quarters might reflect Arthur Morris's notions of a local outlet, but they did not fit the picture Tom Boushall had in mind. A fresh start was indicated. All he really wanted was the use of the Morris Plan diamond. To an adamant Oliver Sands he offered a suggestion. He would give five thousand dollars for a half interest in the Morris Plan franchise provided Fidelity would never use Morris Plan in its name, and he could call the new bank The Morris Plan Bank of Richmond. Sands agreed.

The next day Tom Boushall set out to find a location. His own choice was the first floor of the old Stumpf's Hotel on the northwest corner of Eighth and Main, as close as he could get to banking's nerve center a block east. The building was being remodeled into law offices. Arthur Morris was coming down to help with the selection. As a precaution Boushall had picked out several less desirable locations. Saving his own preference until last, Boushall proudly pointed out the choice corner location and the chance to begin in newly refurbished quarters, even though the rent would be nine thousand dollars a year. Morris preferred a small vacant store front between Seventh and Eighth on Main at a hundred dollars a month. For the second time Boushall threatened to resign. He would have nothing to do with such unimpressive surroundings. If that was the kind of bank Morris wanted, he could have it and run it to suit himself. In a second tactical withdrawal, Morris said he would go along if Boushall would come to New York and convince the board of directors of Industrial Finance. Boushall would and did.

In Richmond fixtures and furnishings were ordered and remodeling began. Back in New York, Tom Boushall was finding out for the first time what the Morris Plan was really all about. To a man schooled in big-time commercial banking, the cumbersome circumventions by which Arthur Morris had arrived at his "hybrid and mongrel institutions" in 1910 seemed impossibly obsolescent in 1922. Where Morris had envisioned a respectable loan company, Boushall had in mind a full-fledged consumer-oriented commercial bank. Things would have to be changed, and they could not wait until he was safely back in Richmond with his own banks to run.

The savings certificate device meant no demand deposits, no checking accounts, and no commercial loans. The usual one-year limitation on repayment ruled out many small loan possibilities. The requirement for two comakers in the easier credit conditions of the 1920s was a serious handicap. Finally, paying 5 percent interest on paid-up certificates made it impossible to make money without the investigation fee and insurance discounts.

To horrified cries of heresy from the assembled Morris Plan executives, Boushall began altering forms, language, and procedures to suit the new Morris Plan Bank of Richmond. Abolished were all references to certificates. Instead, savings passbooks were ordered. Certificate redemption records became savings accounts. The Morris Plan's cumbersome certificates were reduced to a straightforward paragraph: "You assign your savings account as collateral to your loan, build it up to a sum equal to your loan and the savings account wipes out the loan at maturity. And we will pay you 3 percent interest per annum on your assigned savings deposits on a quarterly basis provided you make the required deposits regularly and on time. In the quarter in which you are delinquent or late in making your required deposits, interest will not be figured on those deposits made in the quarter where you were delinquent."

These things accomplished, Boushall headed for Morris's private office. The argument waxed hottest over the idea of paying interest on deposits assigned to loan repayment. Boushall pointed out that the Morris Plan in effect required the borrower to open a savings account at The Morris Plan Bank. It prevented him from depositing in another bank that would pay him interest.

"Paying interest on assigned deposits takes the fiction out of the Morris Plan and makes it a fact," he said.

This argument impressed Morris. Besides, the payment of interest on deposits removed any suspicion that Morris Plan banks were violating usury statutes. In the end Morris agreed to all the changes.

Aside from the obvious honesty of his convictions and his prestigious banking background, Tom Boushall laid out for Arthur Morris two enticements. The first was that Morris Plan companies might become fully respectable members of the banking fraternity. The second was that they might make more money. However, the idea of paying interest on assigned deposits won for Tom Boushall a host of enemies among Morris Plan executives in New York as well as among most Morris Plan managers across the country.

From the start he made a few converts. His words at times might appear caustic, but there was a warmth to them when they were spoken, and a missionary zeal behind them that attracted others. Also he had dared to question Arthur Morris, a fact which commanded respect. Still, as they were to learn, he was a Morris man.

Undeterred by the controversy he left behind, Boushall headed for his wedding in Charleston, a honeymoon in New Orleans, and the gentility of the Chesterfield Apartments in Richmond. From the perspective of twenty-eight years, the prospect was bright. He was about to realize his dream of "banking organized down to the needs of the people" and spread through branch banking over five states. This was in March 1922. Before a year was out, an unsuspected blow would almost end his career before it was well begun.

Meanwhile he first got in touch with his old university roommate, Philip Woollcott, who also wanted to get married, but who could not see his way clear to do so on a languishing income as a bond salesman in the investment department of the American Trust Company in Charlotte, North Carolina. Woollcott had gained a reputation during the war by selling Liberty Bonds through banks. Boushall's idea was that he might do the same with U.S. Savings Bonds to be paid for on Morris Plan instalments. It was agreed that Woollcott would join the bank on July 1, several weeks before the opening on July 17. When Woollcott finally got to Richmond, it took him two days to find Tom Boushall. He never did sell bonds.

Boushall himself was busy with arrangements. He called on all the prominent bankers and businessmen he could catch, hoping, without notable success, to locate receptive board members. He arranged with Industrial Finance Corporation to send in a team on opening day to sell savings accounts with a gift of a pocket savings bank, the first of many gimmicky but successful promotions. As the bank's accountant he hired Luke Harvey Fairbank, who set up the initial books from a running record Boushall had kept in a notebook in his pocket. In mid-July the record showed five thousand dollars spent for organization costs, printing, and stationery, and five thousand dollars for furnishings and equipment. With the commitment to purchase Morris Plan Bank stocks, this left eighty-five thousand dollars to commence operations.

At 9:00 A.M. on Monday morning, July 17, 1922, The Morris Plan Bank of Richmond opened its doors, with Thomas C. Boushall as president; Philip Woollcott, cashier and secretary; Luke H. Fairbank, bookkeeper; Clyde M. Hull, new business solicitor; Temple Carter and Viva VerMette as tellers, and Virginia Lishman, stenographer and staff secretary. The board of directors had been hand-picked by Arthur Morris, who had serious reservations about a second Morris Plan Bank in Richmond with such a high overhead and fancy trimmings. It consisted of Morris himself; Boushall; John Markle of New York, the nation's largest coal magnate and a long-time Morris supporter; Vere Brown, also of New York; and W. S. Royster and L. R. Shulman, two of Morris's Norfolk business friends. The first board meeting had been held in New York on July 5. The second occurred the morning the bank opened. Philip Woollcott was elected cashier and secretary. Royster, as inactive vice-president, filled out the list of officers.

Opening day also included a luncheon to which the presidents of most of the twenty-five banks in Richmond were invited and to which a majority came and extended their good wishes. There was a place, they felt, for the Morris Plan type of service. At the end of the first day, $1,460.12 in savings deposits had been received. The first board meeting had formally authorized the purchase of outstanding stock in Fifth Federal Reserve Morris Plan companies and banks, and shortly after the bank opened the transaction was completed. But not before the new president had astounded his new staff.

Industrial Finance, he knew, was hungry for liquid assets. Although New York owned 100 percent of his own shares, he insisted that the stocks in the other banks be in his hands before sending the $280,000 to New York. As carried on the books of Industrial Finance, these were:

Asheville Morris Plan Company	5 at $117.40
The Charlotte Morris Plan Company	125 at $110.00
The Morris Plan Industrial Bank of Durham	147 at $109.29
The Morris Plan Industrial Bank of Greensboro	385 at $122.74
High Point Morris Plan Bank	100 at $100.00
The New Bern Morris Plan Company	100 at $101.66
The Morris Plan Industrial Bank of Raleigh	100 at $105.13
The Morris Plan Company of Rocky Mount	100 at $112.52
Morris Plan Industrial Bank of Winston-Salem	400 at $122.02
The Homestead Bank of Columbia	230 at $ 23.64
Citizens Savings and Loan Corporation of Lynchburg	329 at $ 11.29
Morris Plan Bank of Norfolk	444 at $136.71
The Morris Plan Bank of Portsmouth	5 at $180.40
The Morris Plan Company of Baltimore	100 at $121.17
Industrial Savings and Loan Company of Wheeling, West Virginia	250 at $114.36

If the Richmond bankers who had wished him well on opening day expected little from a young man with big ideas, they were in for a surprise. In its first six months, the fledgling Morris Plan Bank of Richmond opened a branch in another city and one in a local furniture store, established its first line of credit to automobile dealers, increased its authorized capital to $1 million,

The top officials of Bank of Virginia Company comprising the office of the chairman are (left to right): R. Norris Hatch, vice-chairman; S. Wayne Bazzle, executive vice-president; Frederick Deane, Jr., president, and Herbert C. Moseley, chairman.

It Ought To Be Called Off

Cartoon by Fred O. Seibel, which appeared in the January 23, 1948, issue of the Richmond *Times-Dispatch*.

William F. Kelly (right), vice-president of The American Bankers Association, presents to Thomas C. Boushall a plaque "in recognition of his distinguished contributions to commercial banking, especially in the field of instalment credit." The presentation was made at the ABA's National Instalment Credit Conference on April 1, 1963.

Bank of Virginia Company was listed on the New York Stock Exchange on
January 4, 1971, becoming the first newcomer to the Big Board that year.
Left to right, NYSE President Robert W. Haack welcomes Chairman Herbert
C. Moseley and President Frederick Deane, Jr., to the trading floor.

Board of Directors, Bank of Virginia Company, July 17, 1972

borrowed $150,000 from local commercial banks to keep up with loan applications, and felt the first breath of resentment from other lending institutions. There were also three more attempted resignations by President Boushall in the next few months.

In August, Anton C. Adams was hired at twenty-seven hundred dollars a year as an interviewer and assistant to Philip Woollcott in the proposed sale of government bonds on the instalment plan.

A branch in Petersburg opened for business on November 23 at 1011½ North Sycamore Street, with W. M. Eller as manager. This was to prove the first move in a long and sometimes bitter controversy over branch banking in Virginia, which was finally settled forty years later. At the time its significance went unnoticed.

What troubled the banking fraternity immediately was the opening of a branch in the Phillip Levy & Company furniture store at 305 West Broad Street. The idea of a branch bank inside a retail store was too much. As complaints mounted, the commissioner of banks rescinded the authority and the branch closed October 7, 1922. The Levy account continued to provoke controversy. The original contact had been made by Arthur Morris himself, who spent a good deal of 1922 lending a helping hand to the new bank. A contract was signed under which The Morris Plan Bank of Richmond discounted trade acceptances, since Phillip Levy had no charge account system. On each hundred-dollar purchase, the bank would advance fifty dollars. Since Levy's markup was about 100 percent, things worked out fairly well initially. The bank collected the acceptances for a percentage. Morris saw in Levy a chance to build volume. Levy saw an easily handled instalment plan of payment and a prestige connection with a bank. Tom Boushall saw trouble.

Returning from a board meeting in Norfolk in October, he met Morris and Levy at the Jefferson Hotel. Morris showed him a two-page spread, scheduled for the morning paper, which to Boushall implied that Phillip Levy had practically taken over The Morris Plan Bank of Richmond as its financing agency. His reaction was explosive.

"If that ad appears in tomorrow morning's paper, I shall not be president of the bank at nine o'clock," he said. "You, Mr. Morris, will be president."

There were more heated words on both sides, but the ad was modified. Twice more in the fall of 1922 the president was to

tender his resignation over the Levy account. Time was to prove
him right in his skepticism.

Meanwhile he pursued his own conception of The Morris Plan
Bank of Richmond. At his suggestion the September 26 board
meeting voted the authority to do a trust business, although there
was no immediate thought of a trust department. The same meeting saw unveiled one of the bank's many firsts—the selling of
savings stamps. Pasted in specially printed books, they could start
a savings account when they totaled a dollar. This was one of the
many hard-sell promotions that marked the entire progress of the
bank. It reflected the wisdom of Boushall's early estimate that his
problem would not be finding borrowers but attracting depositors.

Between its opening in July and the following September, the
new bank had already loaned out all its free capital and all its
savings deposits and cash receipts from the beginning of loan
repayments. To keep on making loans, it would have to borrow
money. Boushall went to see Henry Litchford, a former Raleigh
bank official and contemporary of his father, who then headed the
Federal Trust Company in Richmond. Obviously The Morris
Plan Bank could not borrow at the customary commercial rate
of 6 percent with a 20 percent balance on deposit and lend the
money at 6 percent, but he had another idea. Litchford agreed to
lend him $10,000, collateralized by $12,500 in notes from Morris
Plan borrowers. Tom Boushall was not primarily interested in
making money. He was building a bank. This was the first of
several similar borrowings, which by December 1922, totaled
$159,000 from four banks and the Industrial Finance Corpora-
tion.

Commercial banking practice and what was considered sound
business would not let established banks lend money to consumers
as The Morris Plan Bank of Richmond did, but they recognized
its objective as worthy. Besides, their loans were secured by a 25
percent margin in consumer notes. One reason for the borrowings
was Phillip Levy & Company, which by the end of 1922 was
feverishly generating conditional sales paper. Discounting this
was straining the resources of the bank. Levy would go into re-
ceivership in 1924. In October the bank had agreed to handle
accounts from the Washington store, in addition to those in Richmond, Norfolk, Roanoke, and Newport News. The Washington
store had been handled through The Morris Plan Bank there.
Another was a twenty-five-hundred-dollar line of credit to Coburn

Motor Company, Richmond's Studebaker dealer, following the floor plan financing arrangement worked out by Arthur Morris. Even before the bank opened, the board had authorized renting a rear portion of the ground floor at an additional cost of fifteen hundred dollars a year; and in October, the balance of the ground floor was added to the bank's operations.

Despite the forcefully expressed doubts of several contemporary bankers, The Morris Plan Bank of Richmond in just five and a half months had firmly implanted "banking organized down to the needs of the people" in the public consciousness of Virginia's capital city. Every sort of human need was brought to its doors. Giving as references some of the most prominent names in town, a gambler asked for five thousand dollars to buy out a crooked partner. John Powell, student of Elizabethan music, wanted five thousand dollars to underwrite the Society of Anti-Miscegenation. But the great bulk of the bank's loan customers were little people, their stories reflecting stoic resignation in the face of adversity by those with limited incomes, and the desire for a better life by those who could hope for it for the first time. Their sympathetic reception, in contrast to the austere atmosphere of commercial banks, built for The Morris Plan Bank of Richmond a following whose loyalty extended even into the dark days of bread lines and bank holidays in the 1930s.

Loyal, too, was the bank's staff. Each of them had caught some of President Boushall's sense of mission. All had been charmed by a personality that made both men and women admire the man, even if they disagreed violently with his opinions. A conspicuous and highly significant trait was his sense of humor, which was often in evidence, even during some of his most bitter controversies. Long association kept Philip Woollcott close to the president as the number-two man. Tall, spare, often austere in demeanor, Woollcott was a necessary conservative counterpart to the president's obsession with innovation. "I sit at my desk," he used to explain, "and try to keep Tom Boushall's ideas from wrecking the bank." Quickly absorbing the bank's philosophy, Luke Fairbank filled lobbies with flowers, dropped leaflets from an airplane over Petersburg and administered one new branch after another. Although he had had no schooling in bank credit, Tony Adams had an infallible instinct for people and their reliability. Customers to whom he loaned money felt they were doing the bank a favor with their borrowings. As the bank's chief

counsel, Grayson Dashiell provided legal balance, and proved a
repository of ideas for getting the president's experiments out of
the binds they sometimes produced.

In the office the president never raised his voice. Where bank
personnel were concerned, he was a firm supporter, avoiding the
unpleasantness of reprimands or demotions. But there was never
any doubt that The Morris Plan Bank of Richmond was Thomas
C. Boushall and vice versa. Officers learned early to check with
the president before any major move was made and to expect a
new idea before the last one had quite taken shape. Each day's
work revolved around the president's memoranda, scratched on
a pad beside his bed each night, and emptied from a battered
briefcase each morning on the desk of Mrs. Lishman, who alone
could decipher them.

In the crush of opening and running a new and expanding
bank in Richmond, Boushall had not forgotten the bigger picture
of a branch banking empire blanketing the Fifth Federal Reserve
District. By October 1922 he and Philip Woollcott had organized
The Morris Plan Industrial Bank of Burlington, North Carolina.
Although the Richmond bank owned no stock in the new venture,
Boushall, by power of persuasion alone, convinced local investors
that Richmond should have 51 percent of the voting power on the
board of directors as a condition of receiving a Morris Plan charter.

When Tom Boushall had called on most of the Richmond bank
presidents before The Morris Plan Bank of Richmond opened,
all but one received him cordially and agreed that the city needed
an institution of the kind he described since they could not duplicate its services themselves. But they had expected a limited lending agency, satisfying a growing community concern, not an active
competitor who skated along the edge of accepted banking pro-
priety and paid 5 percent on deposits, as contrasted to their 3
percent.

From the time the bank opened, Boushall was advertising
heavily in newspapers, on the sides of trucks, and on streetcar
cards, emphasizing the 5 percent theme with eye-catching copy
that was a radical departure from their own formal announce-
ments. The new bank's giveaways and gimmicks were an affront
to many staid bankers, most of whom hardly advertised at all. In
ads and in brochures, The Morris Plan Bank's nickname was
"Character Corner," and spread across a handsome pamphlet was

Tom Boushall's familiar phrase, "Banking organized down to the needs of the people." In the eyes of his commercial counterparts, these slogans seemed to imply that their own institutions lacked the same qualities. When some of them undertook to educate the high-flying young banker from Raleigh and New York, Boushall's responses only added a personal note to their resentments.

In mid-October two presidents of local banks and the ranking vice-president of a third made an appointment, on behalf of the Richmond Clearing House Association. If Boushall was going to advertise that he paid 5 percent interest, they suggested, he ought also to state the reason, namely Arthur Morris's "unbreakable bank" provision, reserving the right not to pay out in any one month an amount greater than the previous month's income. Boushall agreed. But in fairness, he would have to advertise that their passbooks contained no such provision, and that their banks could therefore be closed by withdrawals, whereas The Morris Plan Bank could not. That ended the initial attempt.

Another attempt the following month did nothing to smooth ruffled feelings. The Morris Plan Bank had been using in its ads a cut of the Law Building the ground floor of which it occupied. Early in November, the Executive Director of the Better Business Bureau called with a complaint from one of his banker members. The ad implied, he said, that the bank owned the building. Would Mr. Boushall please remove the cut. He would be happy to, the president of The Morris Plan Bank of Richmond replied, if the First National Bank, Richmond's largest, would remove the cut of its building from its ads, since it owned only half of it.

Whatever the views of local bankers, there was no denying the new bank's balance sheet. At the end of 1922 it showed a total of $756,000, with savings deposits of $112,000, loans of $421,000, and $150,000 in borrowed money. In five and a half months, with no budget, no estimate of expenses, no hope of profit, and no idea whether he could modify the Morris Plan by paying interest on loan payments, Tom Boushall had more than doubled the total resources of the new bank. He had also established principles that would serve as subjects of lively, if not bitter, controversy both within and without The Morris Plan Bank of Richmond for many years to come.

The first year's books showed a loss rather than a profit. This could be forgiven in any bank's first year. But his officers, his stockholders, and Arthur Morris were soon to learn that growth came first with Tom Boushall. Profits would come later, if at all. For three decades he would hold fast to his priorities in the face of internal intrigue and sometimes outright opposition. Even in the free-wheeling atmosphere of the day, insiders worried over borrowing money to lend in such large amounts. They shuddered at virtually nonexistent reserves, even with risks widely spread over many small borrowers and backed by the "unbreakable" Morris Plan feature. More determined as time went on was the opposition from the outside to Boushall's undying commitment to branch banking. Breaking into the open, it would result in restrictive legislation that would retard the progress of Virginia banking for many years. The issue would be joined in Virginia primarily because Tom Boushall's vision had focused on that state almost from the beginning.

All of the large and most of the small decisions were Boushall's. He alone was willing to take on Arthur Morris or another Richmond bank president. Bank policy was Boushall policy. Thus it was a major blow when, on the first working day of 1923, the president was too ill to go to the bank. Marie's thermometer registered a high and persistent temperature. Finally a doctor confirmed her initial diagnosis of influenza.

A weak passed with no improvement, and the annual board meeting was held in the Chesterfield Apartments. Downtown Philip Woollcott was running the bank. The January board meeting elected Tony Adams and Luke Fairbank as assistant cashiers and R. Grayson Dashiell as counsel.

February came, but Tom Boushall's high temperature continued. Dr. James H. Smith, concerned over the continued fever, brought a portable X-ray machine to the apartment and soberly confided to Marie the real trouble—tuberculous pneumonia. At St. Luke's Hospital, Boushall's left lung was collapsed by a new technique, resting the infected organ by inflating the surrounding pleural cavity with normal air. By the February board meeting, it was clear that the bank would be without the services of its president for some time to come, if not permanently. To lend banking experience to the new officers, Luke Fairbank persuaded his friend and a bank customer, Charles C. Barksdale, president of the Union Bank of Richmond, to go on the board as chairman of a newly created Credit Committee to pass on loans.

April came, but brought no improvement. Marie sublet the apartment and made arrangements at Hilltop Sanitorium in Asheville, North Carolina, then the mecca for the tubercular. Arthur Morris came to reassure Marie and assure continuation of Boushall's salary of six thousand dollars. Borrowing three hundred dollars from his own bank, Tom Boushall left Richmond. Philip Woollcott kept bank reports flowing to Asheville and after a few weeks at Hilltop, the president was able to sit up in bed and resume his memoranda. For a year and a half, his suggestions still dictated major bank policy.

It would be a long road back, and there would be a somewhat uncertain reception after his extended absence. It was six months from the time Tom Boushall had left his desk before the turning point came—for him and for The Morris Plan Bank of Richmond. The staff was still loyal, but doubts were growing. John Markle, the rough-hewn coal magnate and financial angel of Arthur Morris, had several times upbraided Morris for retaining Boushall as president.

"There is a million dollars in my will for you," Markle told Morris, "but I'm cutting you off without a cent if you keep a sick man as president of that bank."

Angered by the threat, Morris refused, and in July 1923 Markle resigned from the board of the Richmond bank. Morris was to remind Boushall many times of that million dollars.

Boushall languished in Asheville, working over his bank reports and the comparatively cautious management of Philip Woollcott. Aware that the bank's board and Arthur Morris had already extended his leave more than generously, he felt helpless, his dream rapidly disappearing. At this point Dr. Charles Minor, the senior doctor in Asheville, recognized the symptoms from long experience and applied some extramedical therapy. It consisted of an angry lecture to the effect that his patient was a quitter and was surrendering to his disease without a battle. To Tom Boushall, these were fighting words. From that day on he began to improve.

On September 16 a daughter, Frances, was born to Marie. A week later her father was strong enough to be carried in a wheel chair from the sanitorium to the hospital to see the child. By the first of November he was able to join Marie and the baby in the apartment across from Hilltop, his ten-month fever gone. By Christmas 1923, they were planning a visit to Richmond in the spring. In mid-April on a six-week visit, Tom Boushall was back at his desk from ten until two each working day. Returning to

Asheville to escape the heat of Richmond, he resumed a limited schedule on October 1, 1923.

But tuberculosis was not through with Tom Boushall, nor he with it. Recurring bouts would come and go for several more years, causing him to doubt his capacity as president of the bank until they brought him to the brink of semiretirement.

With backstopping from the Credit Committee and with the Morris Plan as their Bible, Woollcott, Adams, and Fairbank kept the bank going. Late in the spring of 1923, the president had suggested by memorandum to the board that Woollcott be elected vice-president, Adams cashier, and Fairbank assistant cashier and auditor.

The savings stamp solicitation had been expanded to twenty-five drugstores around Richmond by this time, and lines of credit continued to be advanced to nearby automobile dealers and one line to the Sydnor Pump and Well Company. In the summer of 1923, optional credit life insurance was offered borrowers through The Morris Plan Insurance Society at the standard rate of 2 percent of the face value of the loan.

In the seclusion of the sanatorium, two modifications of his dream had solidified in the mind of the president of The Morris Plan Bank of Richmond. The first one was that the Fifth Federal Reserve District was simply too large an area for practical administration of a branch banking system. Accordingly his board, on the president's recommendation by memoranda, sold the minority stock in Wheeling, West Virginia, and Rocky Mount and New Bern, North Carolina, back to Industrial Finance Corporation. The immediate advantage was more money to lend from Richmond. The second conclusion reenforced an earlier conviction that minority stock ownership in the remaining Morris Plan banks or companies could be more of a liability than an asset. The parent bank had the responsibility that accompanied stock ownership without the authority to control the policies and actions of local management.

Late in 1923 the board authorized still another branch in Richmond at 1202 Hull Street to serve the former suburban community of Manchester across the James River from the downtown area of the capital city.

In January of 1924 the board acted on an earlier Boushall suggestion and purchased thirty-nine thousand dollars' worth of stock in The Morris Plan Industrial Bank of Raleigh, which Boushall had pulled off a side street and renamed on the tenuous strength of a management contract. The additional stock meant a controlling interest by Richmond in the Raleigh bank. In turn the Raleigh bank bought ten thousand dollars' worth of stock in the High Point and Durham, North Carolina, Morris Plan companies, giving Richmond a profit on the sale of the High Point and Durham stock.

The Hull Street branch opened in February 1924. In May another branch opened its doors on Fifth Street between Broad and Grace, designed to serve Central Virginia's major retail shopping center revolving around Thalhimer Brothers and Miller & Rhoads department stores just to the east of the new branch. By July the Petersburg branch had outgrown its initial quarters and was relocated in the offices of a local bank that had been merged.

Although no master plan had crystallized in the president's mind as yet, these moves set a pattern of restricting out-of-state operations and expanding those in Virginia. With additional moves that soon followed, they also began to consolidate opposition to The Morris Plan Bank of Richmond.

Immediately upon his return to his desk in October 1924, the president of the bank had launched a home-state expansion program. Letters went out to all the industrial loan associations in Virginia, asking point-blank if they would like to become branches of The Morris Plan Bank of Richmond. Predictably most did not even reply, and those that did refused, but the seed had been planted. The following month it sprouted.

Into the president's office walked Allan D. Jones, a Newport News attorney.

"I am the answer to your letter," he said. Jones was chairman of the board of the twenty-year-old Merchants and Mechanics Savings and Loan Association, originally chartered in 1904 as a cooperative by craft union members working at the Newport News Shipbuilding and Dry Dock Company. Still a one-room bank after two decades, the Association was interested in Boushall's offer. In January 1925 it became the Newport News branch of The Morris Plan Bank of Richmond, with Litt Hardy Zehmer as manager.

CHAPTER IV

Branch Banking: The Lines Are Drawn

T HUS FAR Virginia's banking fraternity had not seemed overly concerned, but they were soon to take notice.

In May 1926 another Morris Plan branch opened at 1724 East Main Street. By the end of June, Community Savings and Loan Corporation of Petersburg had been purchased, adding sixteen hundred loans to Richmond's fifteen hundred. By mid-October the Fifth Street branch had outgrown its quarters and was moved to 408 East Broad, only to outgrow this new location by the following year. Earlier in 1926 the Systematic Savings Corporation of Richmond was purchased. This small association had operated like the Morris Plan, but stalled at $150,000 in assets. As each new location was added, the irritation increased among traditional bankers over the Morris Plan's hard-sell promotion and advertising methods, which they regarded as unorthodox and which they had tried to forestall from the very beginning.

Luke Fairbanks had flowers growing in the new lobbies and even put bowls of tropical fish on view. Prizes and premiums were routine. College boys were hired to solicit accounts over the summer and experiments were undertaken with full-time commission salesmen. New branches also pushed hard on Christmas Club accounts, which paid 5 percent against the regular 3 percent offered by most other banks. This triggered the first overt move against The Morris Plan Bank of Richmond.

Several of the larger Richmond banks began to apply pressure to have the new bank and its branches join them in abandoning interest payments on Christmas Club savings. These were short-term accounts for all participating banks, and even 3 percent was a losing proposition. The Christmas Club had been a prize promotion for The Morris Plan Bank of Richmond. Although it made no money at 5 percent interest, it did attract customers. In the face of growing pressure, the president executed a finesse. The Morris Plan Bank of Richmond would eliminate interest on

Christmas Club savings if the three largest banks in town—First and Merchants, State-Planters, and American National—would each deposit fifty thousand dollars in The Morris Plan Bank of Richmond, to remain there from December 1927 to March 1, 1928. Somewhat to Boushall's surprise, the three agreed to the bargain. The mutual concession by three banking giants indicated that along with its growth in loans and deposits, the new bank was putting on political muscle through its growing support by small savers, but even Tom Boushall had not yet realized the extent of its potential.

On the heels of the deal concerning Christmas Club interest, a letter was distributed by the Virginia Bankers Association, stating that the VBA had unanimously agreed to introduce a bill in the 1928 legislature limiting interest on savings to 4 percent. By return mail Sam Keyes, the legislative committee chairman, got a letter from President Boushall. Mr. Keyes was totally incorrect, the letter declared, to proclaim the decision unanimous. The Morris Plan Bank of Richmond had not been consulted, had not voted on the question, and was heartily opposed to it.

Back came a five-page reply. Boushall took it to Grayson Dashiell.

"When anybody takes five pages to prove he was right, something must be wrong," said Tom Boushall.

Both Boushall and Dashiell knew what it was. Colonel Thomas B. McAdams of State-Planters had constantly reminded Boushall that if he kept on paying 5 percent the banks of Virginia would legislate him out of business. Then in late January 1928, Dashiell called to arrange an interview with Keyes and Scott Irby, secretary of the VBA legislative committee. Keyes opened the conversation.

"Mr. Boushall, we know you can defeat the limitation on interest. We also know you would like to have branches in Norfolk and Roanoke. Would you consider joining us in supporting the 4 percent limitation if we support you in a section of the code that would permit you to establish branches in these two cities?"

Despite its growth on paper, The Morris Plan Bank of Richmond had been in a slowly tightening vice, paying 5 percent on savings while most Virginia banks paid 4 percent and Richmond banks 3 percent. Here was a way to get off the hook, with two branches thrown in.

"We'll have to think about it and let you know this afternoon," he said.

The VBA delegation left. Boushall, Woollcott, and Dashiell conferred briefly, waited anxiously until an appropriate interval had passed, and then called to accept the offer. That evening, by prearrangement, Tom Boushall and Scott Irby walked into the joint hearing of the house and senate committees on banking and insurance with Boushall's arm around Irby's shoulder. Waller Holladay, vice-president of the American National Bank and a Richmond state senator, held up a copy of the new code.

"Mr. Boushall, do you support the wording of this code as now amended, including specifically the clause on the limitation of 4 percent interest that can be paid on savings accounts?"

"I do," said Tom Boushall.

The committees reported the bill, and it was passed the next day.

It had been news to Tom Boushall that he could have defeated the limitation on interest payments, but the elaborate preparations for the joint committee hearing indicated that the older VBA heads were better politicians than he was.

A pact among bankers to limit the interest paid their constituents was not calculated to warm the hearts of legislators, and The Morris Plan Bank of Richmond was already established as the financial champion of the little man. Of this, Richmond bankers had been advised by the highly influential Dr. Douglas Southall Freeman, editor of the Richmond *News Leader,* who had editorially advocated more banks like The Morris Plan Bank of Richmond to serve the creditless public. Along with other newspapers in the state, the News Leader emphasized the point by loudly proclaiming in the wake of the 1928 act that a deal had been made between the state's leading banks and The Morris Plan Bank of Richmond. There had indeed been a deal, but its implications went much deeper than bank officers at Eighth and Main quite realized.

Branch banking was anathema not only to most commercial banks in Virginia but to most of the rest of the nation as well. In 1922 the American Bankers Association had passed a resolution proclaiming that "branch banking is contrary to public policy, violates the basic principles of our government, and concentrates the credit of the nation and the power of money in the hands of a few." One troublesome complication was that state-chartered banks in most states, including Virginia, could branch by starting new banks anywhere almost at will, while national banks, which included Virginia's largest—First and Merchants National Bank—were prohibited from branching by the National Bank Act of 1864. To end this discrimination, national banks elsewhere had tried since 1921 to acquire at least limited branching authority from Congress, but the best they had been able to get was authority to branch in the head-office city granted by the McFadden Act of 1927.

Consistently denied branching authority and generally opposed to branch banking in principle, national banks had led a campaign in state legislatures to limit branching rights by state banks. Where only eight states prohibited branching in 1910, twenty-three states had prohibited or limited branching by 1930. The 1928 Virginia act had been a compromise. The banks of the state had removed the thorn of 5 percent interest paid by The Morris Plan Bank of Richmond in exchange for branches in two additional cities. The more the Morris Plan continued to flourish, the more its competitors were convinced that this was the limit. No additional cities would henceforth be invaded by the flag-waving troops from Eighth and Main. The act itself would finally precipitate the next skirmish over branch banking. Virginia's constitution prohibited special legislation applying only to a specific city or county. To get around this stipulation, the 1928 act authorized branching by any bank into cities of fifty thousand or more, which included Norfolk and Roanoke. But it would shortly include other cities as Virginia's urban growth gained momentum, and once more raise the question.

Another provision of the 1928 act enabled all banks to react to suburban growth by permitting mergers or acquisitions at will in the bank's home city or county and within twenty-five miles of the parent bank, provided the merged bank had been in operation two years or more. In some cases the State Corporation Commission, which regulated banking, could waive the two-year provision. Initially the suburban branching authority was as much a boon to The Morris Plan Bank of Richmond as to any other bank, but it would prove troublesome later on.

Meanwhile the 1928 amendments established The Morris Plan Bank of Richmond as the only banking enterprise encompassing Virginia from Norfolk on the East Coast to Roanoke at the edge of the mountainous southwestern end of the state. To capitalize on this unique status, the bank changed its name to The Morris Plan Bank of Virginia.

In addition to adding new prestige, the reduction of interest payments from 5 to 4 percent, the new legal limit, seemed to reassure depositors. It removed any public suspicion that something must be wrong with a bank that paid 5 percent while others paid 4 or 3 percent. To offset any possible withdrawals when the interest rate dropped, the bank put on a campaign advertising that it would pay 5 percent on deposits received before the new law became effective in late June. These new deposits, plus new money at 4 percent, enabled the bank to cover some $500,000 in withdrawals from the 5 percent backlog of deposits, plus another $150,000 in special deposits received late in 1927, and still end the year 1928 with a net increase in savings of $750,000.

With a new name, new prestige, and a 20 percent reduction in interest costs, the bank was in business as a savings institution. Savings deposits increased each year until the bank holiday of 1933.

The changes also pumped new enthusiasm into bank personnel. Luke Fairbank put on a campaign in the name of The Morris Plan Bank Club, one of his major promotion ideas. Philip Woollcott went to Roanoke to open the new branch by July 1. Tom Boushall tackled Norfolk where he was a board member, and where the management and directors of the original Morris Plan Bank were reluctant to lose identity in a merger with the burgeoning younger Richmond institution.

By virtue of the original agreement of 1921, the Richmond bank owned 40 percent of the stock in the Norfolk bank, although not enough to force the issue. But Industrial Finance Corporation, now renamed the Morris Plan Corporation of America, also owned stock. Arthur Morris agreed to vote this stock in favor of the merger, and with some reluctance, the Norfolk interests went along. On December 1, 1928, the merger was completed, and another balance sheet of approximately $1 million was added to The Morris Plan Bank of Virginia. With the openings in Roanoke and Norfolk, the six-and-a-half-year-old bank headquartered in Richmond increased the number of its savings accounts in calendar 1928 from 11,886 depositors to 34,545. Loan customers increased from 15,213 to 24,884, to give a total year-end customer account figure of 59,429. During the year, total bank resources increased 60 percent, and the number of customers, 109 percent. At year-end, the bank stood fifth among all Morris Plan banks in the country. The interest rate agreement also enabled Tom Boushall to resume interest payments at 4 percent on Christmas Club accounts. A new club promotion brought in 15,708 new customers during the year.

To support larger deposits and two new offices, the capital account had to be increased. Four thousand shares with par of twenty-five dollars were offered at fifty dollars and were oversubscribed well before the closing date. As part of the price of new branches in Roanoke and Norfolk, Myon E. Bristow, state banking commissioner, required the phasing out of the not too successful Eighteenth Street and Hull Street branches. This proved to be an added bonus to the code amendment.

Even before the 1928 branch banking amendments, there had been evidence that the Morris Plan and consumer banking were attracting more concerned attention from commercial lending sources. In the free-spending, anything-goes atmosphere, combined with the low commercial interest rates of the late twenties, bankers were generally reappraising the profit possibilities of consumer lending. In Richmond The Morris Plan Bank was about to face its first real competition since its founding in 1922.

On June 27, 1927, the city's morning newspaper carried a large display ad announcing a personal loan department at the American National Bank. Appearing without warning, the ad caused consternation at The Morris Plan Bank of Richmond. The officers met President Boushall at his office door in a body. How, they asked, could their own bank compete with the third-largest bank in town? By way of response, Boushall made an impromptu speech.

"Gentlemen," he said, "this is the best thing that could have happened to us. For over five years we have been desperately paddling a small canoe upstream. Now we have a large tugboat pushing us from behind."

Walking to his desk, he wrote out an ad for the next morning's paper, welcoming American National to the fold of consumer banking "in which this bank has long pioneered." As Boushall had hoped the ad took a good deal of the steam out of American National's announcement. Subsequent events demonstrated that there had not really been a major threat from that quarter. American National had opened its new department on a side street, safely clear of its prestigious main lobby. In charge was Littleton Fitzgerald, from whom Boushall had tried to buy the old Fidelity Loan and Savings Company in 1921. When American

National, renamed American Bank and Trust Company, failed
to open after the bank holiday of 1933, The Morris Plan Bank of
Virginia bought its entire consumer loan portfolio sight unseen.
During the almost six years of its operation, it had accumulated
total outstanding loans of only $126,000. This insignificant
result indicated another reason why commercial banks has not
entered the consumer credit field earlier and why they were not
initially successful when they did.

Experience had taught Morris Plan bankers that they had to
set up complete and rapid servicing of loans for individuals not
accustomed to dealing with banks. Borrowers had to be thoroughly
briefed on repayment procedures. Notices of payments due had
to be mailed promptly and followed up personally, if necessary.
Payments had to be posted daily. In short, rapid cash turnover
made consumer loans potentially profitable, but they required
much more attention to detail and therefore a far larger personnel. Nevertheless consumer financing by commercial banks had
arrived in the late 1920s. In 1928 Boushall's old alma mater, The
National City Bank of New York, announced a personal loan
department. In Richmond six commercial banks followed suit
in rapid succession.

The entry of commercial banks into consumer lending precipi-
tated a countermove by Morris Plan bankers, especially the president of The Morris Plan Bank of Virginia. If other banks moved
into their field, they would move into the commercial bankers'
exclusive domain of demand deposits and checking accounts. This
would take some time. Demand deposits would turn Morris Plan
companies into full-fledged banks, affected by all banking laws.
Besides, Arthur Morris was adamantly opposed to the move. Demand deposits would have to wait, but they would also have to
come.

Meanwhile Richmond's Morris Plan president was called on
the carpet to defend a practice that he alone followed—the payment of 3 percent interest on deposits assigned to repay loans.
From New York, James A. Hoyt, president of The Morris Plan
Corporation of America, which had succeeded Industrial Finance
Corporation as the parent of Morris Plan companies, issued a
directive to Boushall. The inconsistency of paying interest to a
man repaying his debts had to cease. Boushall's reaction was
characteristic. The Morris Plan Bank of Virginia would talk
about the 3 percent interest inconsistency, he wrote back, when

Mr. Hoyt cleaned up all the other inconsistencies in the Morris Plan. Hoyt called a meeting of corporation bank managers in his office. Boushall was to state his case and abide by a majority vote. Boushall repeated the arguments he had used on Arthur Morris. Not a single fellow Morris Plan banker voted against the Richmond president. But there were other Morris Plan bankers who belonged to their own organizations. They challenged Boushall to defend the interest payments before the annual convention of The Morris Plan Bankers Association. This second audience was hostile from the beginning. Boushall was known as a Morris man. Furthermore he had the unwelcome habit of jabbing with unerring accuracy at uncomfortable truths. His auditors were frankly incredulous when the Richmond president cited chapter and verse to prove that the 3 percent interest payment actually amounted to only a fifth of 1 percent on the face of the bank's total loan portfolio.

Interest was paid quarterly. On a loan taken out January 1, no interest was therefore paid until April 1, and then only on the amount of the monthly payments for the balance of the year, or nine months. On July 1 interest was paid on second-quarter loan payments for six months. On October 1 it was paid on third-quarter payments for three months. No interest was paid on the final three months of payments. The agreement with the borrower also stated that no interest would be paid for any quarter in which payments had been delinquent, which occurred in at least 25 percent of the loans outstanding.

The sixteen management members of the parent Morris Plan Corporation of America were to have their innings. They had never favored Boushall's scheme for controlling all Fifth Federal Reserve Morris Plan banks from Richmond. In order to achieve that control, Boushall had to have parent corporation approval and money. Toward the end of 1926, it became clear that neither would be forthcoming. It was also clear that the Richmond bank's primary need was for money to continue its own spectacular expansion and to meet the steady demand for new loans. If, instead of buying more stock in some of the district's Morris Plan banks in order to gain control, the parent corporation would buy back some more of the stock the Richmond bank owned, Richmond would acquire much needed cash and Arthur Morris could heal a sore spot on his New York board. Accordingly in mid-November 1926 Richmond sold back to New York all of its minority holdings in Durham, High Point, New Bern, Columbia, Lynchburg, and Portsmouth, together with 5 of the 125 shares in Charlotte and 5 of the 100 shares in Rocky Mount, for a total of $133,520.57 book value. This left Richmond with minority holdings in Charlotte and Rocky Mount, which eventually were also sold to New York, and majority control in Raleigh, Greensboro, Winston-Salem, and Asheville. The last would be sold and then repurchased, and finally figure prominently in the history of The Morris Plan Bank of Virginia.

The growth of the Richmond-based enterprise in Virginia and its unique status as the only branch banking system in the state were focusing the president's sights on the Old Dominion as the locale of his contribution to banking organized down to the needs of the people. He had never been satisfied to have the Richmond bank remain within the narrow confines of the Morris Plan. But to compete successfully with entrenched banking empires in the financial center of his adopted state, all things had to be sacrificed to growth, and innovation was essential.

Whether it was conceived by Arthur Morris, Tom Boushall, a staff member, an officer, or simply borrowed lock, stock, and barrel from some other institution, any new means of building volume or building employee incentive was worth a try. Some were successful, some languished for lack of attention, some expired almost at birth.

In 1926 bank advertisements urged home improvement loans, with twelve months to pay, thus anticipating the Federal Housing Administration by about six years. The following year Arthur Morris advanced a plan for the purchase of small homes with loans up to 80 percent of appraised value.

A management training institute was started in the John Marshall High School auditorium, with assistance from the U.S. Department of Commerce, for family grocery store operators. It was not too successful. The families kept eating up the groceries, and the stores collapsed and closed.

Taking a leaf from Boushall's own experience at the National City Bank of New York, the Richmond bank in July 1927 recruited its first college trainee, Ernest P. Mangum. A full-fledged training program was to come much later. Also from the National City Bank came the idea for The Morris Plan Bank Club of 1927. All employee loans were made through the club, and employee savings were paid 7 percent. The club also engineered a heavy calendar of employee social events.

As he passed by the Emigrant Industrial Savings Bank in New York in June 1928, Tom Boushall noted their sign, "Interest from Day of Deposit to Day of Withdrawal." When he got back to Richmond, The Morris Plan Bank of Virginia adopted the practice, continuing it until the bank holiday year of 1933. Also in 1928, the bank joined the Travelers Insurance Company in setting up a plan for group employee coverage, beginning at a thousand dollars for the lowest-paid employee and graduating to officers at five thousand. The insurance program was a lesson in employee relations. The bank was footing the entire bill, but the employees did not respond in appreciable numbers. When in 1933 they had to begin paying fifty cents a month, with the bank paying the rest, the number of policies increased.

In 1927 a bonus of 1 percent of annual salary for employees of one year or less, graduating to 2 percent for those with at least two years of service, was inaugurated. Appreciation was heightened by the stipulation that officers got their 2 percent only if bank earnings did not fall below 14 percent. Nor were customers forgotten. Late in 1929 Philip Woollcott arranged for borrowers who were covered by Morris Plan Insurance Society Life Insurance and who became ill to call members of the Instructive Visiting Nurses Association free of charge. The president himself was still preaching doctrine well ahead of his time, and it usually fell on deaf ears.

With a politely applauded speech to The Morris Plan Bankers Association convention in Richmond's Jefferson Hotel, he launched a long, if lonely, campaign for bank research. But neither he nor Philip Woollcott would buy innovation for its own sake. Despite pressure from The Morris Plan Corporation of America, they refused to commit the Richmond bank to allout participation in Arthur Morris's plan for a national trade acceptance operation, an extension of the Phillip Levy idea. As a result the Richmond bank was later saved substantial losses suffered elsewhere by more pliable Morris Plan management.

The continual launching of new ideas and the periodic defense of existing practice would have taken their toll on a man in perfect health. After five months back on the job, the fever returned and the doctor once more put Boushall to bed for two months, while Philip Woollcott again ran the bank. Besides the physical strain, these recurring illnesses kept the Boushalls in financial straits. Dealing in small personal loans, Morris Plan bankers were seldom offered stock or financial connections with business enterprises they loaned money to, as were commercial bankers. Even when his own bank finally moved into the commercial field, the president frowned on the practice. While he spent full time on the financing of other families, Tom Boushall spent little time on his own.

In 1928 he purchased a lot on Rio Vista Lane with a check not to be cashed until payday. The house itself he financed with both first and second mortgages, paying off the latter and providing money for furnishings by playing the stock market on margin. Between periodic bouts with his illness, he continued to keep respect in the eyes of Arthur Morris himself.

Early in 1928 he went to Florida at Morris's request to check on several Morris Plan banks that had been having difficulty in the wake of the 1925 land boom in that state. The following November he sailed for England at Morris's request to look into the problems Morris was having in pursuing his ambition to become an international banker, having first talked Morris into paying Marie's expenses for the trip. He returned to advise Morris to fire his two representatives in Paris as untrustworthy and to forget about sinking five hundred thousand dollars in an attempt to start a Morris Plan Bank of England.

Richmond's commercial bankers were becoming increasingly concerned by the competition they were getting from The Morris Plan Bank of Virginia. In late 1928 and early 1929, a group of them raised a seventy-five-hundred-dollar pool to finance a series of newspaper advertisements aimed at the bank. The ads sounded the theme that business could succeed best by sticking to old-line commercial banks. Except for its automobile lines, the bank had touched only lightly on the commercial loan business. The general public, in its native wisdom, took the ads to mean that the commercial banks were concerned over the new bank's growth. Hearing that his competitor's advertising fund had been exhausted, the puckish Mr. Boushall sent word to the agency involved that The Morris Plan Bank of Virginia would put up the next seventy-five hundred dollars if the sponsoring banks would continue the ads.

The automobile, more than any other factor, shaped American life in the late 1920s. With a view to enlarging its own relatively small dealer floor plan financing, the bank in 1928 arranged to buy out S. R. Brame, who had been operating a local dealer finance company under the name of General Finance Corpora-

tion. With the purchase came S. Mayo Shugart, the previous manager of General Finance. Shugart knew the business. He also
knew most of the dealers in central Virginia by their first names.
These characteristics were not unique, but Shugart's arrangement with the bank was. He ran the automobile finance department on a profit-sharing basis. Initially this proved a mutually
beneficial system. Dealer financing grew apace, but like the bank
itself Shugart's was a one-man operation. The profit-sharing feature was also contrary to Morris Plan practices. It would finally
help bring about a day of reckoning for the Richmond bank and
its president.

The acquisition of General Finance Corporation was only the
beginning of the bank's next period of expansion. The president
was determined to take full advantage of its unique status as the
only bank in Virginia with statewide branches. In Norfolk an
inflated stock swap and sixty thousand dollars in cash exchanged
the 1928 building of the old Merchants and Mechanics for new
quarters in the former Norfolk National Bank building. In Petersburg, where the branch had been leasing the Mortgage Guaranty
Company building, the purchase of the structure was arranged.
The building was outgrown twice in subsequent years. In Roanoke, where the Richmond bank had picked up the personal loan
department of the Roanoke Securities Corporation, new offices
were rented at the corner of Jefferson and Luck. In Richmond,
headquarters had moved up through the fourth floor of the old
hotel building and spread over more space on the ground floor as
well. There was still room in the former hotel, but the president of
The Morris Plan Bank of Virginia had decided that the state's
only branch banking enterprise was worthy of its own headquarters building. Few suspected that the 1929 Wall Street crash was
in the offing as he began a search for a construction site.

By late 1929 physical expansion, acquisitions, and the president's plan for the new building had brought the need for more
capital to the critical point. The implications of the October 30,
1929, stock market crash were slow in reaching the South. Morris
Plan bankers felt secure in any event, behind their "unbreakable"
feature. Their risks were spread over many small borrowers, and
few of their loans were secured by stock shares. But it was not a
good time to float new stock issues. In New York The Morris
Plan Corporation of America was short of ready cash and could
not have subscribed to its share of another issue, as it had done

so often before. Additional shares sold by The Morris Plan Bank
of Virginia would have reduced New York's stock holdings below
the current 57 percent, and forced it to relinquish control of the
bank. But New York did have shares in a number of Morris Plan
banks outside of Virginia. Boushall had started the Richmond
bank on just such a base. Now he prepared a similar series of
maneuvers to finance its continued growth.

The immediate object was $800,000 in added capital and sur-
plus for Richmond. The president went after it in three steps.

The bank issued the $800,000 in new stock shares, selling
$400,000 worth on the open market. The Morris Plan Corpora-
tion of America subscribed to the other $400,000 to preserve its
57 percent interest in the Richmond bank. In order to give the
parent corporation its money back. Richmond bought for $400,-
000 cash New York's 99 percent ownership in The Morris Plan
Bank of Washington, D.C., and its 51 percent ownership of The
Morris Plan Bank of Wilmington, North Carolina, which Boushall and Woollcott had organized in 1928. To get Richmond's
$400,000 back, the bank organized The Morris Plan Regional
Investment Corporation. To this new agency were pledged Richmond's stock holdings in Raleigh, Greensboro, Winston-Salem,
Washington, and Wilmington. In exchange for these bank stocks,
Richmond took all of the stock of the regional investment corporation. But the bank stocks were transferred to the new corporation at a figure $400,000 above their value as carried on Rich-
mond's books. Reflected in the value of the new corporation's
stock, this gave Richmond a $400,000 paper profit, which could
be listed as capital. The net result was that Richmond got its
$800,000 in hard cash, an additional $400,000 added to assets, and
picked up majority holdings in Washington and Wilmington.

It also produced a liability that loomed significantly a few
years later. In the bank's year-end report to the State Corporation
Commission, the transaction showed at a $400,000 profit. State
Banking Commissioner Myon E. Bristow took immediate exception. The bank would have to reverse the entry in its 1930 statement. Thus while the bank in 1929 showed an extra profit of
$400,000, its 1930 statement showed a corresponding $400,000
loss. Boushall could never make Arthur Morris understand that
the bank had not actually lost money in 1930. As a consequence,
the $400,000 was added to a growing black book of sins compiled
against the Richmond president by New York.

CHAPTER V

Damn the Torpedoes

ALTHOUGH IT PRODUCED scare headlines and sui-
cides in New York, the stock-market crash of October
1929 produced no panic in Richmond or in other areas of
the country far removed from its financial heartbeat. Between
the first market break in October and the second break in the
late spring of 1930, Dashiell, Woollcott, Adams, and Boushall had
floated a fifty-thousand-dollar loan in New York to buy Richmond
bank stock and had resold these shares to pay off the loan. While
the 1930 break awakened the country to what was really happen-
ing to its economy, southern business did not really feel the pinch
for almost a year. Bank failures did not reach catastrophic proportions for almost two years. The Morris Plan Bank of Virginia
continued to act as if nothing had happened, plowing ahead with
by far its largest expenditure in the form of a new Richmond
headquarters.

For the year 1929, when many of the country's commercial
banks had shown decreases in total savings, the seven-year-old
bank in Richmond had a net gain of $650,000. Total resources
were up $2,980,000 for the year, or 24.1 percent of the aggregate
gain for all 323 banks in Virginia. By the end of the year, the
bank and its branches had become the eighth-largest banking
enterprise in the state. Its individual segments ranked fifth in
Richmond, third in Norfolk, second in Roanoke, and largest of
all in Petersburg and Newport News. Against these impressive
growth figures, the bank had shown a very modest $103,896 in
net earnings after taxes and reserves, partly because it kept its
loan interest rate steady at 6 percent, while ninety-day commercial
borrowings had been requiring higher and higher rates.

The 6 percent rate convinced many more small borrowers that
The Morris Plan Bank of Virginia was indeed their bank, but as
time went on and earnings dropped still further, the parent
corporation in New York, and even the bank's own directors,
began to harbor serious misgivings.

The market crash and the black days that followed demonstrated the basic strength of Morris Plan banks. As banks toppled across the country, they remained on a whole, sound. Their faith in the basic honesty of the little man was returned with interest. As stocks continued to plummet, speculators were jumping out of windows in New York and Chicago and bread lines and bankruptcies became common, but even the jobless borrowers came in to make their loan payments or to seek the bank's help in working out their financial difficulties.

In Virginia The Morris Plan Bank was taking advantage of the merger of weaker banks into stronger ones by moving its branches into the vacated quarters. When Luke Fairbank's promotions had crammed the Broad Street branch with 890 customers per front foot, the former quarters of Central National Bank at the northwest corner of Third and Broad streets were leased. Bank buildings were also purchased or leased in Norfolk and Petersburg. Before construction started on the new headquarters building at Eighth and Main, the bank was offered the Richmond Trust Company building at Seventh and Main, rescued from difficulty by the American Bank and Trust. It was rejected as being off the main line of bankbound traffic.

During most of 1930 economic paralysis spread slowly southward, but even in early 1931 it had not depressed real estate prices in Richmond. In January 1931 the bank completed the purchase of the northeast corner of Eighth and Main streets, a block from Virginia's financial crossroads, where Burk & Company operated a clothing store that had resisted the exodus of retail establishments up the hill toward Grace and Broad streets. For 103 feet on Main and 108 feet on Eighth, the bank had to pay three thousand dollars per front foot with a year's notice before possession.

In the spring of 1931, Morton G. Thalhimer came to Tom Boushall. O. H. Berry & Company had put up a new building at Sixth and Grace, but its customers, more aware than some businessmen of coming events, had reduced their level of purchasing. The company was about to go bankrupt. This, Thalhimer argued, would be a hazardous development for Richmond business. Five thousand dollars would make possible a merger with Burk & Company and prevent failure. In exchange for such a contribution, The Morris Plan Bank of Virginia could have its corner without waiting a year. The result was Berry-Burk and a start on the new bank building which, as it turned out, probably would never have been built had the original terms of the purchase remained in force.

Physically drained from an operation that had given him a permanently collapsed lung after a recurrence of his illness, the president of The Morris Plan Bank of Virginia took on a new set of antagonists, bank architects. He and two board members, Allen J. Saville and Edward Simpson, had agreed that the building should be large and impressive enough to dominate the corner, even if it meant initially renting out space to someone else. Saville recommended an architect who produced sketches of the traditional columned entrance and arched lobby fronting on Main Street. Boushall exploded. The last thing The Morris Plan Bank of Virginia wanted was to look like every other bank. Besides, the president wanted a corner entrance.

The architects were adamant. So was the president. Finally he resolved the impasse in a typical move. Writing off a six-thousand-dollar architect's fee, Boushall fired the architects. Sick at heart, he drove with Marie to her home in Charleston for a long weekend. The next day, sitting in bed waiting for breakfast, he fished an envelope out of his coat hanging on the chair and drew a design for a building with a corner entrance. Thus was born the architectural trademark that distinguished The Bank of Virginia and many of its branches until banks everywhere adopted contemporary design. But not without another architectural argument. From New York, at Boushall's suggestion, came representatives of Hoggson Brothers, respected bank architects. Boushall showed his sketch. This time the architect threw up his hands.

"All bankers want corner entrances," he said, "but it won't fit with what you need."

"Thanks for coming down," said Tom Boushall. "We'll look for another architect."

The man from Hoggson reconsidered. An elevation of the new design appeared in the Richmond paper on July 2. But the bank building was not yet out of the woods. Arthur Morris had opposed from the beginning the idea of an expensive new building in the midst of a national economic crisis. In the summer of 1931, Austin Babcock, representing The Morris Plan Corporation of America, had resigned from the bank board in protest over the new building plans. As late as October, with the foundations laid and steel girders lacing the sky, Morris himself, in a despondent mood, had ordered Boushall to halt the work. All of Boushall's persuasive powers had been needed to make him change his mind. Morris had troubles of his own, and they influenced his thinking when he directed that construction of the new building be halted.

Under the mounting pressure of the times, The Morris Plan Corporation's chronic money problems had been intensified until Morris had been forced to borrow money from his member banks. While the new building was under construction, he and Boushall had skirmished verbally over a requested loan of one to two hundred thousand dollars from Richmond. Despite charges of ingratitude, the president stood firmly against "upstream" loans from child to parent. Finally Grayson Dashiell proposed a solution. The Richmond bank would pay a one-time, flat sixty-thousand-dollar fee and the parent corporation would cancel the royalty of a half of 1 percent of sales finance volume that Richmond, like other Morris Plan banks, had been paying the corporation each year since its founding in 1922. Morris took the cash in hand, and the bank was free of one more tie to the parent corporation—one that, over the succeeding years, would have cost many times the sixty-thousand-dollar redemption.

Pressure was also mounting on Tom Boushall. In April 1931 overexertion had filled his pleural cavity with fluid, and this had to be periodically drained. The process kept him in and out of bed for the balance of the year.

Not only Morris, but some of his own board members were wavering on the question of overexpansion in perilous economic times. Constantly emphasizing the savings in new building costs made possible by depressed business conditions, the president had so far kept the dissatisfaction from breaking into the open. By midsummer 1931 bank failures were increasing, lines of the jobless were lengthening, businesses everywhere were suffering, and the weak were going under in a dismal procession.

The Carrier Corporation installed air conditioning in the first floor of the new Morris Plan Bank of Virginia building for one half of its original bid. The supplier of Indiana limestone for the front of the building went bankrupt after delivery. At ten thousand dollars, the new vault was a duplicate of one that had cost The Central National Bank twenty thousand in 1928. Although the bank had paid a total of $303,000 for the land, the entire building, including the air conditioning, came to only $360,000. Meanwhile new alarms over the solvency of the bank and the competency of its president had arisen to haunt Arthur Morris and The Morris Plan Corporation of America directors.

Boushall had chosen March 1931, with the market crash of the previous October still reverberating like receding thunder, to propose that the Richmond bank do what no other Morris Plan bank had ever done—accept demand deposits and service corresponding checking accounts. To ensure safety and acceptance in Morris Plan circles, the innovation would be tried out first in a small way at the Newport News branch. Arthur Morris would have none of it. Demand deposits would cancel the "unbreakable" feature of Morris Plan banks. They would wreck everything that he had tried to build over the past twenty years. And of all people his protégé was the one to propose the move. The argument generated more heat than the many that had preceded it. In the end Tom Boushall had to compromise.

Newport News would experiment with demand deposits and checking accounts, but the Morris Plan Bank of Virginia and its branches would have to set aside 25 percent of demand deposits as a cash reserve, another 25 percent in bonds as a further reserve, and lend out only 50 percent of the demand deposits. At first both Morris's fears and Boushall's hopes proved unfounded. Checking accounts grew slowly, even after they were offered in Petersburg and the new service was featured when the building at Eighth and Main was opened. It was not until September 1932, when the bank offered employees a dollar for each new checking account they could acquire, that business began to pick up. Eventually Morris was converted to the idea, but as the storm clouds gathered over The Morris Plan Bank of Virginia, demand deposits loomed as an unprotected liability.

The real reasons for Boushall's insistence were two. The first was that checking accounts were one more step toward the full-fledged banking institution Boushall had always visualized. The second was that Mayo Shugart's automobile financing was taking larger and larger chunks of available cash. Demand deposits would provide new cash without borrowing. But with demand for new loans constantly shrinking, the idea of accepting vulnerable new liabilities in order to get money to lend seemed incongruous to Arthur Morris, especially against the backdrop of the times.

In July 1931 the president of The Morris Plan Bank of Virginia could look ahead to December and see an impending crisis of major proportions. Its cash position weakened by extensive outlays for new buildings, the bank would have to pay out some six hundred thousand dollars in Christmas Club savings. The grapevine was no doubt aware of some of the bank's internal troubles. It would be a good idea to check out lines of credit long established with sources in other cities. Routinely Tony Adams mailed off a note for fifty thousand dollars to Billy Augustine, who was then a vice-president of the Shawmut National Bank in Boston—far enough away so that a negative reply would not set the rumors flying. Back came a wire from Augustine: "Note not discounted. Have Boushall come to Boston at once."

Here was the tip-off. The line of credit was canceled. Undoubtedly lines in other cities would be as well. There would be little use in trying other banks for new loans.

Giving the matter some thought, Tom Boushall went to see A. E. Duncan, president of the Commercial Credit Company in Baltimore. Duncan began the interview by calling in a vice-president.

"Henry," he said, "I want you to meet your alibi for getting so little business in Virginia. This is the president of The Morris Plan Bank of Virginia."

Over luncheon the two worked out an arrangement. Commercial Credit would open a $1 million line of credit to the Richmond bank, secured by $1,250,000 of the bank's retail automobile paper. It was the same formula Boushall had used in the early twenties to borrow money for lending purposes from Richmond banks. To a lending agency specializing in automobile financing, the collateral was unquestionable. Saying nothing about the new line of credit except to his own bank associates, Boushall prepared to execute still another time-honored maneuver. To show $1 million in new borrowings when the word was out that the bank was in trouble would be extremely hazardous. Instead he fell back on the technique of creating another holding company, this time the Old Dominion Acceptance Corporation.

First the bank bought $250,000 in Old Dominion stock. This provided the cash margin for the Commercial Credit loan. Then the bank sold Old Dominion $1,250,000 in automobile paper. Old Dominion used this as collateral to borrow from Commercial Credit. The transactions then showed on the bank's books as increased investments, rather than as increased borrowings, as assets rather than as liabilities. Actually only $600,000 was borrowed from Commercial Credit—just enough to pay off the Christmas Club members. With new loan volume shrinking and old loans being paid off, cash flowed into the bank in increasing volume. By April 30, 1932, Commercial Credit had been paid off, as well as some $500,000 in previous borrowings from other banks. Having served its purpose, the Old Dominion Acceptance Corporation was subsequently dissolved, and Tom Boushall faithfully promised his board he would never again ask to borrow money to lend. But trouble loomed from a familiar source—thin reserves and even thinner earnings. Loans were being paid off steadily, but few new ones were being made from which the bank could deduct its 6 percent and pay its expenses.

Banks everywhere were suffering in the same fashion. More than thirteen hundred had suspended operations in 1930 and another two thousand in 1931. In a vicious circle the nation's economy slid deeper into the morass. Banks dumped their securities to prevent additional losses, depressing the market even more. As banks continued to fail, depositors withdrew their money from those remaining in business, thus increasing the panic. Looking for cash to meet withdrawals, banks pressured borrowers to repay short-term paper, and distrust of banks brought more withdrawals.

Their loans called, business firms were forced to liquidate their inventories. Plain citizens tightened their belts, and the demand for consumer loans dwindled to a trickle. Caught between reduced income from a slack demand for loans and the need to pay higher interest rates to attract depositors, banks everywhere were feeling the pressure on earnings.

The Morris Plan Bank of Virginia was still paying 4 percent on savings deposits and 3 percent on assigned deposits. Month by month earnings declined as interest fell on a shrinking volume of new loans. There was mounting apprehension that the bank would be unable to pay its staff and carry the building at Eighth and Main.

His left lung still draining, Tom Boushall lay awake nights wrestling with the problem. By the time of the board meeting in January 1932, he was ready with an answer. From its founding the bank had operated according to the Morris Plan on a cash accounting formula, discounting loans in advance and listing the total deducted interest less expenses, as monthly income. Under this cash accounting system, earnings fluctuated month by month with the volume of new loans. As long as loan volume was increasing, there was no problem. But when loan volume was dropping sharply, while expenses remained constant, a low loan month might find the bank without any appreciable income. Banks operating on the more conservative unearned discount level reserve method added the interest to the face of the loan and only drew down the aggregate monthly interest as earned every thirty days. This system stabilized monthly earnings and spread them over the entire loan portfolio.

The problem was how to make the transition. The unearned discount reserve system required using the monthly interest on all loans outstanding. But the bank had already deducted the interest on all its then outstanding loans. The only possible answer was to create an unearned discount reserve. Accordingly the bank took a hundred thousand dollars from surplus and a like sum from undivided profits and set up an unearned discount reserve of two hundred thousand dollars. As each new twelve-month loan came in, the interest was deducted and added to this reserve. Each month one-twelfth of the interest on that month's loans, plus one-twelfth of the interest on all loans outstanding, was drawn down to meet expenses and add to earnings. Not all the board members understood the implications of the new discount reserve. If some of them saw that the transition from the old system meant counting the interest on loans outstanding twice, they said nothing. The bank was in trouble and they trusted the president when he said this was the way out. Low-volume loan months would be cushioned by increments of interest from previous months and from the total loan portfolio. Fluctuations in earnings would thus be compensated for.

Two impending disasters at least temporarily averted, Tom Boushall headed for Walter Reed Hospital and the last and by far the most devastating battle with his illness. For nine years infection had been eating away at the inside of his chest. Fluid continued to build up in his pleura at the slightest exertion. Arresting the progress of the disease and effecting a permanent cure would require drastic surgery.

In January 1932 Boushall was admitted into the crusty presence of Colonel William L. Keller, chief of surgical services and commanding officer at Walter Reed Hospital. After extensive tests and examinations, the Colonel pronounced the verdict. In four operations over a three-month period, he would cut through all the ribs on the left side, remove the top of the pleura and treat the bottom half until it was completely healed.

"You have one chance in twenty to survive," the Colonel said in summary, "but what's that to you? You're no good as you are. If I kill you, you'll be no worse off."

Shaken, Boushall called Grayson Dashiell. He requested that the bank's attorney make out his will and suggested to the board that he resign or take a leave without pay. Dashiell subsequently brought word that the board's only wish was for the president's recovery. Arthur Morris wired the corporation's blessing from New York. Once more Philip Woollcott took over the operation of the bank, this time without even the benefit of memoranda from the president.

For three months Tom Boushall, in constant pain, was wheeled from operating to recovery rooms during the series of operations in which Colonel Keller cut away much of the left side of his chest as orderlies fainted at the sight of the gaping hole. Finally, as the last wound began to heal, Colonel Keller called on Marie.

"I'm sending you two home," he said. "You can look after him. If he doesn't get out of here, he'll wind up in the psycho ward."

It was a physically and mentally exhausted Tom Boushall who was pushed up the ramp into Broad Street Station on April 15, 1932. As his wheelchair approached, Luke Fairbank turned to Tony Adams and said, "He's a goner. He'll never make it to the bank again."

Sensing their doubts and harboring some serious ones of his own, Boushall made himself go to the bank an hour or two each day. Philip Woollcott continued to run the bank, carefully maintaining a sound cash position, building up savings accounts with an incentive program among bank employees, and checking details of the new building now approaching completion at Eighth and Main. With the president a semi-invalid, the stage was set for those outside the bank who had always opposed what they considered his high-handed tinkering with Morris Plan machinery, his insistence on expansion at all costs, and his brinkmanship with reserves and earnings.

These policies were in glaring contrast to steadily worsening economic conditions. After two and a half years, it was all too obvious that the nation's economic setback would not be temporary. All across the country, factory wheels had slowed. New orders had dried up. The armies of the jobless were grim reminders to those still drawing pay. One after another, banks continued to topple like forest giants in the quiet after a storm. The depression had acquired a capital *D*.

Early in 1932 Walter Head became president of The Morris Plan Corporation of America. At the April board meeting of The Morris Plan Bank of Virginia, he met the shadow of Tom Boushall, two days out of Walter Reed Hospital. Calling Philip Woollcott aside after the meeting, he suggested they talk at Broad Street Station when Head would be passing through a few weeks later. When they met again Head bluntly suggested that Boushall was through. Perhaps he should be pensioned off to one of the North Carolina banks, the one in Asheville perhaps, and Woollcott could then become president in fact. Here was real temptation. Off and on for years, Woollcott had acted as president, although he had always consulted Boushall on big decisions. After ten years he felt himself ready to run a bank on his own. But he and Tom Boushall had been friends since boyhood. Boushall had given him his big chance. Boushall's sense of mission had inspired him. Philip Woollcott rejected Head's suggestion.

Meanwhile the president slowly recuperated, issuing periodic suggestions from his office as the vice-president continued to run the bank. Boushall himself was at a low ebb in body, mind, and spirit. Word had come to him of Head's suggestion, which he knew must have been discussed both in New York and among some of his old supporters in Richmond, where there was growing concern over his ability to resume active management. Once again Tom Boushall's future at the bank he had founded was squarely up to him.

In August he and Marie made a two-week visit to Virginia Beach. Timid about his appearance and the thin layer of unsupported flesh over his left side, he entered the surf. Now the waves became his adversaries, and he fought them, left side exposed. Slowly his confidence returned.

Back in Richmond he strode briskly to Philip Woollcott's office.

"Philip," he said, "I'm ready to assume full responsibility as president of the bank."

For Woollcott still wondering whether he himself had made the right decision in rejecting the presidency, it must have been

Fifty Years of Leadership—The four men who have served as president of
The Bank of Virginia (left to right): William T. Gordon (1969–   );
Frederick Deane, Jr. (1967–1969); Herbert C. Moseley (1959–1967); and
Thomas C. Boushall (1922–1959).

The Bank of Virginia's headquarters is located on the corner of Eighth and Main streets in the financial district of Richmond. The adjoining building on Eighth Street houses the corporate offices of Bank of Virginia Company in addition to many of its affiliates.

The Morris Plan Bank, forerunner of The Bank of Virginia, was first located on the northwest corner of Eighth and Main Streets in Richmond.

Board of Directors, Bank of Virginia-Central, July 17, 1972

a difficult moment. But at least, he now had peace of mind. The matter had been resolved.

Not so the basic problem. Loan volume and earnings remained dangerously low. In its attempt to get into the commercial loan market, the bank had picked up some risks turned down by other banks, and a few of these had been written off in red ink. It also faced a paper loss of twenty-five thousand dollars after liquidating the Industrial Bank of Richmond, reorganized successor to the original Richmond Morris Plan unit, which still carried the Morris Plan diamond in order to keep it from going under.

To the bank's directors the opening of the new building at Eighth and Main on June 28, 1932, was confirmation of their fears that Tom Boushall had overreached himself. While smiling businessmen, bankers, and housewives crowded the flower-decked lobby and mezzanine, the board gathered dourly in Boushall's new office to predict that this final extravagance would break the bank. Their conclusion was more a reflection of general pessimism than a considered evaluation of the evidence. Both in Virginia and in North Carolina, each time an affiliate had moved to more elaborate quarters, it had prospered as a result. People might want small loans, but they felt insecure about making them in small offices. With banks failing everywhere, they seemed reassured by the new building and by the thought that The Morris Plan Bank of Virginia might be the exception.

Internally the bank had cut salaries 10 percent in May and again in September. Dividends had been reduced to 1 percent. In its investments the bank had steered clear of corporate or government bonds, which might be adversely affected by the coming election. Larger commercial accounts had been reduced after a few fingers had been burned. The books showed $1 million in cash. In September 1931 holdings in The Morris Plan Company of Asheville, North Carolina—of which the Richmond bank had bought control in 1929 to save it from collapse—were sold for thirty-five thousand dollars. Control would return later to Richmond.

Reviewing the bank's first decade, the 1932 annual report could say with justifiable pride that The Morris Plan Bank of Virginia had shown more rapid growth in customers, assets, and geographical distribution than any other banking institution in the state. From $375,000 in assets, it had grown to $10.4 million as of December 31, 1932. From two officers and four employees, it had spread to six offices in five Virginia cities, with a total staff of 106. It had made 224,000 loans, totaling $66.8 million and accumulated deposits of $5.9 million in 29,400 savings accounts.

To Morris Plan loans and savings certificates, the bank had added Christmas and Vacation clubs, retail and wholesale trade acceptance discounts, traveler's checks, cashier's checks, safe-deposit boxes, payment of gas, water, telephone, personal tax, and electric bills, and finally personal checking accounts. Proving the soundness of the bank's management and philosophy, losses on loans amounted to an infinitesimal one-tenth of 1 percent. But to the principal stockholders, Arthur Morris and The Morris Plan Corporation of America, these glowing statistics translated into fixed costs and frozen assets at a time when the flow of new loans had slowed until only the priming from the unearned discount reserve kept earnings above expenses. Net earnings in September 1932 totaled $447, the smallest figure in two years. Apprehension in New York was fueled early in 1933 by reports from Fred Roberts, who was sent to Richmond as an auditor.

"If you take out the premium paid in on the sale of capital stock," Roberts said, "and if you take out the transfer of capital to an unearned discount reserve, I don't believe this bank has earned a dollar since it was organized."

New York was further upset by Roberts's suggestion that Boushall be fired.

"A nice southern gentleman," Roberts had told his superiors, "who knows nothing about running a bank."

Roberts had not been quite fair and certainly not discreet, but his reports had their effect. Their impact was heightened after the bank holiday of 1933.

CHAPTER VI

Called to Account

M ANY STATES were closing their banks because of the crisis. On March 4, 1933, Franklin Delano Roosevelt was telling America in his inaugural address that "we have nothing to fear but fear itself," but even as he spoke, news wires reported that all New York banks had been closed by the governor's order, including the Federal Reserve Bank of New York. The next day the Federal Reserve Bank of Richmond closed. That day and the next, Richmond bankers talked only of what they should do. In every neighboring state except North Carolina, all banks had ceased to do business. On Sunday evening the immediate problem was solved. The new president declared a bank holiday beginning Monday morning, March 7.

For a week Main Street hummed with rumors. First and Merchants and State-Planters were sure to open. So was The Morris Plan Bank of Virginia. Odds-makers were less certain of some others. On Friday, March 11, John M. Miller, Jr., president of First and Merchants, called every Richmond bank. Each bank, it was hoped, could open on at least a 15 percent basis when the week's holiday ended on Monday. Miller called again on Saturday with new instructions from Washington. All banks would open on Monday, but on an unrestricted basis. State bank examiners would have to certify that each state bank was financially able to do so. The Morris Plan Bank of Virginia was high on this list. On Sunday evening the officers gathered at The Morris Plan Bank of Virginia for a rehearsal. The lobby was rearranged with more tellers' windows. If they could keep lines of depositors from forming, perhaps a run, if there was one, could be broken.

Someone turned on the radio. The President was speaking on a nationwide hookup. Everything is going to be all right, the hypnotic voice assured the populace. All the good banks would be wide open Monday morning. Only the bad banks would be closed. Monday dawned. Marie drove the president to the bank, then cruised Main Street with instructions to report periodically on how long the lines were at other banks. In the lobby every-

thing was ready: cash was neatly stacked where depositors could
see it, tellers were poised. At 9:00 A.M. sharp the doors of The
Morris Plan Bank of Virginia opened. Nobody was there. At 9:05
Marie called to report no lines at any bank. At 10:00 a lone customer entered sheepishly to make a deposit. There were no withdrawals all morning. The Roosevelt magic had done its work.
Every bank in Richmond, except the American Bank and Trust
Company, opened on one of the calmest days in the city's banking history.

The picture was somewhat different in Newport News and
Petersburg. There branches of The Morris Plan Bank of Virginia
were the only ones to open for several weeks. Norfolk and Roanoke had opened with the parent bank, but there was trouble in
North Carolina. Unless Richmond would guarantee deposits at
Raleigh and Greensboro, Gurney Hood, North Carolina's commissioner of banks, would keep them closed. Raleigh had made
a number of questionable, and now uncollectable, mortgage
loans. Greensboro directors had borrowed from that bank to pay
off loans at other banks.

Here was a real dilemma. Two banks carrying the Morris Plan
diamond were in jeopardy, both of them under the jurisdiction
of The Morris Plan Bank of Virginia. But if they were to open,
Richmond would have to assume a risk of unknown proportions.
If Raleigh and Greensboro did not open, Richmond stockholders
stood to lose a hundred-thousand-dollar investment, plus another
hundred thousand dollars under North Carolina's double in-
demnity clause. Either way, bank officers would not appear in a
favorable light. In the end the board took the safer course of
accepting a known liability. Raleigh and Greensboro remained
closed—another black mark, it appeared, against the leadership
of Richmond's president, for across the country only a handful
of Morris Plan banks had failed.

In contrast to the other entries in New York's black book,
Boushall had not been directly involved. In fact local management in Raleigh and Greensboro had acted in violation of specific directives. But these violations had proved to be the last
straw. For some time the parent company had been concerned
about Mayo Shugart and his automobile finance business. Auto
loans were holding volume better than the rest of the bank's portfolio, but under the profit-sharing arrangement the bank was not
getting the full benefit. Nor were the parent corporation's direc-

tors reassured when four days after the bank holiday, Tom Boushall purchased another automobile finance company, American Ideal Credit Corporation, from the Seaboard Citizens National Bank of Norfolk. This time there was no profit sharing. O. B. Wooldridge, the manager, became assistant cashier in charge of automobile finance in the Norfolk branch.

Other attempts to build loan volume had been ingenious but unproductive. An arrangement to have Western Union deliver a loan application in response to a telephone call had not produced results, nor was the response impressive to a home improvement loan promotion, featuring two years to pay, instituted the previous July.

In pre-Depression times the bank's growth figures had justified Tom Boushall's innovations and his insistence on going his own way, but when he continued blithely ahead in the face of repeated crises, New York decided it was time for the checkrein or perhaps a more drastic crackdown.

From New York came a committee of three old Morris Plan hands, Austin L. Babcock, Frank J. Scott, and Ralph W. Pitman. Babcock had resigned from the Richmond board over plans for the new building. Scott was a certified public accountant and former auditor of Chase National Bank's accounting division. Pitman had been with Morris Plan banks since college days, and was currently president of the one in Philadelphia. The committee had been empowered by the New York board to make a thorough investigation, suggest improvements, and see that they were carried out. For weeks the trio pored over bank records. As the subject of their investigation, the president was largely excluded from their sessions. Philip Woollcott, always somewhat reserved, answered questions with obvious resentment. In early May the report to the parent company directors was ready. Boushall and Woollcott were called to New York for an accounting.

The bill of particulars was extensive, but not completely damning. There were write-offs from unproductive negotiations to buy the Law Building, which had been the bank's original quarters; there was an empty gravel pit, foreclosed in an early experiment with commercial loans; and there was a twenty-five-thousand-dollar paper loss when the bank liquidated the old Fidelity bank, later reorganized into the Industrial Bank of Richmond. There was renewed criticism over C. C. Barksdale, who had helped the bank out in the early days of Boushall's illness and who had been hired when his own bank got into trouble. There were also fees for architects dismissed as well as the high overhead for the new building at Eighth and Main.

It was a troubled Arthur Morris who sent for Tom Boushall before the session with the committee. The man he could trust to tell him the truth, the protégé he had tried to persuade to become president of The Morris Plan Corporation of America, had let his own bank get into trouble. And what bank was not in trouble in 1933? Boushall wanted to know. Unbeknownst to him The Morris Plan Bank of New York, largest of them all, was in more serious difficulties than Richmond, even as they were speaking. To Arthur Morris this made the Richmond situation worse.

"That's just the point, Tom," he said. "This was no time for you to let your bank get in trouble."

There might still be a way out. Morris put a question.

"On whom," he said, "do you place responsibility?"

"Mr. Morris," he said, "you're embarrassed to ask for my resignation. Now you have it. I'm responsible for every error, every loss, every mistake. I hired everybody in the bank. I assigned every duty. I supervised every action. Now you can start out fresh with a new president who can run a bank without error or loss."

He got up and held out his hand. For a moment Morris sat still. Then he said, "Sit down, Tom. I never had more confidence in you than I have at this moment. Let's see what the committee says must be done."

With Morris won over, the session with the three trouble shooters was somewhat less severe than it might have been. Their fire was turned largely on Philip Woollcott. The bank was to amend the profit-sharing contract with Mayo Shugart, whose income at times exceeded Boushall's. It was to collect eighty-four thousand dollars in outstanding loans to key officers, directors, and employees. Finally Woollcott was to be relieved of his title as senior vice-president and of most of his responsibilities.

A chastened pair of bank officers returned to Richmond, still under the watchful eye of the parent corporation's committee. In a few weeks Philip Woollcott came to Tom Boushall. He wanted a bank of his own to run, a smaller operation with less pressure. Richmond now had a two-thirds interest in The Morris Plan Company of Asheville. Woollcott would like to take over that four-hundred-thousand-dollar operation, form a syndicate, and buy out Richmond's holdings.

"Philip," said Boushall, "as far as I'm concerned you can have anything this bank has to offer."

And so Philip Woollcott became president and chief executive officer of the bank to which he had once been tempted to retire Tom Boushall. Less than a year later, he had made good his promise and put together the necessary cash to buy out Richmond's interest. Applying what he had learned in Richmond, he built the Asheville bank into a replica of The Morris Plan Bank of Virginia, without as many far-flung branches.

Woollcott's departure left a place that was difficult for Boushall to fill. A close friend and confidant, the vice-president had also been an effective counterweight to the high-flying founder. When put to a severe test, his loyalty had been unquestionable. Intermittently during the president's nine-year illness, Woollcott had stepped aside when Boushall's strength returned. Throughout the years following his departure for Asheville, the two remained fast friends, each continuing to respect the other's abilities and preserve the warmth of long association.

By now the Richmond headquarters of The Morris Plan Bank of Virginia employed a total staff of a hundred people. To fill the void left by Woollcott, Tom Boushall went beyond the immediate staff, as he would do on many future occasions in filling top-level executive posts. Over luncheon in the middle of the March bank holiday, he, Grayson Dashiell and Gaius Diggs, who had joined the board, had hired Malcolm C. Engstrom to organize the bank's growing mountain of records and set up a statewide system of accounting controls. Now in July executive responsibilities were split. Engstrom was elected vice-president and secretary of The Morris Plan Holding Corporation, which owned the bank's buildings; the Regional Investment Corporation, which owned the affiliates; and the General Contract Purchase Corporation, a local branch of the Fifth Federal Reserve District Finance Company, which had been Arthur Morris's idea for expanding trade acceptance business. This brought the ancillary corporations under one head. There remained Woollcott's duties of running the bank while Tom Boushall kept making it bigger.

The shadow of the parent corporation's watchdog committee over his shoulder had not pleased the Richmond president, but it was obvious that New York was going to maintain a special interest in his affairs. During the committee's investigation he had been impressed with Ralph Pitman. He was a Morris Plan career man, a fact that would reassure the parent corporation. He was an able operations man, whose time was not fully occupied with running The Morris Plan Bank of Philadelphia and with his duties as president of The Morris Plan Bankers Association. Boushall went to Morris. Would he lend Pitman to the Richmond bank for, say, three days a week?

It was a calculated risk. Pitman had been openly critical of the bank's skimpy reserves and paper-thin earnings. A blunt thirty-one-year-old, who worked hard and played hard, he personified the notion that a bank should make money. But Boushall was certain that New York was going to put somebody in the Richmond bank. He preferred to pick his own man. Pitman agreed, provided his authority as executive vice-president was equal to Boushall's, even though he remained on The Morris Plan Corporation of America's payroll. But Morris, foreseeing a clash of personalities as well as philosophies, arranged for Gaius Diggs as chairman of the executive committee, to be an arbiter between the two. Boushall agreed to both conditions; then he went to Pitman.

"Ralph," he said, "you know me and I know you. So help me, I'll never go with you to ask anyone to decide between us who is right. If we can't agree in reasonable and friendly fashion, neither of us deserves his job."

But Tom Boushall was not to win over Ralph Pitman without a test of strength. At thirty-one, Pitman had a record in the Morris Plan to match Boushall's. A football fullback at Morningside College Seminary in Sioux City, Iowa, he had gone to work in the Morris Plan Bank in Denver, Colorado, while studying law at night at the University of Denver. In 1924 he earned his law degree at twenty-five. Already a vice-president of the Denver bank, he became president shortly after graduation. From Denver he went to the St. Louis Morris Plan bank and finally to Philadelphia as president of the Morris Plan bank in that city. In 1928 he became secretary of The Morris Plan Bankers Association and was later president. In Richmond he became the focal point of the parent corporation's continuing concern about the low state of reserves and earnings and Tom Boushall's insistence on running things to suit himself. From Arthur Morris, Pitman had the word that he would be president of the Richmond bank in six months. The first test came even earlier.

As an economy move Pitman proposed closing the branch at

Fourth and Grace. To Tom Boushall the branch had served the shopping area that surrounded it, as distinct from the financial district down the hill on Main Street. To Pitman it was another office only six blocks away. The issue split the board, with Grayson Dashiell and Gaius Diggs voting with New York interests in Pitman's favor. It was the first time the board had ever repudiated Tom Boushall's position. Dashiell expected Boushall to resign. But this time, the president would have been tendering his resignation to his own board not to Arthur Morris. Acceptance would have been a foregone conclusion. Tom Boushall was not about to throw away twelve years of his life's work. The branch was closed. Pitman set up a series of charts to check the results. They showed that in six years customers who moved their accounts to Eighth and Main just about offset accounts closed.

Meanwhile Pitman persuaded the Southern Bank and Trust Company to take over the old quarters and their eight-thousand-dollar rental. Southern Bank and Trust blossomed at that location. In the months that followed, the rift deepened between Pitman, the operator, and Boushall, the builder. By December 1934 Dashiell and Diggs had proposed to Arthur Morris that Boushall be made chairman of the board and Pitman become president of the bank. An informal meeting of the board at the Richmond Hotel found local board members split, with Dr. Carrington Williams, John Cecil, and Allen Saville opposing the move.

Before the January board meeting, Arthur Morris confronted Tom Boushall on the subject. Boushall, as usual, was adamant. He would not accept the chairmanship. He would not stand for reelection as a director or an officer. He would not resign. Nor would he modify his stand for growth first and profit later. The board and Arthur Morris would have to choose. There was a good deal at stake. Richmond was the second-largest bank in the Morris Plan system. At the 1933 convention of The Morris Plan Bankers Association, Boushall had been elected first vice-president. To force his resignation would raise questions well beyond the growth-versus-profits issue. And Tom Boushall was capable of forcefully articulating just what the issue had been. So might some of the board members, who could be counted on to resign in protest.

Arthur Morris went to Dashiell and Diggs. He could not support their plan to make Boushall chairman and Pitman president.

Now Allen Saville came to Tom Boushall. By withholding the voting proxy that came to the president from the parent corporation, Boushall could remove Dashiell and Diggs from the board and perhaps end the controversy. But to Tom Boushall this would have been an act of vengeance. Besides, if he were proved right in subsequent years, Dashiell and Diggs would be even stronger supporters.

With the issue resolved, there began to develop once more a bond between two strong men, with a fundamental difference of philosophy. As time went on Boushall charmed Pitman, as he had so many others, but did not change his views. From time to time Pitman would exclaim in exasperation, "I would rather run a profitable hock shop than an unprofitable bank!" Of the 3 percent interest on loan payment deposits, Pitman exclaimed, "It's crazy, paying a man to pay his debts." When Richmond's Morris Plan joined a prestige group of national banks in sponsoring the Philadelphia Symphony Orchestra over Radio Station WRVA, Pitman, though an accomplished musician, objected on the grounds that it brought in no business.

"We were all right until Christmas," he told Boushall, "then our listener died."

After board meetings Pitman and some of the younger officers would retire to the club for the evening while Boushall, who neither smoked nor drank, played bridge at his home with Marie and Arthur Morris. During one such meeting at the Hermitage Country Club, the president posed an inquiry. Drawing Pitman aside, he asked, "Why do the boys call you Ralph and me Mr. Boushall?"

"Because," said Pitman, "they respect you and they just tolerate me. It's one of your assets," he continued. "Hang on to it."

Unlike one another in so many ways, Boushall and Pitman had banking minds tuned to the same wave length. Day after day they would bring to the office memoranda on the same subject. In conversation they would often start to speak simultaneously of the same problem.

"He is not worth a damn at running a bank," Pitman summed up to associates, "but at developing a bank nobody can touch him."

One of Pitman's early priorities was to move in on Mayo Shugart and his automobile dealers. With New York's blessing, he began personal cultivation of dealers themselves, bringing their business directly into the bank. Shugart's profit-sharing agreement could not be attacked directly, but Shugart himself could be discouraged.

After 1933 it was increasingly The Morris Plan Bank of Virginia that Tom Boushall concentrated on developing.

By July the following year, Philip Woollcott had formed his syndicate and was ready to work out arrangements for taking over the Richmond bank's holdings, beginning a career in Asheville analogous to Boushall's. In the fall of 1934, Winston-Salem stock was sold to a North Carolina group. In July 1937 holdings in The Morris Plan Bank of Wilmington were sold to the new young president, Emsley Laney. With Raleigh and Greensboro already charged off following their failure to open after the bank holiday, Richmond was left with only the profitable Washington, D.C., operation.

Although Franklin Roosevelt came to power on the promise of recovery, the main thrust of the New Deal was reform. After a dozen years of backing business, the national government reversed this trend. "Rugged individualism" gave way to "the forgotten man." The Public Works Administration, the Agricultural Adjustment Act, and the National Recovery Act were followed by Social Security, the Wagner Labor Relations Act, REA, and TVA. In financial circles the restoration of banks as instruments of credit was accompanied by stiffer regulations for bankers and easier instalments for borrowers. The Federal Reserve System was reorganized and given additional powers. Commercial banks were barred from marketing corporate securities. Tough bank examiners discouraged risky loans and questioned banking practices. Gradually, most of the commercial banking system was brought under federal supervision.

Reluctant to make the old ninety-day renewable business loans at enforced low interest rates, banks turned toward term loans to industry and moved heavily into consumer finance and home mortgages backed by federal guarantees. Bank failures and greater banking restrictions made state and national banking authorities more reluctant to approve new banks, but branch banking became more prevalent. The result posed something of a philosophical dilemma for Morris Plan bankers in general and Tom Boushall in particular. A proliferation of New Deal agencies vindicated their pioneering in consumer credit and home improvement loans, but it also threatened them with restrictions. Men who had spent a lifetime extending credit to the little man did not appreciate the federal government's telling them how to do it.

Called to Washington to help iron out details of the home improvement section of the Federal Housing Act, Tom Boushall challenged Roger Steffan of the National City Bank of New York on the rate of interest to be charged, with Boushall winning support for a higher charge.

Once this issue was settled, The Morris Plan Bank of Virginia was an enthusiastic participant, since it had been in the business of home improvement loans before the federal program became law. It made the first loan under the home improvement section of the law and was the first bank in Richmond to qualify for the regular FHA home purchase program of 80-percent twenty-year loans. In a few years the bank was making more home improvement loans than all other Virginia banks and finance companies combined.

While it generated no great enthusiasm among Virginia banks generally, the FHA put the federal stamp of approval on the Morris Plan Bank of Virginia. Its president was asked jointly by the American and Virginia bankers' associations to be liaison officer between the FHA home improvement plan and banks in the Commonwealth. Boushall, Luke Fairbank, and Ernest Mangum stumped the state as federal emissaries.

Another battle was joined when The Morris Plan Bank of Virginia undertook to cover accumulated losses by selling three hundred thousand dollars' worth of preferred stock to the Reconstruction Finance Corporation, which had been rejuvenated to supply capital for industry, business, and banking. What Boushall saw was a chance to recoup the two-hundred-thousand-dollar charge-off in the failure of Raleigh and Greensboro, the loss on the Law Building negotiations, the defunct gravel pit, and various other red ink items that caused The Morris Plan Corporation of America's investigating committee to complain.

Boushall drew up a proposal. The bank would write down the par of its capital stock shares from $25.00 to $16.67. This would reduce stated capital from $900,000 to $600,000. The bank could then sell $300,000 of preferred stock to the RFC, restoring par capital to $900,000 and picking up $300,000 in cash. But Sam Husbands of the RFC saw things differently. The bank could go ahead and write off the $300,000 and still be solvent, he said.

"All you want is to get $300,000 preferred stock at 6 percent and lend it out at 12," said Husbands, "and that is not the purpose of the RFC."

But in the end the sale was approved.

The bank's move went virtually unnoticed. Major banks were also issuing preferred stock. State-Planters had issued some $2.5 million, largely to write down a heavy investment in its new building at Ninth and Main.

There were more difficulties when the Morris Plan Bank of Virginia applied for membership in the new Federal Deposit Insurance Corporation, reenforced by the Banking Act of 1933. Government officials raised the old question of whether Morris Plan companies were banks or loan companies, especially since all their deposits were savings. But the Virginia banks alone among all Morris Plan banks and companies also had demand deposits. After some delay it was approved for membership in the FDIC.

The philosophical dilemma remained. As a banker Tom Boushall could see the need for, and utilize, the Federal Deposit Insurance Corporation and the RFC. Simultaneously he could and did oppose many of the aims of President Roosevelt—so effectively, in fact, that he was one of two Virginia members of the South's Committee to Uphold the Constitution, an organization aimed at stemming the incoming tide of the New Deal.

CHAPTER VII

Still More Innovation

THE BANK'S CONTINUED GROWTH and the new prominence accorded its president combined to bring greater recognition from the Virginia banking and business fraternity. At the 1935 Virginia Bankers Association convention, Boushall was elected to the board of directors. He renewed the campaign for a formal program of bank research, which he had first urged upon that organization in 1930. When concrete results were still not forthcoming, he began in January of 1936 a series of twelve articles for *Bankers Monthly* on research possibilities. Two years later, still pursuing the subject, he wrote the Library of Congress for a bibliography.

"All we have on the subject," replied the librarian, "was written by you."

The bank would finally contribute heavily to the support of the Graduate School of Business Administration at the University of Virginia in order to realize this goal.

As vice-president of the Richmond Community Fund in 1935, Boushall found proof of what a number of family assistance loans at the bank had indicated. The depression was bearing down hard on the sick and those attempting to help them. Hospital beds were empty because those who should have been occupying them could not pay the bills.

Faced with the same problem, a group of school teachers in Texas had contracted with Baylor University Hospital in 1929 for the prepayment of hospital bills. A similar plan was in operation in Washington, D.C. With doctors Carrington Williams, Joseph Geisinger, and Henry Fletcher, he visited Washington to study the plan and became convinced that the idea was feasible. T. Norman Jones, vice-president of the Virginia Electric and Power Company, and several concerned doctors were recruited to form the Richmond Hospital Service Association. The bank loaned the association five thousand dollars. The Medical College of Virginia, St. Elizabeth's, Johnston-Willis, Retreat for the Sick, and Stuart Circle Hospital joined in sponsorship. Later on, Grace and St. Luke's hospitals became members. Boushall was the first president, Jones vice-president, and Dr. Fletcher secretary-treasurer.

Twenty-five years earlier, the problem of an unpaid hospital bill had launched the Morris Plan. Now, as the problem became greatly intensified and national in scope, The Morris Plan Bank of Virginia made possible the organization that has become the $100-million-a-year Virginia Blue Cross.

To remove any suspicion of self-interest, Boushall, as president of the new association, would not permit its funds to be deposited in his bank until 1946.

At the bank itself the "Farragut philosophy" was resumed. By the end of 1933, checking accounts had grown in number to 4,040, with $509,000 in demand deposits. But the volume in Norfolk was relatively static at 500 accounts.

In a deliberate attempt to screen out portions of the port city's transient population, Norfolk banks, prompted by Robert Beaman, president of the National Bank of Commerce, had drafted stringent rules for both borrowers and depositors. Perhaps as a result the Norfolk branch had been unable to build new checking accounts. Once the problem was identified, orders came from the president in Richmond to use Richmond Clearing House rules instead. Fearful of Beaman, Norfolk branch officers called for reenforcements. Boushall went to see the National Bank of Commerce president.

"Who does the Richmond president think he is," Beaman snorted, "trying to dictate what rules should be used in Norfolk? I wrote those rules myself in 1921. If you try to introduce your Richmond rules here, we will not clear your checks."

Outside Boushall called the two Norfolk branch officers aside.

"You will announce the new rules as we planned," he said. "The same day we will have three hundred thousand dollars in cash here from Richmond. We will clear our own checks against cash. The other Norfolk banks will have to pay us in cash."

The cash indeed came down, but Norfolk banks had gotten the word. Norfolk branch checks were cleared as usual, and within six months, Norfolk had adopted Richmond's rules. Checking accounts began to pick up. But loan volume languished at The Morris Plan Bank of Virginia and all its branches. Although earnings improved slightly, they were unsatisfactory.

In 1935 the average citizen was still hanging on to his money. The average savings deposit at the bank rose to $420.96.

The bank had been making over-the-counter loans to purchasers of new cars without collateral or endorsement. Now it began making loans to buyers of used cars, taking a lien on the car as collateral, an unheard-of move at the time. Launching a direct mail solicitation for all bank services, a special appeal for loans on both new and used cars was included. Not only were used car loans an unknown risk, but there was the danger that dealers who were selling their own loan paper on new and used cars to the bank might take offense. Some dealers did but the bank persuaded the rest that the new move would expand the overall automobile market and demonstrate the value of used cars as collateral. While this type of loan on a used car was an innovation for Virginia banks, it was in reality an extension of the Morris Plan basic philosophy. The bank would lend a responsible borrower three hundred dollars on a three-hundred-dollar car, but it would not lend an irresponsible customer a hundred dollars on a thousand-dollar car. The bank imposed conditions conducive to wise use of the new credit. With the rarest exceptions the automobile purchaser had to put up at least 25 percent of the purchase price to keep him from making too big an investment with too little equity.

New-loan volume was still low, and the bank had quantities of cash on hand from repayment of old loans. But it could be made to work harder. Capital gains were also earnings. Anticipating this development, the bank in 1931 had hired Edwin Hyde from Inglehart Investment House on Wall Street. Hyde and Boushall went to New York and opened an account at the Bank of New York, with its extensive research and investment departments and conservative advice. With a wide-spectrum portfolio of government and corporate bonds, the bank began its first true investment program, slowly building capital gains to help pay off the three-hundred-thousand-dollar preferred sold to the RFC and restore the par value of its common stock.

The investment program pointed to another idea. If the Bank of New York could attract deposits from The Morris Plan Bank of Virginia in exchange for its expertise in the bond market, why couldn't the Richmond bank merchandise its own expertise in consumer loans? Hyde collected the bank's bookkeeping and credit forms in a loose-leaf binder and set out to gain deposits from other Virginia banks in exchange for teaching them the Morris Plan system. More head-shaking ensued. Other bankers wondered why The Morris Plan Bank of Virginia would build up competition among the other banks of the state. Within the bank itself, Hyde's binder was dubbed "Morris Plan Banking in a Hundred Easy Lessons." Again the president had taken the long view. If consumer loans were generally stimulated, the Richmond bank would get its share. Meanwhile, by 1938, it had collected seventeen correspondent bank accounts, a firm foundation for a future correspondent bank division.

Allen J. Saville provided the lead for another means of building earnings by the use of banking services rather than loans. Throughout the Midwest and South, the simultaneous growth of new industry and old cities had been accompanied by a host of small, independent utility companies. In the 1920s many of these had been welded into utility holding companies, which in turn had suffered from the stock market crash and the subsequent slowdown of the economy. As utility holding companies grew bigger, specialized corporations developed to manage their holdings, including the sale of home appliances on instalment. One of these was Stone & Webster, a Boston corporation, with offices in Roanoke, Virginia. Its problem was keeping track of consumer appliance loan paper.

Boushall's solution was a refinement of the old Phillip Levy trade acceptance agreement and the bank's automobile financing for dealers. By December 1, 1935, details had been cleared with the various holding company officials, and the bank had a highly profitable operation going. It was collecting 5 percent interest each year on total appliance loan volume, but advancing only 75 percent on three-year loans, or 70 percent on four-year loans, and finally 65 percent when Stone & Webster extended loan life to five years. With Stone & Webster drawing up the monthly listings, one secretary in Roanoke could handle the paper work in a few minutes each day. Considering the bank's experience with consumer loans, risks were amply protected.

After a few years it dawned on Curzon Hoffman, the Roanoke manager of Stone & Webster, that he was doing the work and the bank was making the money. The interest rate was reduced in periodic negotiations from 5 to 3½ percent, and finally to 3 percent, when another bank solicited the business. Eight years later the holding company had sold off all the small gas companies to local interests, but the bank followed Hoffman to the Carolina Coach Company and financed his purchase of buses until competing banks pushed the interest rate below the profitable level.

The business with Hoffman illustrated the long lead The Morris Plan Bank of Virginia continued to enjoy in instalment lending and the reason it could so successfully ride the new wave of consumer financing.

While most commercial banks had moved in this direction, they could not bring themselves to believe that the risk on consumer loans was as low as The Morris Plan Bank of Virginia had so often demonstrated it to be. Furthermore it took two or three times as many man-hours to keep records on a large volume of small loans. This problem, the Stone & Webster business had shown, could be solved as far as a discount business for another firm was concerned, by means of the reconstructable record. The holding company maintained the individual records in case something went wrong with a single account. All the bank had to do each month was post totals and write a single check.

This was the exception. The greater part of the bank's business with retail or wholesale concerns, as in the case of most commercial bank consumer loan business today, went back to the Phillip Levy system. In this the bank kept the individual records for a fee in addition to discounting the paper.

Although the Stone & Webster arrangement was profitable, it was a side issue. The bank's principal business was loans, which by 1936 were improving but somewhat sluggishly. By now the bank was lending the average citizen money to meet family crises, finance the family car, furnish the house, install central heating, or add a room. One more market remained—the house itself.

The Depression had collapsed the boom in three- to five-year, nonamortized mortgage loans. Lending institutions of all kinds had been caught with reams of uncollectible paper. Foreclosures had given banks a black name almost everywhere. Even the great mutual savings banks, a prime source of home mortgage money in pre-Depression days, had cut these loans by one-third. The demand was there, intensified for several years by tight mortgage money. Meeting it was "a natural" for The Morris Plan Bank of Virginia, with its consumer orientation and its profile as primarily a savings bank. But this time there was no question of plunging into an uncertain new territory. The directors were asked only for an initial $50,000. Loans were to be insured. In charge would be Bernard LaPrade, who had come to the bank in 1935 with prior mortgage loan experience at the defunct American Bank and Trust Company. The first $50,000 was quickly exhausted, and the limit was increased, first to $100,000 and then to $250,000. Mortgage loans directly increased earnings and brought in new customers who could not find this type of financing elsewhere. But growth was still foremost among the bank's concerns, and innovation was the demonstrated technique for achieving growth.

One or two New York banks, among them the National City Bank of New York, had inaugurated the special checking account, charging five cents per check, with no minimum balance. To New York once again went President Boushall. He came back with the entire National City package procedure—accounting, promotion, selection, and screening. On October 26, 1936, The Morris Plan Bank of Virginia launched its own popular checking account service, previously unknown in the South. The customer could open an account with five dollars; he bought a book of twenty checks for a dollar; there was no other charge and no minimum balance. The original checking account requirement had been fifteen checks per hundred dollars of deposit. The more liberal popular checking account opened bank doors to many more people. It also brought the Morris Plan Bank of Virginia additional recognition. Stories were carried in Richmond and Petersburg papers and in the *American Banker*. Perhaps not the least of the dividends was that Virginia's commercial bankers were aghast. But a year later Harry Augustine, then ranking vice-president of State-Planters Bank and Trust Company, and John White, ranking vice-president of First and Merchants National Bank, called on Tom Boushall.

"If we adopt your program of twenty checks for a dollar, will you cut the price below five cents?" they wanted to know.

"We will not reduce the price below five cents, but we may raise it above five cents," said Tom Boushall.

Shortly after the innovation five cents a check became standard among Richmond commercial banks. In just a year's time, however, the bank had seen that five cents a check carried no profit, and the price was gradually raised to ten checks for a dollar. Finally a flat twenty-five cents a month stand-by charge was added.

By 1937 the banks of Virginia had changed their minds about automobile and appliance loans. Desperate for loan volume, they had entered the field without the benefit of Morris Plan know-how. State bank examiners were concerned lest this new volume of small loans get completely out of hand.

Finally Myron E. Bristow, state banking commissioner, called on Boushall and asked him to call a meeting of representatives from all Virginia banks engaged in consumer lending. A considerable number came to The Morris Plan Bank of Virginia board room. Bristow addressed the group. If they would adopt a code of procedure for these small loans, including down payment and length of term, his examiners would use it for regulatory purposes instead of asking the legislature for new legal restrictions. Before the meeting adjourned, the group had elected Boushall chairman of a new Bankers Discount Conference and adopted a code that faithfully reflected Morris Plan Bank of Virginia practice.

The following year the Virginia Bankers Association proposed that the conference become the consumer credit committee of the association, Boushall remained as chairman, and he and Ed Hyde put on a consumer credit luncheon at VBA meetings until the committee was abolished several years later. As a footnote, in 1942 the Federal Reserve System promulgated regulations covering the same field, but with restrictions somewhat more lenient than those originally drawn up by the conference.

Innovation and promotion continued at the bank. Direct mail solicitation was expanded by cross-checking automobile accounts with those of other bank borrowers and depositors, including the new mortgage loan customers, to encourage users of one banking service to take advantage of them all. Sponsorship of the Philadelphia Symphony gained prestige for the bank, but no new customers, while a dramatic travelogue over WRVA, under the bank's exclusive backing drew a gratifying response from educators and school children. The state itself circulated a bank-sponsored movie in color, produced by the State Department of Conservation and Economic Development. The bank's lobby continued to be enlivened by events under the sponsorship of local organizations, among which one of the most successful was the weekend rose show arranged by the Richmond Federation of Garden Clubs. Nor were bank employees neglected. A special booklet for them relating the bank's story was included in a review of progressive employee relations in the *American Banker*.

But the most spectacular promotional results were largely unintentional. A customer brought to Tony Adams, then vice-president and cashier, a copy of a letter Thomas Jefferson had written, while President of the United States, to a man to whom he owed five hundred dollars, advising that he would pay the obligation "in monthly portions." It was too good to pass up. Gary Underhill, in charge of advertising and publicity, took the letter to Whittet & Shepperson, which did most of the bank's printing. Treating a reproduction by dipping it in tea, the firm came up with virtually an exact duplicate. The bank ordered thirty-six thousand copies. The Washington affiliate ordered another thirty thousand. The fun began. Dr. Douglas Southall Freeman wrote an editorial in the Richmond *News Leader,* taking the bank to task for so faithful a reproduction. A Washington antique dealer threatened to sue, after almost paying five hundred dollars for a copy. Periodic "finds" kept the story going for years. The *Saturday Evening Post* carried a résumé. As late as 1961 *Newsweek* reviewed the affair.

The year 1937 brought virtually full vindication of Tom Boushall. The New Deal and finally Virginia bankers themselves had copied Morris Plan Bank of Virginia innovations one by one. The bank's president himself had been elected to positions of prominence in the Virginia Bankers Association and to several national organizations. While gains were not spectacular, loan volume was growing steadily and so were earnings. Deposits were on the increase. Success and prominence had even confirmed The Morris Plan Bank of Virginia as a leader among Morris Plan banks. Joseph E. Birnie, a former Richmond officer and now secretary of The Morris Plan Bankers Association, undertook a campaign that elected Boushall as a director of the United States Chamber of Commerce. Ralph Pitman was already president of The Morris Plan Bankers Association.

Tom Boushall now decided it was time to lay a ghost. For fourteen years, whenever a disagreement arose, Arthur Morris had thrown in his face the million dollars supposedly cut from John Markle's will by Morris's support of Boushall. Boushall drew up a balance sheet. In one column were his debts to Morris; on the other were Morris's debts to him. Armed with the document Boushall went to New York. As usual Morris opened the conversation.

"Before you start," he said, "I want to dictate a letter to your board."

While Boushall sat in silence, he gave his secretary a letter recommending that Boushall's salary be raised from twelve to fifteen thousand dollars, the first net raise in seven years. But the

Richmond president was not to be turned aside. He had not come for a raise. Thanking Morris, he said what he had come to say.

"I'm tired of hearing about John Markle and his million dollars," he said. "It means you feel I'm now and forever in your debt. You fail to recognize what I've done for your simple Morris Plan idea or how The Morris Plan Bank of Virginia has progressed compared to the rest of your banks. I've added up what I owe you and what you owe me. They balance exactly. Unless you agree today that you will never mention John Markle to me ever again, I offer you now and irrevocably my resignation."

But Morris had a bill of particulars of his own. There was the matter of checking accounts and demand deposits in the precarious days of 1931 and 1932. There was the building program threatening disaster in those same years. There were the branches, which represented an overextension of resources in Depression years.

From the vantage point of 1937, Boushall argued that each move to which Morris had taken exception had proved a long-run benefit to the bank and to the Morris Plan generally. With the ultimatum not to mention Markle again still plain on Boushall's face, Morris gave his word. Except for a casual reference in 1960, he kept it. Boushall's arguments were sustained by the position of The Morris Plan Bank of Virginia at the end of 1937, its fifteenth full year.

Loans and discounts in the year increased by $3,949,615 to a total of $15,187,900, and there was a $1,515,591 gain in savings. The number of popular checking accounts had risen from 531 at the beginning of the year to 3,939, and regular checking accounts had shown a modest increase of 304. Safe-deposit box rentals had increased from 958 to 1,027. Losses had run consistently below the one-half of 1 percent loss reserve, which had shown a net gain of $26,918 during the year. While loan volume was increasing, the unearned discount reserve had swelled from $439,411 to $586,948 —enough to cover earnings for several months. As the balance sheet increased to $20,281,723, the bank's staff rose from 135 to 166. Retained earnings from loans and earnings from the revitalized investment program had made it possible to pay off the $300,000 in preferred stock sold to the Reconstruction Finance Company. The following year the bank would not only pay another dividend, but would add enough to par capital to round it out at $1 million.

With a continuing policy of high interest payments on deposits and low operating charges, the bank in 1938 showed the most modest earnings of any bank in the United States of comparable size. Thus it demonstrated once more its deemphasis on profit in favor of growth and service. Earnings were largely from loans, and by 1938 76 percent of deposits were out in loans, with only 20 percent invested in bonds. Ranking fifth in total assets of all Virginia banks, The Morris Plan Bank of Virginia stood second in the number of loans by the end of 1938, with 43,969 outstanding.

As of December 31, 1938, the six largest banks in total assets in Virginia ranked as follows among the three hundred largest banks in the nation:

First and Merchants National Bank	97th
State-Planters Bank and Trust Company	125th
National Bank of Commerce, Norfolk	171st
First National Exchange Bank, Roanoke	226th
Central National Bank	264th
The Morris Plan Bank of Virginia	276th

But whereas the first five had increased their size by merger and consolidation from outside, The Morris Plan Bank of Virginia's growth had been largely from the inside and stemmed from a faster rate of expansion in banking services.

The prewar and war years were marked by continued expansion, but even more by a swing away from the bank's original concepts.

By now the satellite system embracing the entire Fifth Federal Reserve District had solidified into the central bank with one branch in each of its five Virginia cities. Only Washington, D.C., continued in its out-of-state orbit, but it too was operated as a branch. The break with the Morris Plan on checking accounts was followed by a full-blown return to commercial banking, Federal Reserve membership, and finally the gradual elimination of the Morris Plan from the bank's name, signs, and stationery.

The Petersburg branch had again outgrown its quarters and moved into the Virginia National Bank building, where two banks had previously failed. The Washington branch was moved to rented quarters in the former home of the defunct Commercial Bank of Washington, and $250,000 in preferred stock was issued to add to its capital. Like the headquarters bank Washington was able to cancel out its royalty payments to The Morris Plan Corporation of America in exchange for releasing the corporation from its guarantee of an uncollectible note carried over from the original Fidelity Loan and Savings Company that Arthur Morris had set up. Washington also began automobile sales financing after Tom Boushall insisted on the move over the objections of counsel for the bank.

Following the recommendation of The Morris Plan Corporation of America's investigating committee, Ralph Pitman had been curtailing Mayo Shugart's somewhat freewheeling operations with automobile finance. By 1939 the bank was ready to hire Jay E. Rauch, who had handled the Roanoke area for Commercial Credit Corporation, as head of automobile finance there. In 1941 Shugart resigned as vice-president in Richmond, and Rauch took over this phase of the business in all five cities. He switched to used cars as the war curtailed new production and greatly expanded the business by buying up portfolios of nervous competitors anxious to unload.

The following year began a two-year battle to establish a Morris Plan Bank of Virginia branch in Portsmouth, the only remaining city of more than fifty thousand that was open for such a move under the 1928 amendments to the Virginia banking code. George Whitehurst was executive vice-president of the Commercial Exchange Bank of Portsmouth, the third Morris Plan bank to be established that had held its franchise since 1912. He had developed a heart condition, and his competitors in Portsmouth banking were moving in. However, he preferred the Morris Plan Bank of Virginia as a successor. Catching wind of the plan, Whitehurst's competitors went to court to block the move and gain control of the Commercial Exchange. Not until November 25, 1944, did Whitehurst win control. Commercial Exchange stockholders were credited with $750,000 in deposits at Richmond. In turn Richmond had to increase its capital by $250,000. That amount in preferred stock was sold directly to the Life Insurance Company of Virginia.

The Richmond bank and its president had their own troubles with the Federal Reserve Board. Boushall had persuaded most of the officers and board members that the bank must soon come to commercial banking and that Reserve Board membership would be a decided asset.

The Morris Plan Bank of Detroit was in the process of changing from a state to a national bank which, with some charter changes, would mean automatic Federal Reserve membership. Boushall persuaded Morris that The Morris Plan Bank of Virginia should follow suit.

Owning 57 percent of a Federal Reserve member bank would have placed severe holding company limitations on the parent Morris Plan Corporation of America. Maxwell Wallace, a counsel for the Federal Reserve Bank of Richmond, suggested a solution. The law recognized a difference between a man and a corporation, Wallace said. If Arthur Morris would buy 17 percent of The Morris Plan Bank of Virginia's stock from the parent corporation in his own name, the parent company would no longer own control of Richmond and thus be subject to Federal Reserve restrictions.

Henry Johnson, a lawyer and member of the parent corporation's board, objected to the legal reasoning and to loss of control in Richmond by The Morris Plan Corporation of America. Federal Reserve counsel in Washington upheld Wallace, but Johnson blocked the move with the board of The Morris Plan Corporation of America in New York. Not until 1954 was the Richmond bank able to establish Federal Reserve membership. The Morris Plan in general and Tom Boushall in particular lost another initial round when they took on the Federal Reserve Board itself.

Anticipating a shutdown of civilian production, particularly appliances and items purchased on the instalment plan, the board in the late summer of 1941 called a meeting of lending agencies to discuss the forthcoming Regulation W, designed to limit consumer loans and brake inflation when supplies of hard goods dwindled. Boushall represented The Morris Plan Bankers Association. The board's approach was to require a minimum down payment and limit the length of the loan for various categories of appliances and other hard goods. Commercial loans were limited only as to the total money to be loaned by any one bank.

Boushall and other Morris Plan bankers argued that consumer and commercial loans should be treated alike, with limits on the money to be loaned and bankers determining who got it. Otherwise, they pointed out, arbitrary requirements on the borrower would discriminate against the very people who most needed consumer loans. Regulation W was adopted largely as originally drafted, but Boushall kept up the fight. Before Federal Reserve Board members, the Richmond Federal Reserve Bank officials, and the Senate Banking and Currency Committee he presented his case with a homely example. A bachelor who wanted a refrigerator to cool his beer and who could meet Regulation W requirements could get his loan. Yet the head of a large family who wanted a refrigerator to cool his children's milk, but who couldn't pay 10 percent down and the remainder in eighteen months was denied one. It was not until after the Korean War that the board and Congress finally modified the application of consumer credit regulations.

Even more troublesome than Regulation W was the excess profits tax, enacted as a wartime antiprofiteering measure. The theory was that if a corporation made considerably more money than it had the previous year, part of the excess must be war profits. The Morris Plan Bank of Virginia's rapid growth placed it in the 83 percent bracket. The result was that although the bank earned $334,350 in 1942, federal taxes took $239,500, leaving only $94,850 in earnings after taxes. But bank officers immediately began studying the new tax law and adjusting accounting procedures, so that by 1944, with less earnings before taxes than in 1942, earnings after taxes were $240,956. The excess profits tax figured in the bank's decision to maintain interest payments on deposits at a rate higher than most other banks.

As wages and salaries rose, deposits increased, loans were paid off, and new loans declined. Banks generally were increasingly burdened with interest payments on deposits. They soon discovered, furthermore, that people would keep their reserve cash in the bank without worrying too much about the interest it earned until total savings reached the point where the money would earn substantially more elsewhere. Then they would invest it. As cash accumulated, banks themselves ran into investment problems. Interest on ninety-day treasury bills, which were standard short-term outlets for idle funds, dropped to thirty-five-hundredths of 1 percent. Faced with paying out more interest on deposits than the deposits themselves could earn, banks began cutting their own interest rates from the prewar 2½ percent to 1 percent in most cases.

By December 1942 The Morris Plan Bank of Virginia had reduced its interest rates to 1½ percent on deposits up to $2,500, 1 percent from $2,500 to $5,000, ½ percent from $5,000 to $7,500, and no interest above $7,500. Officers, directors, and stockholders wanted to know why the bank should stop at 1½ percent on smaller deposits. The president had the answer, down to three decimal points. If the bank dropped to 1 percent and saved a half of 1 percent, the excess profits tax would take 83 percent of the savings. The bank would reduce its costs by only seventeen-hundredths of 1 percent, but depositors would lose a half of 1 percent in interest.

"Gentlemen," said Tom Boushall, "I favor our customers over the federal government."

One federal program was a tremendous assist to the bank—the Federal Housing Authority, with its guarantee of loans for the purchase of low-cost homes selling at about twenty-five hundred dollars. Here was Morris Plan philosophy in action. The loans required no down payment beyond ownership of a lot worth three hundred dollars, and even then the prospective homeowner could lease the land with option to buy. Thus for less than the cost of an old home or an apartment a man could buy a new home, pay for it over seven years, and even borrow and amortize the cost of the lot.

The bank moved cautiously into the field in 1939 and then heavily as the war effort created a housing boom in Richmond and in the seaport cities of Norfolk, Portsmouth, and Newport News. Recognizing this unparalleled contribution, the Reconstruction Finance Corporation offered to buy the loans from the bank and pay the bank a half of 1 percent for servicing them, releasing bank capital for more home loans. By June 1941 the bank had financed so many of these homes that the officers began to worry. If economic conditions after World War II were similar to those that followed World War I, it might mean a mass exodus from the new housing developments, and The Morris Plan Bank of Virginia might be accused of misleading the RFC into buying the loans. To cover that contingency, Boushall wrote a letter to George B. Williams, president of the RFC, saying, in effect that the bank did not represent these home loans as permanent investments that would stand up in the postwar period. The bank showed no loss on the loans. In fact the $2,500 homes soared in value to $5,000, $7,500, and finally $10,000 in postwar years.

While higher salaries and wages and limited supplies of consumer goods reduced the average citizen's need to borrow from banks, a peripatetic wartime civilian and military population and hard-pressed farmers created a boom for small-loan companies. With no deposits these companies were constantly in need of capital. Searching for loan volume wherever it could be found, the bank, which had once borrowed money to lend itself, now extended money for others to lend. Lines of credit were extended to small loan companies operating around Pittsburgh, Albany, New York; and in Vermont, New Hampshire, South Carolina, and Alabama, totaling well above a million dollars. These were withdrawn after the war ended. But the most significant move for the bank's future began in September 1942, when J. Joseph May, an investment banker, was elected a vice-president in charge of developing commercial accounts.

From its early days the bank had engaged in automobile financing and even extended twelve-month instalment loans to small business enterprises. Petersburg and Newport News had handled routine commercial accounts after the banking holiday of 1933, but had little or no experience with unsecured and seasonal loans. The new policy was another departure from the Morris Plan and a direct encroachment upon a field long held by well-endowed commercial banks. Deposits were mounting, but so were interest costs. Mortgages alone were showing appreciable growth. Consumer loan volume was not keeping pace. The time was ripe for the countermove conceived when commercial banks had offered The Morris Plan Bank of Virginia its first competition in consumer loans ten years before. At first new commercial loans were slow. In mid-1943 Joe May was given a three-month leave of absence to promote the sale of government bonds in Virginia. Late in 1943 the figures showed a lifelong total of 30,000 commercial loans out of an aggregate of 665,000.

The die was cast and with it the last procedural link with the Morris Plan. Beginning with revised nomenclature for Morris Plan forms and interest paid on assigned deposits, The Morris Plan Bank of Virginia had added checking accounts and demand deposits, safe-deposit boxes, popular checking accounts, and finally commercial loans. Assigned deposits were phased out after banking laws were changed in 1938 to permit 6 percent consumer loans by banks.

With the conviction that future loan volume would depend to a large extent on commercial accounts, the bank was faced with another dilemma. The Morris Plan had so long been associated with consumer loans that something would have to be done if the bank was to launch an effective advertising and promotion campaign for commercial business. Toward the end of the war, the words *Morris Plan* had already been placed in small type under the name Bank of Virginia. In June 1945 Tom Boushall had a frank conversation with Arthur Morris, who had complained that his name had been deemphasized.

In their first meeting in 1921, Boushall had questioned Morris's use of his own name in developing his banking system. Now Morris decided it would be an act of personal conceit to insist on retaining the Morris Plan designation, and to do so could conceivably impede the bank's development. But, he insisted, the Morris Plan diamond must continue to be a part of the bank's name. The bank board approved the change at its November 1945 meeting. Following some conversation with the State Corporation Commission, it was made official.

At the end of twenty-three years and six months, The Morris Plan Bank of Richmond, with capital of $375,000, had become The Bank of Virginia, with offices in six cities and a loan portfolio approaching $15 million. A more prestigious name could hardly have been chosen, but once again the bank had defied tradition. Back in 1804 the Virginia General Assembly had legislated out of business the current crop of unchartered banks with their own currency notes and had created the state-supported Bank of Virginia, which had flourished but failed to survive the end of the Civil War. Some months after the change of name in 1945, Eppa Hunton IV, a prominent Richmond lawyer and staunch supporter of Confederate remembrances, reminded Tom Boushall of this heritage of precipitous demise.

"Tom," said Hunton, "aren't you embarrassed by the failure of the old Bank of Virginia?"

"Eppa," said Boushall, "aren't you embarrassed by the failure of the Confederacy?"

"No," said Hunton vehemently.

"Neither am I," said Boushall.

Before the name change had been officially endorsed by the board, a chain of events had begun that would relieve the bank of its last out-of-state holding and make it exclusively a Virginia operation.

Separated from automobile financing when Arthur Morris had moved into that field, The Morris Plan Corporation of America had been left with earnings from Morris Plan banks and companies as its major source of income, and these had not been substantial. Since its first original capital had been exhausted in launching a national system of Morris Plan lending institutions, the parent corporation had been chronically short of funds. The New York law firm of Satterlee, Canfield, and Stone had long represented the corporation. To this firm two young lawyers, Ellery Huntington and David Milton, had returned from wartime service early in 1945 in search of some profitable postwar financing. In a series of corporate maneuvers, they wound up with 20 percent of the questionable but flush Equity Corporation, an investment trust. In return for the cash it had so long needed, Equity was given control of The Morris Plan Corporation of America. Huntington now suggested that the Richmond bank retire the $250,000 in preferred stock, issued when Richmond had acquired the Portsmouth bank, by issuing 15,000 shares of common. The issue was substantially oversubscribed at $39 bid, $41 asked, with the parent corporation picking up its 57 percent and the Richmond bank adding to its capital after retiring the Life Insurance Company of Virginia's preferred shares.

Next, the parent corporation offered to buy its pro rata share of the stock Richmond owned in the Washington Morris Plan bank if Richmond would offer its 94 percent ownership to its stockholders. From this transaction Richmond added to its capital $246,830 after taxes, severed its last connection with an out-of-state subsidiary, and retired the last of its outstanding preferred stock. But the Washington branch story was not closed without another round between Tom Boushall and Arthur Morris. In June 1942 Willard Barker, Washington's president, entered the army. Second in command was Elwood Childers, a young graduate of the Harvard School of Business Administration, and Arthur Morris's son-in-law. Morris recommended that Childers be put in charge in Washington until Barker returned. Boushall flatly refused. Childers had neither the experience nor the following of the Washington bank staff. A countersuggestion was that Linwood P. Harrell, then in charge at Petersburg, substitute for Barker if Boushall would remain as president of the Richmond bank and chairman of the Washington board. The battle went on for two weeks, but before the month was out Harrell was elected executive vice-president of the Washington bank.

The war effort, the swing toward commercial banking, and the passing years brought more changes to the bank than the new name. Despite lowered earnings, employee benefit programs had been steadily expanded until by 1942, they included group life insurance, group hospitalization and annuity, medical examinations for all new employees, a generous sick leave and vacation policy, and tuition costs for American Institute of Banking courses. Commissions were paid on new business acquired with extra effort, and a job classification system instituted. Many of these were Virginia firsts in the banking business.

In addition to reshuffling because of wartime assignments, the bank's top management people changed materially. In March 1944 Ed Hyde resigned to become second in command at the Peoples National Bank in Charlottesville and later moved to Miller & Rhoads department store in Richmond. Ernest Mangum left the Norfolk branch to be succeeded by Litt Zehmer, and O. B. Wooldridge succeeded to the Portsmouth office when George Whitehurst died suddenly of a heart attack.

On October 9, 1944, Herbert C. Moseley was elected assistant vice-president and cashier in Petersburg, whence he was to rise to significant heights. By the end of 1944, the bank's staff had increased to 271, of which 75 percent were women, but the trend toward the distaff side was to reverse itself as personnel came home from the war. Earlier in the same year, Ralph Pitman, who had cut his three days a week in Richmond to one, resigned as executive vice-president to return to Philadelphia. It was two years before Tom Boushall found a replacement for him in W. W. McEachern, who had sold out his interest in Florida banking. Shortly after McEachern's election Malcolm Engstrom, who had been vice-president and comptroller, resigned to assume the same position with the Industrial Bank of Commerce, a former Morris Plan bank.

In July of 1945 Tony Adams, now vice-president and cashier in Richmond and a bank director, died of a heart attack on the bank's twenty-third anniversary.

The Bank of Virginia emerged from the war years with its prestige and influence greatly enhanced and its president a national, if still a somewhat controversial, figure. Its pioneering in the field of consumer finance had been recognized by federal authorities and copied by the more progressive commercial banks. Its prodigious war effort—buying government bonds itself and lending a top official to head a statewide war bond drive—had been greatly acclaimed.

Besides advising on governmental credit regulations, the bank's president had served as chairman as well as a director of the

Committee on Education of the Chamber of Commerce of the United States and pioneered once more with a chamber study demonstrating the direct relationship between education and income level. The result was his appointment as chairman of a National Citizens Committee on Education by the United States Office of Education in 1946. The same year he was invited to present his ideas on freeing the economy of government controls on the front page of the Richmond Times-Dispatch. Appointed to the Consumer Credit Committee of the American Bankers Association in 1944, he began a crusade through that organization for better appreciation of consumer banking.

As a lending institution, The Bank of Virginia was unique. While other banks had developed networks of correspondent banks in smaller communities, it alone had branches in other cities. Their growth was already proving the superior service and earning power of branches versus correspondents.

CHAPTER VIII

Shackling the Octopus

THE IMMEDIATE POSTWAR YEARS were to illustrate graphically how far the tide of consumer credit, which The Bank of Virginia had been riding so long, had finally come in. Wartime savings burst forth into a nationwide buying spree. During the first calendar year after the war, the bank's net deposit gain was only $2,158,000, but its loan portfolio increased by $10.1 million—from $15,608,000 to $25,723,000. By this time the bank was serving the largest number of customer accounts, including the largest number of checking accounts and showed the largest total of savings deposits of any bank in Virginia.

Although it was still consumer oriented, the bank and its branches were now offering every commercial banking service except a full trust department. This fact was not lost on Virginia's banking fraternity. When the branch at Fourth and Broad in Richmond had been closed during the Depression, the bank had been left with one branch in each of its five cities. Under the restrictions of the banking code amendments in 1928, the more apprehensive bankers felt The Bank of Virginia was reasonably secure. But bankers in Portsmouth, the only city of over fifty thousand still available to the bank under the amendments, went to the court and for two years delayed the merger with the Commercial Exchange Bank of that city.

With branches of their own all over town, Richmond's larger banks made no move when The Bank of Virginia in 1945 purchased property on the southeast corner of Fourth and Grace for a new branch to serve that retail sales area. Nor was there an objection when the bank applied for new Richmond branches in South Richmond and far out on West Broad Street, along which business and industry were now extending rapidly. But when The Bank of Virginia requested another branch in Norfolk at Twenty-first and Granby, bankers from that city and from Portsmouth were unanimously opposed.

President after president told a State Corporation Commission hearing in December 1947 that another banking outlet in the area would bring chaos. Finally Judge McCarthy Downs asked Maywood Lawrence, president of the Citizens Trust Company of Portsmouth, whether he would register the same complaint if a local bank had made a similar request.

"No, sir," replied Lawrence.

"Then that is the end of the case," said Judge Downs. "Your objection is obviously to a specific bank and not a judgment as to public convenience and necessity."

The statewide move against The Bank of Virginia had begun the previous June at the Virginia Bankers Association convention. Opposition in Tidewater Virginia had echoed along the Shenandoah Valley when the bank followed the trail that Arthur Morris had outlined and created another separate, wholly owned corporation to handle the automobile end of the business.

From his home base in Roanoke, Jay Rauch had built up auto finance until it represented the lion's share of the Roanoke branch loan portfolio. Late in 1946 he proposed that business could be further expanded if local offices could be opened in cities in the middle and northern areas of the Valley. Under the law The Bank of Virginia could not invest in common stock of other corporations, nor could it engage in insuring automobile loans directly. In a series of corporate maneuvers, a Delaware insurance brokerage firm was converted into Commonwealth Discount Corporation of Virginia with The Bank of Virginia as the sole stockholder. Local Valley bankers saw the new automobile finance offices in their cities as potential branches of The Bank of Virginia, in addition to being aggressive competitors for automobile business. In the latter category The Bank of Virginia already exceeded any other Virginia lending institution.

Commonwealth Discount Corporation came into being early in 1947 at about the time Boushall was negotiating to take over a bank in Alexandria. The alarm among Virginia bankers over branch banking had now become general. It had surfaced by June 1947 during the Virginia Bankers Association convention at Virginia Beach, even prior to the fight over an additional Bank of Virginia branch in Norfolk. The association's legislative committee came in with a recommendation that the 1948 session of the General Assembly be asked to repeal the 1928 provision permitting branches in cities of fifty thousand or more. As Committee Chairman R. F. Burke Steele pointed out, these now included Alexandria and would soon embrace Danville, Lynchburg, and the county of Arlington, which was pressing for city status.

The committee felt it was speaking for the majority of the association when it recommended "that statewide branch banking should be frozen where it is." Tom Boushall made a long and impassioned plea for fair play but fear kindled by visits from anti-branch banking forces had done its work. The committee's report was adopted seventy-eight to two. Both sides made their preparations for the General Assembly session in January. Larger banks made the rounds of their correspondent institutions and enlisted almost unanimous support, which was indeed formidable. A count by The Bank of Virginia officers showed that fifty-one out of the hundred house of delegates members and twenty-one of forty state senators were officers, directors, or counsel for constituent banks. Nine of Richmond's ten-man delegation stood with The Bank of Virginia, plus a handful of others. But most assemblymen—some of whom were stockholders in the bank—reported that home-town pressure was too great.

The bank appealed to the press. As the battle lines were drawn, twenty-one editorials supported The Bank of Virginia. Richmond and Norfolk newspapers particularly were on the bank's side. A brochure was mailed to every member of the legislature. The climax came before the joint house and senate committees on insurance and banking. The house chamber and galleries were packed. But behind virtually every senator and delegate, except those from Richmond, was a home-town banker. Boushall led off and was enthusiastically applauded. Wirt P. Marks, who had succeeded as bank counsel on the death of Grayson Dashiell, stressed the legal dangers. Then David Mays, counsel for the Virginia Bankers Association, walked to an easel and uncovered a chart showing the organization of the Equity Corporation, its control by two foreign-chartered corporations, and how it in turn controlled The Morris Plan Corporation and finally The Bank of Virginia. Would the committee, Mays wanted to know, vote to have a foreign-based, Wall Street-dominated corporation competing with the small banks of Virginia?

"Will you allow this octopus to wind its tentacles around our people, control their money and withhold credit?" he demanded to know in conclusion.

The committee would not. Neither would the house or senate.

The legislation was enacted. Rescinding the right of a bank in one city to open a branch in another city of fifty thousand or more, the new amendments were a three-way check on The Bank of Virginia. Not only was the parent bank in Richmond forbidden to open branches in other cities. The number of its existing branches was also frozen, except for those in the parent bank's city. Two new branches for Norfolk had already been approved by the State Corporation Commission and were not affected.

The code had previously permitted a bank in one city or county to merge with another bank in a contiguous city or county within a twenty-five-mile limit after two years. The 1948 amendments made this five years, all but ruling out any ambitions The Bank of Virginia might have had in the Richmond metropolitan area. Local bankers in the six-branch cities were quick to take advantage of the new legislation. The chairman of the VBA legislative committee, Burke Steele, who was president of the Petersburg Savings and Trust Company, promptly organized a small bank in adjacent Colonial Heights and later another in Hopewell. The Southern Bank of Norfolk opened two satellite branches across the city line.

While the new legislation kept The Bank of Virginia from becoming a truly statewide branch banking system like the Wachovia Bank in neighboring North Carolina or the Bank of America in California, it nevertheless had some inevitable side effects. Preventing other banks from establishing branches in distant cities, it protected The Bank of Virginia's unique position as the sole, though limited, branch banking system in Virginia. It also limited the local response that other major banks could make through their correspondents to the demands of the new industrial plants that had begun to spread across the state. A branch in a small city could call on the total resources of the system to which it belonged. A correspondent bank had to refer to its large city headquarters bank any calls for loans or services it could not perform on its own. Large banks could not count among their total resources those of correspondent banks. While restrictive legislation protected small banks from the aggressive competition offered by The Bank of Virginia branches in their cities and towns, it did not protect them from holding companies, which began buying up banks in the late 1950s. This move by holding companies, plus a growing tendency on the part of industry to look for heavy plant construction financing outside the state, would finally reverse the statute of 1948. Meanwhile the conviction grew among the more far-sighted bankers that the statute had set banking in Virginia back by at least ten years.

In a now familiar pattern, The Bank of Virginia also grew. Increasing its capital by selling more stock in order to keep pace, the bank continued to open new branches authorized prior to 1948 and to enlarge old ones. A new building in Roanoke had been opened in June 1947. Two more Richmond branches, authorized prior to 1948, were opened in rented quarters, one at 1618–20 Hull Street in June 1948 and the other at 2900 West Broad in August. In April 1949 the Norfolk branch at Twenty-first and Granby opened and in November the third Norfolk branch, at Charlotte and Boush. New quarters for Portsmouth opened the same year.

In the first full year after 1948, it picked up 14,659 new customers, gained $4.6 million in resources, and earned $4.90 a share, compared to $4.48 the year before. During 1949 $300,000 was transferred from undivided profits to par capital, restoring par at $20 and bringing total par capital to $1.8 million. At the end of 1949, the bank stood 5th among Virginia banks in total deposits and 297th among all the banks of the nation. Also in 1949 Clark L. Kelly came from Louisville, Kentucky, to head a revitalized correspondent bank section, since the bank was now restricted as to new branches and had to compete on the same terms that applied to other banks.

In January 1950 the Fourth and Grace office finally opened, after construction delays, including the addition of another floor, and in May Newport News opened new quarters. These new outlets, the continuing rush of goods-hungry consumers to loan windows, and finally a buying spree sparked by the Korean War kept the bank growing. By the end of 1950, the effects of the new branches began to make themselves felt. In December a dividend of ten thousand shares at twenty dollars per share was declared, bringing par capital to an even $2 million. With $73 million in total resources, the bank had passed Central National and moved into fourth place among Virginia banks, behind First and Merchants, State-Planters, and the National Bank of Commerce in Norfolk. Earnings increased to $6.50 a share.

The year 1951 brought the greatest growth in the bank's history, a gain of half as much as that for the first twenty years. Demand and time deposits together registered an increase of more than $12 million, and total resources increased by more than

$13 million. Customer accounts increased by 17,230. Net earnings before taxes topped $1 million, although reimposition of the excess profits tax cut net per share to $4.08. By the end of 1951, the bank had made 1,133,489 loans for $783,154,053, with a loss ratio of one-sixteenth of 1 percent.

Most of The Bank of Virginia branches were operating miniatures of the mother bank in Richmond. The exception was Roanoke. Bringing this branch into the fold as a true reflection of the parent bank ultimately produced two far-reaching changes in the philosophy and operation of the overall banking enterprise. A succession of managers had never quite made the Roanoke branch an active participant in community affairs or the aggressive gadfly to local bankers so characteristic of The Bank of Virginia.

In 1947 Tom Boushall had gone to Roanoke for a frank discussion with three board members, headed by W. P. Hazelgrove, who also had connections with the First National Exchange Bank of Roanoke where C. Francis Cocke, a former Roanoke branch board member, was on his way to the presidency. The gist of Boushall's remarks was that the three could not serve two bank masters. The result was three resignations from the Roanoke branch board. A year later Thomas P. Parsley, Roanoke branch manager, turned down an offer to come to Richmond and joined the Mountain Trust Bank of Roanoke, where he became president in two years, after a merger with The Bank of Virginia failed to materialize.

At Petersburg, whence a succession of branch managers had gone on to bigger things, Boushall called Herbert C. Moseley to the Roanoke branch, which had largely become a funnel for Bank of Virginia funds flowing to Jay Rauch's growing automobile financing division. As the division expanded even further with the new business from Commonwealth Discount Corporation offices established along the Shenandoah Valley, automobile finance began to give The Bank of Virginia itself an irregular financial profile. By 1949 the parent bank was allocating $20 million of its $56 million in deposits to automobile financing. Commonwealth Discount's local offices had contributed to the feeling, which several Virginia bankers had expressed to Arthur Morris himself, that if they did not stop "this fellow Boushall" he would take over banking in the state.

Within the Roanoke branch, loyalties were divided between Rauch and the parent bank, and morale was low. The sense of mission and the active sales promotion that were the trademark of other branches were missing. Moseley's job was to build enthusiasm and to make the branch a part of the community, but if this was to be accomplished the branch could not continue as the financial arm of Commonwealth Discount. To the dominance in Roanoke of auto financing was added the outspoken opposition of McEachern who, as executive vice-president, continued to express concern over the hazards of such wholesale underwriting of high-risk loans.

In the fall of 1949, Rauch approached Tom Boushall about a substantial increase in automobile financing. Boushall would go no higher than the $20 million already allocated. Rauch offered his resignation. Rather than accept it, Boushall suggested the bank sell him Commonwealth Discount. At the beginning of 1950, the sale was completed at the purchase price of a hundred-thousand-dollar tax-free windfall. Three Roanoke branch officers went with Rauch, who at first continued to use the Roanoke branch as a source of financing, using lines of credit from New York extended through The Bank of Virginia, but at Moseley's urging these were reduced and finally discontinued. Switching to Mountain Trust, Rauch practically wiped out The Bank of Virginia's automobile business in the Roanoke area, but in five years he was again using the Roanoke bank for a portion of his credit needs.

Having moved away from automobile loan dominance, The Bank of Virginia also gradually slipped clear of FHA red tape and regulations in its guaranteed home improvement loans. Luke Fairbank, who had watched over the FHA involvement since the bank first took state leadership in these loans in 1934, now suggested an alternative. In September 1948 the bank began pushing its own home improvement loans once more—at 6 percent, compared to FHA's 5 percent—but with insurance required on the loans as an additional selling point. In time Title 1 FHA loan volume became nominal, while the bank's own home improvement volume continued to climb. The new loans earned more and were regulated less. They also brought deep satisfaction to Tom Boushall.

For the banking community to recognize and finally to adopt The Bank of Virginia's social consciousness as it had by 1949 was sweet indeed. For government to do so was another matter. At the conclusion of the 1949 annual report of the bank, Boushall unburdened himself on the subject.

"There must be a genuine realization that our country is being led toward the maelstrom of a socialistic state by the promises of the present Federal administration."

The blame, the report said, lay with Washington policy makers, who were acting "in full imitation of the socialistic pattern being followed in England and in direct line with the fulfillment of the Marxist Doctrine.

"Realization must come," the report continued, "that economics is based on far deeper laws and reactions than can be controlled by the semi-illiterate action of men devoted to their own aggrandizement and personal success."

A life-long Southern Democrat, Tom Boushall, like many other businessmen of the South, would express these convictions by supporting Republican presidential nominees in years to come even as they continued to adhere to the Democratic party at home.

As time passed and the bank grew, faces changed. During 1947 Allen J. Saville, R. Grayson Dashiell, Admiral Joseph K. Taussig, who had more recently joined the board, and H. Laurie Smith, president of Lawyers Title Insurance Company and a bank board member, all died. Joining the board during the late 1940s and early 1950s were W. Brooks George of Larus & Brothers Company, and C. Hancock Reed of Williams and Reed. Daphne Dailey joined the staff in 1948, taking charge of public relations and advertising. In June 1950 Louis F. Rahmer came from the Bank of New York to set up a credit analysis division as an adjunct to the commercial loan department. McEachern had resigned the previous March, leaving the bank once more without an executive vice-president. Other officers often resigned to become presidents of other banks. As Ralph Pitman had said in the late 1930s, "the alumni of The Bank of Virginia could run any bank in the country."

As the bank passed the age of thirty-five, there were few signs of middle-age spread. Certainly there was no slackening of the frantic pace. It was still, as one future president described it, "a sales promotion agency with banking on the side." There were small and subtle changes in its philosophy as the little man's bank. There was also ample evidence that other banks had learned their lessons from the maestro at Eighth and Main.

Twice in the period—with the Bank of Commerce and Trusts and the Merchants and Mechanics Bank, both in Richmond—The Bank of Virginia set up mergers, only to be outbid by other banks. With the exception of new locations in Richmond, the bank had to be satisfied with two prospective mergers in the Richmond area under the amended banking code. One was with The Bank of Henrico, with offices in Sandston and Highland Springs, and the other with the Chesterfield County Bank. When the bank sought approval for three in-city branches at Three Chopt Road and Patterson, at Staples Mill and West Broad Street in the burgeoning West End, and on Westover Hills Boulevard in Southside, it was politely told not to compete with already established branches of First and Merchants and State-Planters. The Virginia Bankers Association in 1948 had required proof of public convenience and necessity in new location applications, but there was nothing to interfere with enlarging the Norfolk quarters, constructing a new bank-owned building for the Petersburg branch, which was also bursting at the seams, or completing the new building, with drive-in facilities, in Portsmouth.

Petersburg marked a departure. Up to that time, whenever the bank had built branch offices in other cities, they had been miniatures of, or strongly suggested, the original Boushall design at Eighth and Main. The Petersburg office was a blend of this and the contemporary architecture that banks had generally turned to in order to avoid the forbidding exteriors and lobbies of earlier days. Strictly contemporary design highlighted the new branch further south on Petersburg Pike, a site selected in preference to the one proposed in the West End. Its pleated roof excited discussion in and out of banking circles, but once again other banks were to follow The Bank of Virginia into even more striking designs. The architecture of the branches at Staples Mill and Broad and in the new shopping center at Three Chopt and Patterson was more conservative, however.

The bank's staff was increasing. In 1922 the original Richmond board had authorized a trust operation. In 1956 it became a reality, with Reginald C. Short coming from the Fidelity Trust Company outside Pittsburgh to set it up. He was later joined by John T. McGrann. The following year two trust officers were trained for Norfolk and Roanoke branches. Short established two common trust funds, one in stocks, the other in bonds. This was unique to Virginia, where other banks maintained a mixed common trust fund. Also new to Virginia was the family trust.

Two other experiments, on the other hand, nearly resulted in disaster. From a simple merchant charge plan, W. Albert Hess had branched into factoring accounts of building material suppliers, and the complicated business finally became snarled. Bank examiners declared the fourteen or fifteen accounts involved a potential loss of $650,000, although only $4,000 or $5,000 was finally charged off as uncollectible in the early 1960s.

By 1958 the bank had acquired the accounts of American Coal Shipping, Inc., a $5 million corporation owned by John L. Lewis's mineworkers and consisting of three railroads serving Virginia coal fields, seven coal mines, and two large coal shippers. On this base, the bank prepared to build an entire foreign trade department, but ocean freight rates collapsed and so did prospects for American Coal Shipping. The bank spent several difficult years liquidating its five-hundred-thousand-dollar participation in the $30 million bank syndicate loan that had floated the enterprise.

To boost deposits in the face of government bills offering an alternative at 2 percent, the bank initiated still another innovation. While paying 2 percent on regular savings, a 3-year, 2½ percent savings certificate was issued–the beginning of a now common procedure. Still another first led to some startling disclosures. After years of negotiation, IBM finally installed data processing equipment, making possible in-depth analyses never before attempted. One much-desired tabulation made in 1956 showed all loans by amount discounted and average unpaid balance. The average discounted consumer loan was $250; the average unpaid balance even lower, indicating too many small loans earning less than they cost to administer. In fact the bank had been losing money on 40 percent of its outstanding consumer loans. Many borrowers had several relatively small loans outstanding.

Instead of being the first to extend needed credit to the average citizen, The Bank of Virginia had become a financial court of last appeal. Rather than looking to the bank for their total personal financing as they had in the past, many people had been borrowing or buying on time elsewhere and resorting to The Bank of Virginia for small marginal loans to cover their overextension. Forthwith a new policy was instituted. First, a borrower would have to consolidate his obligations before he could borrow. Furthermore, the bank would not lend less than $500 in cases where the applicant also had other large debts. In twelve months the average discounted loan rose from $250 to $900. In two years the number of small loans dropped from 58,000 to 38,000, although total loan volume and total outstanding loans continued to rise. From then on, the average loan discounted figure was held relatively high, although exceptions were made where the need was justified in accordance with time-honored practice.

At first, competing banks, now fully committed to consumer financing themselves, welcomed the disappointed small borrowers. A Norfolk competitor promptly advertised that it, and not The Bank of Virginia, was the consumer's true friend. But a little experience soon convinced other banks that The Bank of Virginia had been on the right track. In the easy-credit days after Korean War restrictions were lifted, small loans were less a question of rescuing the hard pressed and hard working than encouraging the already debt ridden.

The bank still kept up with the times. Floor plan financing was extended from automobiles to house trailers in September 1951. While competing banks tried to best The Bank of Virginia at its own game, honors continued to be accorded the bank's president.

The Korean War period had seen a return to consumer credit restrictions, but this time in the form of voluntary efforts by banks themselves through the Federal Reserve System, in line with Boushall's suggestion in the early days of World War II. Boushall himself became one of five credit restraint committee members for the Fifth Federal Reserve District. In 1953 Governor John S. Battle appointed him to the State Board of Education. When Governor Thomas B. Stanley succeeded Battle, he reappointed Boushall and added his name to a special commission studying education in the state. In 1956 he became chairman of the Sweet Briar College Board on which he had served since 1950, and the same year he was elected a delegate to the State Constitutional Convention over aspirant Howard Carwile. In April he joined Mrs. Alfred I. duPont in receiving a Virginia Chamber of Commerce award for outstanding civic achievement. His interest in education carried over into the banking field. With Bank of Virginia support, The School of Consumer Banking was established at the University of Virginia, and Boushall was the first chairman of its board of trustees.

CHAPTER IX

Cutting the Umbilical Cord

B Y THE EARLY 1950s the shape of events forecast major moves that would transform the bank and project it into the forefront of a major advance for banking throughout Virginia.

For twenty years commercial banks had been moving steadily into consumer finance as the nation's incredible productive capacity, nurtured by the demands of war, poured out myriad consumer goods and services and business enterprises looked increasingly to other sources and to each other for money to borrow. Distribution, wholesaling, and retailing had revitalized downtown shopping areas, produced the suburban shopping center, increased the trucking industry, and made convenient and easy credit absolutely essential. Commercial-bank credit accounts outstanding numbered twice as many consumer households as businessmen and farmers combined.

Manufacturing giants who in the 1920s had dreamed of a single assembly line that would roll metallic ores into one end and turn out finished automobiles or appliances at the other were now separating production processes and scattering assembly and distribution plants around the country, closer to major markets. Smokestacks clustered in industrial centers were giving way to low, flat, automated plants, dotting the rural countryside and attracting excess farm labor from forty miles around. Industries that had pushed west with the railroads in the latter half of the nineteenth century now pushed into the underdeveloped South in ever-increasing numbers, and southern population and income growth rates far exceeded the national average.

Located at the southern end of the Boston-Washington, D.C., axis, Virginia, with open spaces, water, ports, and political stability, was a major example of the new trend, with all its benefits and its inevitable price. As the state's major shopping area, Richmond's credit demands were tremendous, and the financial heart of the Commonwealth on lower Main Street beat steadily faster.

As other Richmond banks began to look more and more like

The Bank of Virginia, local board members had talked increasingly of severing all ties with the Morris Plan. New York still owned a controlling interest and still opposed bank plans from time to time. Besides, the Morris Plan image was no longer an asset to one of the state's leading banks. Complete independence would be the final step in President Boushall's dream of a complete and self-sufficient banking enterprise, but he refused to initiate the move. Through endless verbal battles and a dozen resignations, he had always been a Morris man, supporting the founder of the Morris Plan in the early days against his local managers and board members, even as he pushed Morris further and further away from his original concepts. In return the parent corporation had repeatedly come to the rescue of its Richmond offspring, financing its share of one capital expansion after another, assisting in the purchase of branches and tolerating, if not enjoying, the president's insistence on growth at the expense of earnings.

For Arthur Morris and his organization Tom Boushall felt a personal warmth and the weight of many obligations. But the Morris Plan and its founder had changed. Across the country, Morris Plan companies had become banks, most of them carrying commercial accounts, and offering a full range of banking services, with the exception of demand deposits and checking accounts. Some had already purchased their independence. Morris himself had suffered reverses in attempts at international banking and intercontinental automobile financing, and his new automobile finance corporation was running into stiff competition, much of it from banks. Control of the Morris Plan Corporation of America was now shared with Equity Corporation interests. In a few years, it would be reorganized as Financial General.

In New York, Colonel Huntington was dismayed at the bank's announcement early in 1953 that it planned to double the West Broad Street office in Richmond, enlarge the one at Twenty-first and Granby in Norfolk by half, and relocate the Portsmouth branch in a new building with drive-in facilities on a block-long lot. Huntington was also strongly opposed to joining the Federal Reserve, which The Bank of Virginia had wanted to do for some time. Morris himself was the key to independence for The Bank of Virginia. He knew Huntington's sentiments, and as a member of the Richmond board, he was aware of the growing spirit in favor of severance. Furthermore, the loyalty that had

kept Boushall from initiating the move was to him. Finally he
stepped into the breach. Drawing the president aside following
the August 1953 board meeting, he volunteered to talk to Huntington about the sale on the open market of the parent corporation's stock. Morris obtained Huntington's consent, and this
was the beginning of a full year of negotiations. Initially a called
meeting of the stockholders authorized the sale of 20,000 new
shares, of which New York took its portion. It was oversubscribed
by Virginia investors at $47.00. But the parent corporation made
an assessment of the bank's net worth and came up with a price
of $90.00 for its own shares, based on the New York market.
Boushall had his heart set on The Bank of Virginia's being owned
by Virginians. Having just purchased 20,000 shares at $47.00,
they would not go for another 68,000 shares at $90.00. Besides,
the accepted formula of capital plus surplus plus undivided
profits divided by the number of shares gave a book value of only
$51.18.

A round of conferences began. Joining in was Frederick Deane,
Jr., a Harvard Business School graduate from Boston's Back Bay,
just released from a tour of military duty as assistant to one of
the deputy directors of the CIA. Boushall had hired him as his
own assistant. Back and forth to New York the two went, but the
best their combined persuasive powers could do was to reduce
the figure from $90.00 to $65.00 a share, still too high a price.
The final solution was two-pronged. First, all the bank's stock
would be split three for one. In order to keep par from falling
too low in the process, one of the three new shares would be
declared as a stock dividend. In this way, 120,000 shares at $20.00
par would become 360,000 shares at $10.00 par. Based on a price
of $65.00 to New York, this would also mean a theoretical selling
price for the new shares of $21.85. But the formula would only
support a book value of between $17.00 and $18.00. To augment
this figure $900,000 was transferred from the now ample un-
earned discount reserve to undivided profits, to give a book value
of around $20.00 close enough to support a $21.85 selling price.

The parent corporation and the bank were now in agreement,
but not the brokers who were to handle the sale. Boushall had
chosen Kidder, Peabody of New York to handle that end of the
underwriting. J. C. Wheat & Company of Richmond, long associated with bank stock issues, would cover Virginia. Late in 1953
the parent corporation was holding out for $21.85 while the New

York brokers were offering from $18.00 to $18.50. Not until February 1954 was a compromise in sight. Colonel Huntington finally agreed to $19.25 a share, close to the brokers' figure. Then another impasse occurred.

James Wheat felt the shares could be sold in Virginia for a differential of $1.00 to the brokers, or $20.25 a share. Kidder, Peabody insisted on $1.25 brokerage, or a selling price of $20.50. Until now Boushall had harbored serious doubts that Wheat & Company could handle the entire 205,000 shares, representing the parent corporation's holdings. But he had become disenchanted with the New York firm's heavy-handed attitude. James Wheat came forward with a proposal. Rather than the underwriting syndicate being managed jointly by Kidder, Peabody from New York and by Wheat & Company from Richmond, Jim Wheat stated that his firm was prepared to be the sole manager of this important issue and would organize the required combination and divide up among the members the total shares to be sold. Accordingly in March thirty investment bankers met in The Bank of Virginia board room. On April 4, 1954, the 205,000 shares were sold to the public in two and a half hours. It was the largest single stock issue ever handled exclusively by Virginia firms.

For Tom Boushall it was the capstone of a thirty-two-year bank-building program. At last The Bank of Virginia, with its branches, and its complete line of banking services, was free and independent. The sale added 1,600 stockholders to the previous 900, no one of whom owned more than 3 percent of the stock. A limit had been placed on the number of shares going to any one purchaser. Some 83 percent of all stockholders now lived in Virginia.

To The Morris Plan Corporation of America, the sale meant an addition of almost $4 million to its cash reserves. Of this, nearly $2 million represented profit above what it had paid through the years for various issues of Bank of Virginia stock. While the bank had severed connection with the Morris Plan, Arthur Morris remained on the board at Boushall's insistence. One of the first moves following the stock sale was to apply for membership in the Federal Reserve System. The publicity surrounding the stock issue and the number of new stockholders was an immediate asset to the bank, now faced with restoring several hundred thousand dollars to its unearned discount reserve. By the end of 1954 book value of the split stock had increased from the selling price

of $20.25 to $20.86, despite lower operating profits. During the
year more than $10 million were added to total deposits.

Now that the bank's pattern of operations was complete, the
president turned his full attention to pressing internal problems.
With more consumer accounts than any other Virginia bank by
far, The Bank of Virginia would have to build up commercial
loans if it hoped to emerge from the Morris Plan cocoon and take
flight.

Early in 1951 D. Robley Wood had come from the First National Bank of Bluefield, West Virginia, to head the Eighth and
Main branch, thus releasing J. Joseph May to spend full time at
his first love, soliciting commercial accounts. In fact new commercial business was the watchword for all concerned. Constant
negotiations over independence from the parent corporation had
piled paper work and home-office decisions high on the president's desk. As his assistant, Frederick Deane had dealt with these
and helped speed up the solutions that a multitude of bank officers continually sought. But one of Boushall's most difficult decisions still had to be faced. A $100 million banking enterprise
with thirteen branches in six cities could no longer function
efficiently as a one-man operation.

Progress was slowed and frustration fanned by the inability of
various officers to get to the president for the decisions they were
accustomed to have him make. Several good men, measuring their
chances for advancement or differing with the president's forth-
right views, had left. In the summer of 1952 Byers Miller, dean of
the University of Richmond School of Business Administration,
had suggested the school undertake a management study of the
bank. Less than a year later, Dean Miller walked into Boushall's
office.

"Tom," he said, "there is a breakdown in the bank's organization and communications that must be corrected before we go
any farther, and the fault lies at the president's door. You have
twenty-three people reporting directly to you, and all twenty-
three can't get to see you to discuss questions and settle their
problems. The whole organization is going nuts."

He spread out the list: thirteen branch managers, the comptroller, the chief credit officer, the personnel director, the advertising and public relations head, the investment manager, officers
in charge of buildings and sales finance, secretaries of the board
and committees, the president's own secretary, and two or three

others. For the first time Tom Boushall could see the problem in black and white. There would be no further work on a new organization chart, he agreed, until at least a part of the difficulty had been removed. The most obvious first step was to select a coordinator of branches, more than halving the number of officers reporting to the president. Within twenty-four hours the president in his own mind had selected Herbert C. Moseley.

In four years as head of the Petersburg branch, Moseley had increased deposits more than 51 percent while The Bank of Virginia as a whole increased about 36 percent. Transferred to Roanoke, he had stabilized that branch, made it a part of the community, and increased deposits more than 75 percent in less than five years, again exceeding the rate of growth for the bank as a whole. Furthermore, having a traditional banking background, he had concentrated on commercial accounts.

In 1944 searching for new opportunity and more money than the Brookneal branch of the Campbell County Bank and his own small insurance agency could provide, Moseley had written Boushall a letter, typing the final draft himself. Their first interview was not five minutes old before he joined those who had been captivated by the charm and the enthusiasm of The Bank of Virginia president. During a second visit a week later, Boushall dictated to his secretary an offer as branch manager in Petersburg, and Moseley dictated an acceptance.

"Herbert," said the president when the secretary had closed the door, "our Petersburg branch has no commercial business. I want you to go there and build it."

Petersburg businessmen still remembered the weeks following the 1933 bank holiday, when the branch of The Bank of Virginia had handled their daily transactions, but told them the bank did not handle commercial loans. Despite the handicap Moseley swiftly developed commercial accounts. Four years later, in 1948, the president called his Petersburg manager, asking him to drop by Eighth and Main streets at the first opportunity. That night Moseley discussed the call with his wife.

"Roanoke is in trouble. Its little more than an automobile finance agency. I think Mr. Boushall wants me to go out there."

Next day the president confirmed this guess. Moseley went to Roanoke, helped to engineer the sale of Commonwealth Discount Corporation and its auto financing to Jay Rauch and then rapidly expanded every aspect of the branch's business.

In the summer of 1953, Boushall made one of his periodic visits to the Roanoke branch.

"Herbert," he said, "I want you to come to Richmond and be branch coordinator."

"What does that mean?" asked Moseley, aware of the president's penchant for running things.

"It means you'll run the branches. I will not interfere," said Boushall.

Leaving Roanoke in the hands of his assistant, Moseley moved his family to Richmond. On September 1, 1953, he became vice-president and coordinator of branches. Although he had been on a bank's payroll since he graduated from high school, Moseley had not attended college. A part of his understanding with The Bank of Virginia president was that he would attend an advanced management course at the Harvard Business School before assuming his new responsibilities. On December 15 he came back from Harvard to find a secretary waiting for him and a desk next to Rick Deane's on the old Eighth and Main mezzanine.

Though entirely different in background, experience, temperament, and perspective, Moseley and Deane were mentally attuned to one another from the beginning. Moseley was the aggressive administrator and banker, Deane the persuasive manager and cultured public speaker. Together they brought to the bank the hard-headed banking realities of Central Virginia and the broad viewpoint of Harvard's internationally known business school, plus the worldwide intelligence-gathering experience that Deane had enjoyed during the Korean War. Relieved of day-to-day branch operations, the president now began to group internal bank functions. At the end of 1953 the bank's quarterly statement of condition had listed eighteen general officers, most of them dependent on Boushall for decisions. By June 1954 the statement listed only four vice-presidents reporting directly and exclusively to the president: J. Joseph May for commercial loans and investments; Bernard W. LaPrade for mortgages; Moseley as branch coordinator; and Rowland A. Radford, vice-president and cashier, for operations. As assistant to the president, Deane was in a special category.

With reorganization well under way, an even more difficult decision confronted Tom Boushall. This time the catalyst was Aubrey Kidd, now a vice-president and veteran of many verbal exchanges with the president over fiscal policy during his ten years as the bank's auditor. Through the mutual respect engendered by these battles, Kidd had become one of the few men with whom the strong-willed chief executive could talk openly.

Early in 1953 before the sale of the bank's shares to Virginians, Kidd expressed a growing bank concensus.

"Mr. Boushall," he said, "you're not being fair to the officers of the bank."

Somewhat taken back, the president asked why.

"The Morris Plan Corporation of America owns 57 percent of our stock," Kidd explained. "If something happened to you, they could send someone down here to run the bank whom we never heard of and who never heard of us. If he didn't like the way we parted our hair, he could fire the lot of us, and we could have worked for this bank for years for nothing."

"What do you want me to do?" asked Tom Boushall.

"Designate a successor," said Aubrey Kidd.

The vice-president's comments had only crystallized the president's own thinking. At his suggestion the board that year had approved a more generous retirement system, compulsory at age sixty-five. With annual board approval an officer could remain with the bank thereafter, but not in the same position or with the same authority. The Bank of Virginia's founder himself would reach sixty-five on March 28, 1959. To assure a smooth transition in top management, a successor would have to be indicated well enough in advance to test the man himself and to enable other officers to adjust to him. The choice was already somewhat limited. May had chafed at his administrative duties while running the branch at Eighth and Main. His first love was commercial accounts. LaPrade's health was not robust; Radford appeared satisfied with his duties; and so the president transferred more and more responsibility to Herbert Moseley.

Early in October he asked the coordinator of branches to accompany him on a visit to the southside branch on Hull Street. During the drive he asked an opinion. For some time he had been planning a trip to Europe with Marie. What would Moseley think of rotating full authority among the four top vice-presidents? To Moseley it was a test.

"If that's what you have in mind," he replied, "count me out."

Tom Boushall thought this over and made his decision. He asked the board that day to designate Herbert Moseley as the bank's only senior vice-president as of October 11, 1955, with full

authority during his absence. The board complied. Shortly thereafter the Boushalls left for Europe. The president had timed the
trip to give Moseley a chance to make his own decisions, no
longer under the shadow of The Bank of Virginia's forceful
founder.

Meanwhile Rick Deane kept a diary, for he knew the first thing
the president would do on his return was ask for a report on the
heir apparent. When the day came, Deane was ready with chapter
and verse. Moseley had had the full cooperation and support of
all the officers of the bank. Satisfied with what he heard, the president made the change official and requested the board to select
Moseley senior vice-president and began to share full responsibility with him. Henceforth reporting to Moseley as senior vice-
president would be the branch managers, Bernard LaPrade for
mortgages and Rowland Radford for operations, John McClure
as senior credit officer, and John R. Baldwin as director of personnel. The pattern was consistent with the president's natural
tendencies. He would continue to be Mr. Outside; Moseley, Mr.
Inside.

With management succession reasonably well assured, two
other developments began to make themselves felt—one pre-
dictable, one somewhat unusual. The first was a shifting of the
bank's key officers. D. Robley Wood had left to be president of
The Bank of Salem. Moseley's choice as a replacement was William T. Gordon, then manager at Fourth and Grace. It was an
early indication that the senior vice-president believed strongly
in promoting from within.

In 1957 the president had discovered Heyward T. Denyes at
the Industrial National Bank of Detroit, a former Morris Plan
bank. Another outside man, Denyes was brought in as regional
vice-president, with overall responsibility for offices in Norfolk,
Portsmouth, and Newport News.

Late in 1956 Rowland Radford resigned as one of the three
ranking vice-presidents to return to the Georgia banking scene.
The following year Bernard LaPrade's health failed. In 1959
William Gordon, as the new regional vice-president for central
Virginia, joined the list of top bank officers. Reorganization was
progressing, and the Moseley men were emerging.

A second and corollary development was the rise of Frederick
Deane. By the time Herbert Moseley became senior vice-president

in 1955, Deane had almost worked himself out of a job as assistant to the president.

Boushall had continued to delegate responsibilities and reduce the number of personal decisions he had formerly made. The stacks of paper on his desk represented current business. Separation from the Morris Plan was complete.

When Rowland Radford resigned, Cashier William L. Tiller had assumed a host of operational duties and had little time to look after investments, which had been one of his responsibilities. Deane went to the president. In addition to acting as assistant, he would like to take on the bank's multimillion-dollar investment portfolio. Although his father had been an investment banker, Deane knew little of this phase of the business. But Tom Boushall had made up his mind to delegate and not interfere. In three years he had come to respect the ability and the broad perspective that Rick Deane had brought to the bank. Here was a chance to make another judgment in the possible line of succession. With two words he turned a multimillion-dollar investment program over to his assistant. From that day investment decisions were referred to Deane. If there was a complaint, the president stood behind his new investment officer. By the end of 1956 Deane was listed among the regular vice-presidents.

With the branches locked in, banking services virtually complete, and a wide range of decisions delegated, the president began spending more and more time outside the bank. Toward the end of 1956, he was convinced that this time he had a potential top executive who was both ambitious enough and capable enough to succeed him. Since MacEachern had left to complete his banking career in South Carolina, the post of executive vice-president had been vacant. Instead of one man next to the top, the reorganization at first had provided for four. As senior vice-president Moseley held a title for which there was no precedent. At the November 1956 board meeting, the president proposed one more step toward a new bank management. Board members, he suggested, "would be wise" to elect Herbert Moseley executive vice-president of the bank. The board agreed and did so.

Moseley continued to absorb more responsibilities within the bank and to take the initiative on some of his own ideas. One of these was the firm conviction that opportunity for advancement should be opened wider to young men. Along with the realization that their services had to be tailored to a rapidly expanding economy, banks generally had begun to realize that in competition with new industry and the growing service segment of the economy, banking as a career was not attracting bright young future executives. The banker's reputation as an ultraconservative financial advisor had begun to change, but banking salaries and opportunities were often less appealing than those offered by other types of business in an advancing Virginia. Back in the 1920s, the Morris Plan Bank of Richmond had made a pioneer effort to recruit promising young college graduates at the suggestion of Boushall, himself the only college-educated bank president in Richmond at the time. But the initial attempt had failed. Now Moseley, with Boushall's concurrence, renewed the effort.

The Wachovia Bank of North Carolina, successful in various directions, had a flourishing recruitment program. On a visit to North Carolina in 1958 Moseley took over the Wachovia plan in its entirety, including Richard C. Buell, who was running it. Buell had his own methods, but under his guidance the bank acquired a full-fledged training program and a system of evaluating existing bank personnel that opened executive eyes. The man himself stayed with the bank only about five years, but the system he introduced lived after him, producing a number of young executives, including three executive vice-presidents who had been members of the initial training class.

Buell was one of the few men that Moseley would bring in from outside, but the move fit his management theory of finding the right man for the job to be done. He applied the same philosophy to another Bank of Virginia innovation. From the days of the old Phillip Levy account in the early 1920s, the bank had experimented with various ways of serving as financial middleman for business and industry, offering its experience with consumer credit for a fee to relieve firms whose primary business was producing or selling. In 1953 the president had come up with an idea, adopted from a New Jersey bank, of providing a consumer credit service to retail merchants, who were maintaining their own credit departments with questionable results and varying reactions from customers. Accordingly the bank launched the Merchants Bank Credit Service. Customers in effect opened a line of credit at the bank in the form of a permanent revolving loan. Against this they could charge merchandise at participating retail establishments, making regular payments to the bank, which billed them once a month for outstanding purchases. On each purchase the bank advanced the retailer his money, less a 6 percent discount, and kept the necessary records. Purchasers had thirty days to pay without interest. After that the charge was 1 percent a month.

With various modifications the Merchants Bank Credit Service became The Bank of Virginia Charge Plan in 1958, when Chase Manhattan Bank in New York and several other large banks initiated a similar service. In 1958 the bank, in association with others, helped form Interbank Card Association, and went national with Master Charge. The original approach through the retailer had resulted in some complications. Little effort was made to educate the customer. Consequently he was sometimes incensed when his account was sold without his knowledge. In his mind, his debt was to the retailer, and edging the bank into the picture seemed somehow to be a reflection on his integrity.

The indifferent success of the original plan prompted some lengthy discussions among the bank's officers. The plan had been test-marketed in Norfolk, and Heyward Denyes, regional vice-president for Tidewater, was against it. One evening in a hotel room, Moseley and Denyes, with the help of several others, reached agreement. The plan deserved a fair trial, but with someone at the helm who understood retail credit. A credit man was accordingly hired from a well-known retail firm, and the service was pushed hard. Credit cards were issued to the purchaser, along with an advertising program to explain the service. While the basic idea did not originate with The Bank of Virginia, it was first among southern banks to adopt the system.

Rick Deane suggested another step toward big-time banking. Several of the nation's larger banks employed economists to forecast business conditions and to pass some of their findings along to bank customers. In the spring of 1959, Dr. R. Pierce Lumpkin of the University of Richmond's department of economics contracted with the bank as a consultant and began lecturing and writing on economic matters. He later agreed to full-time employment at the bank.

On the outside Tom Boushall was expanding his involvement in community, state, and national affairs, fields he had entered well before most bank officials. By now other bank officers were also accepting community assignments, considering them good for business and as an obligation of conscience. Through their banking associations and as individuals, bankers in Virginia and elsewhere were pursuing their interests before legislative bodies and quietly contributing to political campaigns in which they thought those interests were at stake.

The sometimes violent opposition of the business community to the policies of President Roosevelt and in somewhat lesser degree to President Truman formed the basis for the more direct and visible political activity that now began to emerge. Again Tom Boushall was in the vanguard. The 1952 presidential campaign provided the first real opportunity. Early in the year Boushall had made another decision. Senator Robert Taft of Ohio could not be elected. The obvious choice was Dwight Eisenhower. Having reached this conclusion, Boushall went to work with characteristic vigor and singleness of purpose. In May he issued a call to a group of politically sensitive friends to plan strategy. With their support he led virtual insurrections at local and later at district Republican conventions and helped carry them for Eisenhower. Boushall himself went to the state Republican convention in Roanoke as a voting delegate committed to Eisenhower. In the thick of the maneuvering there, he was on the winning side when the final vote was taken.

The Bank of Virginia president was a Southern Democrat by birth and inclination and had always supported the Democratic state administration, led by Senator Harry F. Byrd, as had most other Virginia businessmen who differed sharply with national policy. In the state elections of 1954, he again became an active Democrat. But two years later when Eisenhower ran for a second term, Boushall was a leader among the Democrats for Eisenhower. Although the majority of The Bank of Virginia customers were regular Democrats, deposits in the years 1951 and 1952 showed greater gains than in any previous year.

Boushall's commitment to education continued to project him into more outside work, still greater recognition, and further controversy. After serving on the Richmond City School Board for several years, he was named to the State Board of Education. However, his moderate views during the massive resistance era following the Supreme Court school desegregation decision in 1954 prevented his reappointment to the State Board of Education until the late 1960s. Also continued during the 1950s was his personal and the bank's financial support of the Graduate School of Business Administration at the University of Virginia in Charlottesville. A school of consumer banking had been set up at the university with Boushall's help.

Both the political and the educational involvement were primarily matters of personal conviction. Oriented more toward bank business was the Salute to Industry dinner the president initiated in 1958 in honor of the Reynolds Metals Company, which had moved its major headquarters to Richmond from Louisville, Kentucky. Governor J. Lindsay Almond headed the list of attending dignitaries. The affair was continued with the same theme through the early 1960s.

CHAPTER X

Boushall Steps Down

FOR THE BANK OF VIRGINIA the twenties had been a fight for acceptance, the thirties a struggle for solvency, and the forties a battle over branch banking. The 1950s brought full maturity to a complete banking enterprise. Beginning with a burst of new business from additional branches, the decade ended with the retirement and partial—but far from complete— eclipse of Tom Boushall. As his compulsory retirement date approached, the president moved to ensure Herbert Moseley's succession. Through the bank's attorney, Wirt P. Marks, he let it be known to the board that this was his wish and that it was in the bank's best interest. Prior to the January 1959 board meeting, he approached Moseley with customary directness.

"Herbert," he said, "I want you to become president of the bank."

Moseley wanted no misunderstandings.

"Mr. Boushall," he said, "I think I can run the bank, but I won't run it the way you do."

The Morris Plan Bank of Richmond had been founded by and had prospered under Thomas C. Boushall, an innovator, builder, and humanitarian. Now circumstances had produced to head the fully developed bank Herbert Moseley, a management-conscious team man interested in both growth and profits.

The January board meeting amended the bank's bylaws to accommodate them both. Moseley was elected president and chief executive officer as of April 1, 1959. Boushall was elected to the newly created post of active chairman of the board, with such duties as the board might from time to time assign him, to serve for twelve months, a tenure renewable annually by the board. Compensation would be the president's present salary, less his annual pension.

Boushall's semiretirement acted as a signal to his friends, admirers, and some of his fiercest competitors. In June 1959 the University of Richmond—where Robert T. Marsh, president of First and Merchants National Bank, was chancellor—awarded

Boushall the honorary degree of Doctor of Commercial Science. In March the Newcomen Society chose The Bank of Virginia for national recognition of business and industry leaders, assembling a stellar list of guests from across Virginia to honor Boushall and Arthur Morris, who remained on the bank board. A few days before April 1, his retirement date, he and Mrs. Boushall set sail once more for Europe in order that Moseley might take over his new duties on his own.

Seven weeks later he returned to his old office on the original mezzanine next to Moseley to undertake perhaps the most difficult adjustment of his life—letting someone else run The Bank of Virginia. Moseley was in full favor and fully assured of his officers' support and cooperation. Although the organization chart indicated no specific duties for the chairman and no one reported directly to him, old habits were hard to break. Policy questions still came to Boushall, but they were always referred to Moseley. For his part the new president was careful to consult the chairman when he knew of his special interest in a problem and to avoid anything to which Boushall might take exception. At board meetings Boushall devoted himself to supporting the new management and attempting to transfer to Moseley the confidence the board had had in the founder.

After a year of this hands-off policy, Aubrey Kidd walked across the mezzanine to Boushall's door, his steps loud in the after-hours emptiness. The chairman was writing in longhand on a pad. After a minute he looked up inquiringly.

"I owe you an apology," said his visitor.

Boushall looked puzzled.

"I didn't think you could do it," said Aubrey Kidd, referring to Boushall's relinquishing the executive reins.

There were still the memoranda, at first to Moseley, who quickly sent them on to Kidd, Deane, or other officers. They carried a new note of deference.

"Think about this for a few days. If the idea is no good, forget it. If it is good, act on it."

Still, it was not easy to live under the shadow of the man who for so long had personified The Bank of Virginia. Finally in 1962 at his own suggestion the chairman moved his office from the executive mezzanine to the quiet area of the second floor. The sign outside his door differed from any other identification in the bank. As he had always been known to every bank employee and to friend and foe on the outside, it read simply "Mr. Bou-shall." There was no need for more.

An original thinker by nature, Thomas C. Boushall believed that only innovation could build a strong new bank in Virginia's financial capital, where major banks were already entrenched. Adopting the lonely orphan of consumer lending, he had looked back to see all other banks follow suit, and still The Bank of Virginia grew to be one of the five largest in the state and well within the nation's three hundred largest. Not without cause was it finally advertised as "THE Bank of Virginia."

Few men in recent Virginia history could claim credit for more progress, both inside and outside the banking enterprise than Boushall. Never a faceless committee member, he conceived Blue Cross from the unlikely paternity of a minor Richmond Chamber of Commerce assignment. Offered the chair of the U.S. Chamber of Commerce Committee on Education, he accepted on condition the chamber appropriate twenty-five thousand dollars for a study of the relationship of education to community economic status. Chairing the consumer banking committee of the Virginia Bankers Association, he attached the proviso that at least one luncheon on the subject be held at each VBA convention. Often in the minority—sometimes a minority of one—he was an artist at disagreement, softening with a smile and natural charm words that, in themselves, were often diamond-sharp. In defending the bank and its philosophy, he was a keen and resourceful debater. While he was on trial along with branch banking before the State Senate Committee in 1948, a colleague urged the late Senator Harry Stuart, a committee member and seldom at a loss for words himself, to ask The Bank of Virginia president a question.

"I wouldn't ask that man a question for five hundred dollars," replied the Senator.

As an executive, he was kind to a fault, unable to bear the unpleasantness of a dismissal or demotion within the bank. Only once did he undertake to relieve an officer of his duties. Supremely confident in his own judgment, he imposed that judgment on the bank and all who worked there, and yet those who left as a consequence remained his friends. Intrigued by new ideas, he raised some that would not stay aloft and others that were not properly propelled, but the aggregate of those that did succeed was enough to fill two successful lives and formed a pattern that every bank in the state would finally follow.

 After innumerable heated arguments and a dozen resignations, he remained a loyal friend and supporter of Arthur Morris and enjoyed his life-long friendship in return. Through sheer determination, with only one lung and only half of his ribs, he won a nine-year struggle with a disease that was a major killer in his time. Born in comfortable circumstances and given a college education by his father as a matter of course, he was a constant champion of the less fortunate in this and other respects both outside his business interests and, more significantly, inside them as well. Ahead of his time in public as well as banking matters— even in his later years—he managed to attract increasing honors and admiration while playing the self-imposed role of eternal gadfly. Finally, perhaps as a crowning achievement, he stepped aside while many active years were still left to let others remodel and redirect the enterprise he had built.

 Even in semiretirement he would recast the meaning of that word, following his convictions still. He threw all of his unfailing energy, his prestige, and his contacts into the campaigns of Virginia Democrats and Republican presidential candidates, to Virginia's first Republican governor in eighty-seven years, and finally to a political independent, Harry Flood Byrd, Jr.

 In 1959 he was named to an eight-man commission to study Richmond's tax structure, served as state cochairman of the Crusade for Freedom fund, raising money for Radio Free Europe, and was a prime mover in Sigma Nu, his Greek letter fraternity at the University of North Carolina. The same year he was selected chairman of a committee to celebrate the fiftieth anniversary of consumer credit in commercial banking across the nation and was named chairman of Richmond's first biracial committee.

 When Virginia's state of mind on public schools had caught up with his own thinking, he was again appointed to the State Board of Education by Governor Mills E. Godwin, Jr., in the 1960s and served on the statewide steering committee for a series of Governor's Conferences on Education, still preaching progress others were not yet willing to accept.

 In 1961 the American Bankers Association presented him with a bronze plaque for contributions in the instalment loan field.

The same year he was given the Richmond First Club's good government award; appeared with Ralph Pitman before a United States Senate subcommittee hearing to oppose a "full disclosure" bill as unwarranted federal intrusion; was an honored guest, along with Pitman and Aubrey Kidd, at the tenth anniversary of the School of Consumer Banking at the University of Virginia; and watched the bank cooperate in a college student loan program guaranteed by a new State Education Assistance Authority, an idea he had presented to Governor Colgate Darden about twenty years earlier.

In 1962 he was named to the Virginia Advisory Council on Educational Television by Governor Albertis S. Harrison, Jr., where the following year he argued successfully against acceptance of a three-hundred-thousand-dollar federal grant toward a fund-raising goal, for fear of federal interference. Also in 1962 he was named president of the Longwood College Foundation.

The following year he retired from the chairmanship and board of directors of Sweet Briar College and was honored at a New York dinner by his friends after being awarded the American Bankers Association plaque at the association's Instalment Credit Conference.

In 1964 he was honored by Big Brothers of Richmond, elected chairman of the Central Virginia Educational Television Corporation, and volunteered as State Treasurer of Virginia Democrats for Goldwater and Byrd, as he had been for Democrats for Nixon in 1960. He had also been a prime mover in Richmond Forward, a nonpartisan group backing a city council slate.

In 1966 and 1967 his political activities projected him into familiar trouble. Along with other banks The Bank of Virginia had given its employees a chance to contribute as individuals to the campaign fund for Virginia's junior United States senator, A. Willis Robertson, chairman of the Senate Banking Committee. On the board of the Portsmouth branch was Dr. Russell M. Cox, close friend of William B. Spong, also of Portsmouth, who was running in the primary against Senator Robertson. Dr. Cox dispatched an open letter to Boushall, chastising him for the bank's "coercion and arm-twisting tactics." Dr. Cox resigned from the board, and Spong defeated Senator Robertson by about six hundred votes. At about this time Boushall was appointed coordinator of Governor Mills E. Godwin's Conferences on Education and to the steering committee for the $81-million state bond issue for colleges and mental hospitals.

Over the next three years, he was appointed chairman of the Richmond Public Schools Foundation and the Richmond Area Tuberculosis Association's Christmas seal campaign, resumed his seat as a member of the State Board of Education, was named general chairman of the Capital Region Citizens Committee for Open Spaces and Parks, and was appointed by Governor Holton to the Virginia Public School Authority. Still preaching the future, he told the home builders of Richmond the area still needed five thousand more housing units, and on the Hundredth Anniversary Celebration of Public Education in Virginia he asserted that education in the Old Dominion was still lagging behind other states.

To his other awards were added the Liberty Bell from the Richmond Bar Association and citations from the Richmond Junior Chamber of Commerce, the state chapter of the Public Relations Society of America, the National Conference of Christians and Jews and the Virginia Education Association.

CHAPTER XI

A New Team and New Directions

T O SUCCEED ITS FOUNDER in the president's chair, The Bank of Virginia had produced a man who in many ways contrasted sharply with his predecessor, but whose abilities were well suited to the times and circumstances in which the bank now found itself.

Moseley, having graduated from the Campbell County High School, was faced with the fact that his father had spent the money he had saved to send him to college in seeking a cure for the bone disease young Moseley had contracted after breaking his arm. Young Moseley, traveling in the family Model T, set out to visit Lynchburg College to see if he could get a job to work his way through. On the way, however, he stopped off to see Mr. Anderson, the president of the Campbell County Bank at Rustburg. He had been told that there might be a position open in the bank. At nineteen he was offered the job at forty dollars a month and took it. Two years later Moseley applied for a leave of absence to serve as assistant state bank examiner. After the experience he returned to manage the Brookneal Branch of the Campbell County Bank. Incidentally, the branch's total soon exceeded that of the head office at Rustburg.

Moseley's transfer to The Bank of Virginia's Petersburg branch was an easy one but somewhat reduced in prestige. In Brookneal his authority to lend extended to the full resources of the branch bank, about thirty thousand dollars. In Petersburg he could lend only a thousand dollars without approval from Richmond.

His performance in Petersburg and Roanoke was a model of what he would later accomplish as president of The Bank of Virginia—joining civic and community organizations, aggressively pursuing new accounts, delegating responsibilities to subordinates to enable them to grow and develop.

As president in Richmond, he put in longer hours than anyone else, often arriving at his office shortly after 7:00 A.M. and usually leaving either to attend a civic club meeting or to read through a briefcaseful of papers. To build business he lived by Confederate

General Nathan B. Forrest's admonition, "Get there fustest with the mostest," inviting new business executives transferring to Virginia out to lunch before they found a place to live, calling on newly appointed management men before their furniture arrived. He compensated for being an exacting and demanding executive by moving younger men in the bank along as fast as their demonstrated talents indicated but, unlike his predecessor, never hesitating to correct the mistake of placing the wrong man in a job.

Among other attributes he possessed a fine aptitude for putting management theory into effective practice. Each officer drew up his own objectives for the year and was judged and his salary adjusted on the basis of the results. Moseley's talents fit exactly the organization he inherited. By now all the larger banks of Virginia resembled each other in service profile, although The Bank of Virginia was still far ahead in the number of consumer accounts. For both these and other lines of business, competition was acute. The future of The Bank of Virginia would be built by extending and perfecting current services rather than by pioneering in new ones. And these talents would soon be put to the test in the greatest expansion and stiffest competition that banking in Virginia had ever known, involving changes that would rearrange the ranking of individual banks that had been static for generations and transforming banking patterns throughout the state. As this metamorphosis unfolded the team of Moseley and Deane developed in depth, each complementing the other in philosophy and talent.

A product of Boston's Back Bay—his mother was a Coolidge—Rick Deane went to a New England prep school and Harvard, earning a master's degree "with distinction" from Harvard Business School, where he had been offered a faculty post. Recalled to active duty during the Korean War, he had been an assistant to one of the deputy directors of the Central Intelligence Agency, in which he had served from 1944 to 1946. With his release from active duty imminent, he had already accepted the offer at Harvard, but on the return trip from a visit to his wife's family in Charleston, South Carolina, he stopped off in Richmond for a routine check on the Central National Bank, which had been recruiting at Harvard. The result was a dinner attended by Edward A. Wayne, president of the Federal Reserve Bank in Richmond, and Edwin Hyde, a Bank of Virginia alumnus, then chairman of the board of Miller & Rhoads department store.

Shortly thereafter, Hyde, attending a civic club dinner, sat next to Tom Boushall. Greatly impressed by Deane, he told Boushall about him and handed Boushall Deane's résumé. Boushall called Deane. The Bank of Virginia was not on the exclusive list of possible employers compiled by the Harvard Business School placement service but, like so many before him, Deane was mesmerized by the charm and missionary zeal of Tom Boushall. From assistant to the president in August 1953, Deane became a vice-president three years later and in 1959 was one of three senior vice-presidents recommended to the board by the new president. The other two had served with Moseley as ranking vice-presidents in the reorganization of the early 1950s—J. Joseph May for commercial business, and John S. McClure for credit and loan decisions. Bernard LaPrade's health prevented his continuing his duties among the top bank officers.

Moseley was not long in demonstrating that Deane's advance was not an isolated move. During 1960, his first full year as president, eleven officers and four staff members were upgraded and given new responsibilities. As he had in Roanoke, Moseley also worked to get leading businessmen elected to both the central board in Richmond and those at the branches. The new members were a clear indication of the bank's growing prestige. Other characteristics of the new management were soon apparent. Promotions would come from within. In his first five years as president, Moseley brought in only two officers from outside, both specialists—Jesse H. Ellsworth from the Federal Reserve Bank in 1961 as assistant vice-president and Alfred P. Dodge from the home appliance sales business as vice-president in charge of sales and sales training.

Initiated into banking in Depression days, Moseley had had early lessons in cost cutting and the importance of profits deeply impressed on him. Where The Bank of Virginia's founder had trusted his instincts and poured resources into innovation, Moseley wanted cost studies and market analyses before major decisions were made. Each operation had its budget made up in advance and, more often than not, was reduced somewhat in the process of passing in and out of the president's office. Moseley also insisted that bank management be a team effort. Each Monday, Wednesday, and Friday the new president met with top officers at 7:30 A.M., the group varying somewhat with the items on the agenda. Gradually the discussion sessions were reduced to two a week, then one, as the president's knowledge of banking affairs broadened and new men settled in their jobs. But for a decade Moseley would meet at least once every two weeks with key management. Officers and staff were quick to react to the new president's example of long hours and aggressive pursuit of new business, combined with the new incentive offered younger men who demonstrated ability.

Aided by the opening of the new building in Petersburg, Bank of Virginia deposits averaged $5 million more in 1959 than the previous year. Trust assets were 25 percent higher. But more important, net operating profit showed a 15.2 percent gain. The pace continued in 1960, despite a general slowdown in the nation's economy. Deposits, including the merger into the Richmond bank of the Chesterfield County bank, increased by a modest 6.7 percent, but the average increase by banks in the area was only 1 percent. However, the 1960 increase in earnings surpassed that of the previous year, totaling 17.7 percent, a good deal of it the result of tightened control over expenses. In 1961 earnings again set a record, crossing the $1 million mark for the first time. Deposits increased by $24,472,380 over the previous year and loans by almost $15 million. Growth continued to demand more space. Land was purchased and plans drawn for a new Chesterfield branch in Chester and land leased for drive-in facilities on Staples Mill Road, both in 1961. Net operating earnings increased again in 1962 and in 1963. In April 1964 the balance sheet topped $200 million, just ten years after it had reached $100 million in 1953. The bank itself had climbed to a rank of 202nd in the nation. By 1963 the original building at Eighth and Main required renovation at a cost of $850,000, two and one-third times the building's original cost.

But the main effort of top bank officers, particularly that of Moseley and Deane, was in response to the transformation of Virginia banking as the full vindication of the original Bank of Virginia philosophy of growth through branching exploded across Virginia.

West Germany, Italy, and Japan, having recovered from the ravages of World War II, had emerged as economic powers, stimulating American consumer goods manufacturers with their competition, and providing stronger American markets and profitable new investments abroad.

By the late 1950s and early 1960s, America was becoming ac-

customed to the longest period in her history of unbroken prosperity with relatively stable prices. Spurred by the Cold War defense effort, but unhampered by either major conflict or economic
depression, output mushroomed, technology began in earnest its
transformation of economic life, and suburbia began to emerge
as a social and political force.

The rush for the suburbs and an unending supply of goods
and services placed a premium on convenience in order to attract
customers and increase sales. Shopping centers continued to
spring up at every urban crossroad. Relative income levels moved
steadily upward, particularly in the South. Television's impact
on public awareness and on consumer demand was a leveling
influence.

The South's industrial growth, with all its implications for the
economy, the society, and the citizenry, continued to keep pace
with the eastern part of the nation. Southern cities began to re-
semble their northern counterparts. Southern farms, adopting
mechanization and grassland farming, demanded more and more
city conveniences. As technology and communications pulled the
nation closer together, the South began to emulate the rest of the
country in financial matters.

Savings and loan associations, fueled by a new burst of home
building, cut deeply into the banking market, while the rapid
spread of home-based credit unions in businesses and industries
encroached on consumer lending. Banks elsewhere in the nation
were beginning to follow the industrial trend toward conglomerates. Bank holding company growth in other states had produced
the Federal Bank Holding Company Act of 1956. Merger and
branch banking were the natural consequences of consolidating
industrial ownership and proliferating retail outlets.

The Bank of Virginia and its Richmond competitors were
busy expanding within the limits of the 1948 branch banking
amendments. The bank had been vividly reminded of those limits
when in 1956 it had drawn plans for a branch in the Village
Shopping Center at Three Chopt Road and Patterson Avenue.

The 1948 law had restricted the bank to branches within the
city limits, but the new building straddled the county line. The
result was some prolonged legal hair-splitting over exactly where
a banking transaction took place within a bank building. The
State Corporation Commission finally ruled that banking was
consummated at the teller's window, and the interior of the new

branch was redesigned with the tellers in the city and the customers waiting in line in the county. The same year the commission had reversed a previous ruling against banks operating in state-owned buildings and permitted a branch at the Medical College of Virginia. Halted at the city line as far as its own branches were concerned, the bank turned to a pair of its creatures—The Bank of Henrico and The Chesterfield County Bank.

Boushall had persuaded Colonel Ellery Huntington, as a cooperative courtesy, to finance the two when local interests had approached the bank itself, and Financial General owned two-thirds of Henrico, holding it until it had been in existence five years and could then be merged into The Bank of Virginia. Financial General held 90 percent of the stock of the Bank of Chesterfield.

After the Chesterfield merger, Virginia Standard Corporation stock was distributed to the bank's stockholders and stapled to the parent bank's stock, so that one could not be sold without the other. Virginia Standard, a convenient insurance agency subsidiary, continued to function as the bank's insurance arm for both automobile casualty and borrower's life.

The merger gave the Richmond bank an additional $2,486,324 in deposits, and new branches in Chester, Bellwood Army Quartermaster Depot, and two suburban shopping centers, bringing its offices in the Richmond metropolitan area to thirteen.

The bank, twice before barred from a branch in Southside Plaza Shopping Center, finally received approval early in 1959 and a year later in Stratford Hills Shopping Center, in addition to the branch at the Bellwood Army Quartermaster Depot.

Competitors too had been busy with suburban Richmond branches. In each of its other cities, where its own branches were frozen, the bank was being steadily surrounded by the branches of local banks. The situation was particularly acute in Norfolk and Roanoke, where Bank of Virginia branches were barred from suburban shopping centers.

Other pressures were also building up. During 1959 State-Planters had merged with Citizens National Bank in Petersburg, which was within the twenty-five-mile limitation of the 1948 act. The new Bank of Virginia branch building in Petersburg, completed with appropriate fanfare the same year, now had big-time competition in that city. Also in 1959 First and Merchants National Bank merged first with the Savings Bank and Trust Company on Main Street, the only Richmond bank that was not gaining in deposits, and later with the First National Bank of Ashland, some fifteen miles to the north.

At the end of the 1950s, Virginia's biggest bank could offer only $1,550,000 in industrial credits, and the four largest Richmond banks together could muster only about $4,900,000, whereas in fifteen North Carolina cities, industry could get $5 million from one bank.

And it was not banks alone that were hurting; Virginia's industrial growth was falling behind that of her neighbor to the south. Banks faced an internal threat as well. Unhampered by state legal restrictions, a pair of bank holding companies were steadily acquiring local banks.

One of them was represented by a familiar figure—Arthur J. Morris. He was board chairman of Financial General Corporation, now based in Washington, D.C. With fourteen banks in Virginia, Maryland, and the District, Financial General had become the sixth-largest banking organization in the state by December 1961. Eighth-largest was The First Virginia Corporation of Arlington, also with a Bank of Virginia connection. Bank loans had helped to finance E. T. Holland in moving from a base of several small loan companies into a complex system for controlling several banks in Virginia's Washington suburbs, now one of the fastest-growing metropolitan areas in the country.

CHAPTER XII

The Bank Makes Its Move

THE ECONOMIC NEED was clear, but the Virginia General Assembly had taken action in 1948 that had effectively removed the possibility of further statewide branching. By 1960 the restrictive chickens of the 1948 legislation were coming home to roost with a vengeance. Enjoying fewer branching and merger limitations, banks in Maryland and North Carolina had become several times as large as the largest Virginia bank. Also, in addition to losing industrial loans to out-of-state banks, Virginia bankers feared that a bank holding company from suburban Washington would become the largest banking enterprise in the state.

Something had to be done. In the spring of 1961 the heads of seven large banks assembled in Richmond to decide. They included First and Merchants National Bank; State-Planters Bank of Commerce and Trusts; Central National Bank; National Bank of Commerce, Norfolk; First National Exchange Bank, Roanoke; Peoples National Bank of Charlottesville; and Shenandoah Valley National Bank, Harrisonburg. The Bank of Virginia was kept abreast of the discussions but, since it had been the focus of the 1948 controversy, it would take no part in what was to follow.

The seven bankers produced the Richmond Plan, later renamed the Metropolitan Plan, which sounded better to small-town bankers, always somewhat suspicious of major moves promoted from the state capital. The Metropolitan Plan would have removed some restrictions on branching from city to city. Any bank could merge with any other bank located in a city of fifteen thousand or more and could thereafter establish branches in the new city and within five miles of the city limits.

The seven fathers of the Metropolitan Plan had in mind presenting it for adoption at the forthcoming convention of the Virginia Bankers Association at Hot Springs in June 1961. In the meantime top-ranking officers of the seven banks concerned once more began making the rounds of their correspondent banks as they had in 1947, but this time telling exactly the opposite story.

Where they had been against further branching fourteen years earlier, they were now in favor of wide-open city branching. Their arguments were intriguing to many local bank directors. An exchange of stock with a large and prosperous bank represented a financial windfall for small bank stockholders. Access to the big bank's assets could represent new entree to industries coming to town. On the other hand the plan threatened pressure toward loss of local independence and an end to unfettered management decision-making. For the small bank not wanting to consider merging, it meant the possibility of finding itself surrounded by branches of a large out-of-town bank that had purchased another local bank.

At the Virginia Bankers Association convention, the Metropolitan Plan was the prime topic of conversation, and the discussions were many and heated. Finally the plan was presented to the general business session. The officers of The Bank of Virginia —not without some effort—sat through the debates, listening to all its old arguments now championed by its former opponents. As the debate dragged on, the seven backers of the plan sensed that the convention was not ready to adopt their package. To save the proposal they moved that the convention appoint a committee to study the whole question of branch banking. The committee would then report to a special meeting of the association in November to present a final plan to the 1962 session of the Virginia General Assembly. But Harry Nichols, president of the Southern Bank of Norfolk, proposed an amendment to eliminate the November meeting and have the committee report instead to the regular June convention of the VBA in 1962. More discussion ensued, but the amendment passed.

It meant that there would be no action to liberalize branch banking until at least the 1964 General Assembly session. That evening Herbert Moseley and Frederick Deane sat down in Moseley's room at the hotel. For at least a year, Moseley and Deane had been talking about forming a holding company. They thought that several of The Bank of Virginia's correspondent banks would be amenable to acquisition. The holding company would extend the bank's services into cities from which they were now excluded, and the newly acquired affiliates would be free to branch.

The Virginia Bankers Association action now left the holding company as the only avenue offering the bank a chance for major growth. Other Richmond banks had been talking about such a move. If The Bank of Virginia acted quickly, it could beat them. That evening the decision to form a bank holding company was made. Immediately upon their return home, Moseley and Deane discussed the matter with the directors of the bank, who concurred in the decision. The bank's officers then tried to reach agreement with a sufficient number of other banks, so that the holding company could proceed as soon as possible.

D. Robley Wood, a former Bank of Virginia vice-president, was president of The Bank of Salem. Shown the advantages, he agreed to recommend the move to his board of directors. Besides its downtown headquarters in Salem, the bank had established a branch in a shopping center on the outskirts of town in the suburbs of Roanoke.

At the eastern end of the state, the Bank of Warwick in the county adjoining the shipbuilding city of Newport News had two suburban branches. It had already tried to effect a merger with The First National Bank of Newport News, but it had not gone through. Liaison with this bank, through a director, Virginia Delegate Lewis McMurran, resulted in bringing it into the group.

At the edge of northern Virginia's sprawling series of apartments and shopping centers, The Bank of Occoquan had offices in Occoquan, Woodbridge, and Dumfries, established with financial help from The Bank of Virginia. The Manderfields, father and son, who controlled and operated the banks, were enthusiastic over the prospects, and a short conversation brought this bank into the expanding group.

In the Richmond area the Chesterfield County Bank had already been merged with its parent, The Bank of Virginia, but The Bank of Henrico remained separate. By retaining its separate identity, Henrico's branching rights could be preserved, and its offices in Sandston and Highland Springs would be added to the new banking group.

The keystone of the holding company and the location of its home offices would be The Bank of Virginia, with its twenty-one locations in six cities making the new corporation the largest of the three bank holding companies in the state. On December 22, 1961, The Bank of Virginia board of directors formally approved the plan to form Virginia Commonwealth Corporation as a registered bank holding company under the 1956 federal bank holding company act and voted to recommend to the bank's stock-holders that they accept the offer to be made by the new holding company to exchange its stock for their bank stock. The charter to be requested of the State Corporation Commission called for authority to issue up to 1.5 million shares of common stock at ten dollars par. Of these, 497,783 shares would be exchanged for most of the stock held by stockholders of the individual banks involved, making a total of some thirty-six hundred investors.

The State Corporation Commission granted Virginia Common-wealth Corporation its charter on January 10, 1962, but final authority had to await approval of the board of governors of the Federal Reserve System. On December 21, 1962, this approval was in hand, and the member banks began operations as Virginia Commonwealth Corporation. Initially officers were drawn from The Bank of Virginia. Thomas C. Boushall was elected chairman of the board; Herbert C. Moseley, president and chief executive officer; Frederick Deane, Jr., executive vice-president; Aubrey V. Kidd, secretary; and William L. Tiller, treasurer. The group con-sisted of the following banks with total assets at year-end 1962:

The Bank of Virginia	$ 176,059,000
The Bank of Warwick	18,521,000
The Bank of Salem	11,430,000
The Bank of Occoquan	9,231,000
The Bank of Henrico	3,398,000
Combined	$ 218,639,000

For reasons best known to themselves, 141 stockholders in the five banks did not exchange their stock. Nevertheless, the new corporation owned between 96 and 99.7 percent of each bank's equity. The market price, when the new stock was first quoted over the counter, was 12⅜ bid, 12½ asked, adjusted for sub-sequent stock splits.

Throughout the fall and early winter of 1961, the Virginia Bankers Association Kramer Committee, appointed to study the question of liberalizing branch banking, had met periodically, but could hardly agree on even as much as the shape of the bar-gaining table. Large city banks favored some form of the Metro-politan Plan; smaller bank representatives generally opposed it. The Christmas holidays slipped by as Main Street buzzed with rumors of possible holding company moves by Richmond's other major banks.

By the time the General Assembly convened, the handwriting on the wall was becoming increasingly clear to the large city banks. The die had been cast with the organizational moves for formation of Virginia Commonwealth Corporation. On January 14, four days after the legislative session began, a pamphlet appeared, carrying the names of Robert T. Marsh, president of First and Merchants National Bank; J. Harvie Wilkinson, president of State-Planters Bank of Commerce and Trusts; and W. Harry Schwarzschild, Jr., president of Central National Bank. Citing chapter and verse, with figures, it argued that Virginia industrial development was falling behind neighboring states because her banks could not command the lending power necessary to finance plant construction.

Meanwhile State Senator Shirley T. Holland, president of Farmers Bank of Windsor, Virginia, a small-town bank in Isle of Wight County, and chairman of the Senate Insurance and Banking Committee, had reached his own conclusion. Surveying the realities of the unfolding Virginia banking scene, he concluded that small banks like his own should have a choice between joining a holding company, merging with a large city bank, or continuing as an independent bank. Without prior notice except to a few close advisors, he dropped a branch banking bill into the legislative hopper on January 18, 1962.

On the house side, Holland signed as sponsor Delegate Fred Buck, a small-town banker from southwest Virginia. The Buck-Holland Bill, as it finally came to be called, was something of a compromise, offering banks a chance to merge if they wanted to, but protecting them if they did not. Any bank could branch at will within the city limits of the parent bank and into a contiguous city or five miles out into a contiguous county, or if a county, into a contiguous city, as the Richmond Plan had proposed. Any bank could merge with any other bank in any other city, town, or county, without a population limitation, but there could be no branching from the merged bank. Branching by merger would thus be statewide, but de novo branching would be restricted to the area of a bank's head office. The Buck-Holland Bill threw the banking fraternity into a turmoil. One of the first to react was The Bank of Virginia. Hearing the news, Herbert Moseley called the Richmond newspapers. The Bank of Virginia, with its long support of branch banking, was in favor of the Buck-Holland Bill. The holding company would be developed to the fullest as the major instrument for banking growth, but the merger route would be employed as appropriate in particular situations.

Banks that had preferred the merger route rather than the holding company approach to expansion were in a dilemma. The Metropolitan Plan had been designed to give them the authority to branch de novo in other cities in which they had affiliated banks. The Buck-Holland Bill would not permit this. If a big bank merged with a small bank in another city, there could be no de novo branching from the smaller merged bank. Big banks would thus find themselves in somewhat the same bind they had created in 1948 for The Bank of Virginia.

A small-town banker himself, Holland wanted his counterparts protected. Holding companies had not thus far explored the possibility of branching from their acquisitions in small cities, but Holland could foresee large city bank holding companies buying up a competitor and surrounding the local independent bank with branches that it could not afford to establish itself.

In the General Assembly, opposition from small bankers to the Buck-Holland Bill began to crystallize. Big banks faced the alternatives of Holland's bill or no bill at all. They began to rally to its support. Holland had planned to slip his bill in early, hold hearings, and get the provision passed before the house and senate became embittered by other controversies and opposition had time to form. But he undertook to explain the bill to the Kramer Committee of the Virginia Bankers Association. All it really did, Holland said, was to remove the twenty-five-mile limitation on branching through merger. Everything else in the present legislation was retained. The committee endorsed the bill in a divided vote on February 1. Instead of removing opposition, the Kramer Committee's action solidified it as small bankers reacted to what they saw as railroading by the big banks.

In the senate the powerful Curry Carter, who had banking connections in Staunton, led the opponents. On the house side the veteran Harrison Mann, editor of a conservative banking newsletter in northern Virginia, and James Thomson, who had an interest in plans for a new bank in Arlington, entered the controversy. Thomson introduced a bill to apply existing restrictions against branching to holding companies, putting them on the same footing as banks. This bill was killed in committee, but Holland had to accept a Thomson amendment instructing the State Corporation Commission to disregard the presence of merged banks or holding companies when considering an application for a charter by a locally owned bank. Using his considerable legislative skill, Holland kept his bill in reserve until the confusion of the last days of the session, easing it through to passage in the final crush of legislation.

The new law did not become effective until late June 1962, but its passage set wheels spinning in bank presidents' offices all over Virginia. Electing the merger route, banks in three major cities vied for the title of the largest bank in the state. Reacting to the new competition, holding companies branched out from their home regions into major cities. New holding companies were formed by other major banks. Smaller banks, which had opposed the Buck-Holland Bill, now rushed to join holding companies or merged systems. Over the next four years, the mad scramble caused a major realignment in Virginia banking. First and Merchants lost its place as the state's largest bank, and a holding company emerged as Virginia's largest banking enterprise.

In June of 1962, J. Harvie Wilkinson announced the formation of United Virginia Bankshares, based on State-Planters and including banks in Alexandria, Newport News, Franklin, and Lynchburg. In the same month one holding company, First Virginia Corporation, reached from northern Virginia to acquire the Southern Bank of Norfolk, whose president had offered the amendment at the Virginia Bankers Association convention to put off any liberalizing of bank mergers. The National Bank of Commerce of Norfolk and Peoples National Bank of Charlottesville set out to challenge First and Merchants as the state's largest bank by first effecting a merger to form Virginia National Bank and subsequently in rapid succession mergers of both rural and urban banks across the state. From Lynchburg Fidelity National began picking up small banks by merger, but became a holding company, Fidelity American Bankshares, in the later 1960s after acquiring American National Bank in Portsmouth.

Virginia had come late to the bank merger and holding company race, but she soon made up for lost time. Between mid-1962 and the end of 1966, the rate of increase in bank branches was three times the national average. For the first time in many years, new banks began to appear in major cities, reversing the trend of the previous three decades towards consolidation of existing banks. A total of thirty-one new banks were started, nearly all of them launched by holding companies getting their foot in

the door of new territory. In the same period the total number
of banks in the state decreased from 292 to 251 as a result of
mergers. But the total of branches increased from 367 to 612,
and the total of offices from 659 to 863.

By the end of 1966 First and Merchants National Bank had
added seven banks by merger and was still surpassed by nearly
$1 million in total deposits by Virginia National Bank of Nor-
folk. Sticking to the Washington-Richmond-Norfolk urban corri-
dor, State-Planters had added three more banks to the original
five forming United Virginia Bankshares and had become the
state's largest banking enterprise. First Virginia had increased its
holdings from five to twelve banks and Financial General from
four to ten. By December 31, 1966, holding companies had
amassed 28.1 percent of the state's total banking deposits, and
61.5 percent of total state deposits were held by the ten largest
banking organizations. Like other states Virginia was also re-
arranging the order of both single merged systems and bank holding companies.

As of December 31, 1961, the five largest banks in Virginia
and their total deposits had been:

1. First and Merchants National Bank, Richmond $275,914,000
2. State-Planters Bank of Commerce and Trusts,
   Richmond   237,626,235
3. National Bank of Commerce, Norfolk   197,466,074
4. The Bank of Virginia, Richmond   150,974,217
5. Central National Bank, Richmond   134,856,768

On December 31, 1966, the line-up had changed to:

1. Virginia National Bank, Norfolk $536,086,579
2. First and Merchants National Bank, Richmond   535,156,910
3. State-Planters Bank of Commerce and Trusts,
   Richmond   341,038,058
4. First National Exchange Bank, Roanoke   300,278,779
5. The Bank of Virginia   234,201,957

The line-up of banking institutions in the state, including holding companies, as of December 31, 1966, was:

1. United Virginia Bankshares (State-Planters,
   Richmond) $640,270,348
2. Virginia National Bank, Norfolk   536,086,579
3. First and Merchants National Bank, Richmond   535,156,910

4. Virginia Commonwealth Bankshares (The Bank
   of Virginia)   322,305,972
5. First Virginia Corporation, Arlington   301,494,464
6. First National Exchange Bank, Roanoke   300,278,779
7. Financial General Corporation, Washington, D.C.   235,315,830
8. Central National Bank, Richmond   168,170,865
9. Lynchburg National Bank and Trust, Lynchburg   128,176,433
10. Seaboard Citizens National Bank, Norfolk   110,506,405

Although legally it was a separate entity, Virginia Common-wealth Corporation in its early years was more an extension of The Bank of Virginia in actual operation. The home bank was by far the largest of the combine; in fact it was larger than all the rest put together. Bank officers doubled as holding company executives. Bank policies were instilled through existing divisions of banking services headquartered in Richmond.

Boushall served as chairman of the board of both corporations, although he was inactive in holding company matters. Moseley was president and chief executive officer of both the bank and the holding company. Deane served both as a senior vice-president of the bank and executive vice-president of the holding company. The Bank of Virginia thus continued to provide the manpower, the management skills, the special services, and the philosophy of the holding company.

The pace of mergers and expansions soon dictated an increase in manpower in Richmond. The bank had followed the national practice of proliferating vice presidents, giving this title to at least one operating officer at each major branch and division. Holding company operations were handled by the general officers of The Bank of Virginia at Eighth and Main.

In 1963 Herbert Moseley was elected to membership in the somewhat exclusive Reserve City Bankers Association, whose membership was severly restricted. Annoyance with The Bank of Virginia's fight for branch banking privileges that Boushall had waged over the years had prejudiced some of the local Richmond bankers whose approval of membership was a prerequisite for election. Moseley was not affected by this and, being popular among his contemporary local bank presidents, was readily accepted and elected.

In January 1965 the bank's computers and data processing at 2735 West Broad were transferred to a separate corporation,

Virginia Commonwealth Services, Incorporated, along with computer personnel. William L. Tiller, the bank's vice-president and comptroller, became president of the new corporation. The same year Virginia Commonwealth Properties was incorporated as a legal repository for holding company properties similar to the separate corporation established earlier by The Bank of Virginia. The bank's investment department was transferred to the holding company in 1965 as a service to all member banks. In March 1965 Boushall, having reached the mandatory retirement age for directors of Virginia Commonwealth Corporation, was elected honorary chairman of the board.

CHAPTER XIII

New Forms for Old Principles

THE BANK CONTINUED its erection or acquisition of new buildings. Before it had joined the holding company, a new six-hundred-thousand-dollar building in Petersburg had been opened and another six-hundred-thousand-dollar home for the Portsmouth branch completed. The building at 2735 West Broad had been given a seventy-five-thousand-dollar face lifting and housed the first sophisticated computer installed by a Virginia commercial bank. The new drive-in facilities were already in operation at Staples Mill Road.

In 1963 the branch at Azalea Mall Shopping Center opened, after being served by tellers in a trailer located outside it. A hundred-thousand-dollar home office in Chester for the Chesterfield County Bank was opened and the Highland Springs branch quarters enlarged. Later the bank was to buy from Whittet & Shepperson the building occupying two adjacent lots on North Eighth Street, and early in 1966 it acquired the Sutton Building fronting on Ninth Street next to the twenty-three-story Fidelity Building and joining the printing property between Eighth and Ninth. The Norfolk building and the addition to Eighth and Main were a part of a nationwide phenomenon, the rebirth of Main Street. In every major city, older downtown areas suddenly sprang to life and numerous skyscrapers arose.

In one year, 1964, several new buildings were announced, started or completed within a few blocks of each other on Richmond's Main Street. The sixteen-story Ross Building at southeast Eighth and Main housed a branch of the Central National Bank, which had built a skyscraper eight blocks away on Broad Street in 1930, in anticipation that the city would grow uphill and upstream, as most river cities do. Central National's Broad Street headquarters was the only tall office building erected in Richmond for a third of a century.

In the next few years, in addition to the Ross building, the Fidelity Bankers Life Building towered twenty-three stories high at northwest Ninth and Main, matching First and Merchants' remodeled home. At southeast Ninth and Main, the Mutual Building was remodeled. Richmond Federal Savings and Loan renovated the old Bank of Virginia headquarters at northwest Eighth and Main, and one block to the west the tall 700 Building took shape, while to the north behind it in the same block still another office building of the same height was begun.

In Norfolk the city had leveled acres of downtown slums and shoddy shops to build its new civic center complex, and Roanoke was beginning to refurbish the clutter of buildings beside the downtown Norfolk and Western Railway tracks.

As the 1960s neared their close, the capital city had under construction a new city hall across from the gray stone eminence adjacent to the state capitol, and a huge coliseum. A new public safety building, federal office building, a continually expanding Medical College of Virginia complex, and new state office buildings had reshaped the skyline and rearranged traffic arteries downtown to keep pace with the sprawling suburban growth.

The South was rising again. In Virginia a thousand miles of interstate highway were two-thirds completed. Almost half finished was a state-financed, four-lane divided arterial highway system linking the interstate to every city and town of five thousand or more. The ports of Hampton Roads, pioneering in container handling of ocean freight, were surpassed on the East Coast only by New York City. The state's college enrollment had doubled in the decade, all twenty-two of the projected two-year community colleges, enrolling well over thirty thousand students, were in actual operation by mid-1972.

Divided during the Eisenhower and Nixon presidential campaigns, the solid Democratic South had sprouted a new growth of state Republican officials, including Virginia's first Republican governor in eighty-seven years, Linwood Holton, who took office in 1970.

A rising tide lifts all boats, and finance in Virginia and the South joined the growing rush of change that inexorably remodeled every phase of Southern life. As the new pattern continued to unfold, it bore a striking resemblance to the principles that from the beginning had guided The Bank of Virginia— branch banking, proliferating bank-connected corporations, convenience, catering to consumers, and hard-sell advertising and promotion. Internally Virginia banks adopted management training programs, banking research, active community involvements, and continued to emphasize education. The Buck-Holland Bill was the catalyst that transformed stiff and formal banking atmosphere and service. Fierce competition for mergers and acquisitions generated a parallel race for customers and their loans and deposits, which were the measure of progress and success.

As late as 1959 Boushall was telling state bankers, assembled at the Newcomen dinner in his honor, to drop their aloofness, quit standing and waiting for business, and take a more active role in the community. Two years later an article in Richmond newspapers by Moseley called for a new type of bank executive attuned to service and solicitation of new customers. The bank itself continued to provide an example. In 1959 a training program for bank tellers emphasized that the customer is always right, and regular sales staff meetings played variations on the same theme.

A display of money made the rounds of the bank's offices, and a Home Builders Association exhibit was set up in the lobby at Eighth and Main. In 1962 an ancient Model T in the lobby promoted auto loans. The Petersburg opening offered a ten-dollar savings account toward a college education to each baby born in that city during a twenty-four-hour period. This was followed the next year by the fourth edition of a booklet on financing a college education with bank savings and loans. A weather forecasting book by local amateur weatherman Louis D. Rubin was another giveaway. Female bank personnel donned grass skirts for a Hawaiian salute promoting Vacation Club savings, on which the bank paid out $298,373 to 3,090 members in 1962. Silverware was given away with new accounts to members of the Silver Savings Club in 1963, followed in 1966 by Lollipop checks, cashable by children for lollipops while Mother did her banking. The following year a local actor in a Scrooge costume, visited branch lobbies as Mr. Shrewd Saver. Another promotion offered winners a Great Art Tour for Two to Europe. A "Carefree 65" promotion gave retired customers a free checking account with no minimum balance and no limit on checks. In 1966 Daphne Dailey was elevated to vice-president and was placed in charge of an entire Women's Division, with red carpet days and special promotions aimed at this market. The same year the bank's management training program was opened to women. In 1970 Edward B. White, Jr., brought in as marketing director in charge of advertising and sales promotion, updated one of Luke Fairbank's promotions by giving away ceramic cookware in a "Fancipans" campaign.

"Loans by Phone" were available in 1961, as was a "Thrifticlub" organized with twelve specific saving goals instead of one and a choice of club-type deposits, each with coupon books and mailing envelopes. Free checking accounts were offered to college students whose parents had accounts at the bank in 1966. Precredited bankbooks mailed to selected potential customers in 1959 were followed in 1970 by Blue Ribbon Passbook accounts.

A "Charge-a-Loan" option providing a cash advance of fifty to three hundred dollars on Charge Plan accounts began in 1963 before the bank's own merchants credit service joined Master Charge, but in 1966 the entire plan ran into a Justice Department antitrust suit. When it first offered its own Charge Plan seriously, the bank had inserted a clause in the agreement with the retailer that he would use only The Bank of Virginia plan and no other. By the mid-1960s, other similar plans had entered the market, but were theoretically excluded from serving many retailers signed up with The Bank of Virginia. The case was settled by a consent decree under which the bank withdrew its exclusive provision, which had not been strictly enforced. Two years later, when the fifteen-year-old plan joined Interbank Card Association, to become Master Charge, the service included fifteen banks at ninety locations, enrolling more than three thousand retail establishments and over three hundred thousand individual customers.

While the bank's showmanship was varied and continuous, it was well above carnival quality. The booklet produced for the Salute to Industry dinner in 1959 won first prize in the annual competition by the Virginia State Printers Association. In 1965 the bank's annual report won first place in the *Financial World* nationwide competition for the third straight year.

The tactics continued to pay off throughout the 1960s in terms of growth, earnings, and relative rank for the bank among chartered banks in the nation. Increases in net operating income occurred each year, ranging from 12 to 24 percent. Total deposits followed suit, but by lesser percentages, indicating the new stress on earnings. In 1963 the bank made its two-millionth loan, with loss ratios still amazingly low, in spite of leading the state in the ratio of loans to deposits with 61.7 percent. After forty-one years, credit losses in 1963 on the loan portfolio were less than fourteen-hundredths of 1 percent of the total volume of loans made. On consumer loans the overall loss ratio was only slightly higher— about one-fifth of 1 percent.

The mid-1960s brought to all Virginia banks a switch in emphasis from demand to time deposits, on which higher interest rates were paid, but despite greater interest outlays earnings kept climbing. One reason was the push behind investments, particularly the aggressive pursuit of municipal bonds, issued in greatly increased numbers by Virginia municipalities, seeking to keep pace with their own growth and the greater expectations of a citizenry inspired by growing incomes and a new awareness of standards of living and education elsewhere in the nation.

Reflecting the largest one-year growth in the bank's history, the year 1965 represented the harvest of organized planning and budgeting on the part of top management. Savings and time deposits increased by 19 percent to a total of $83,956,342 as of December 31. Stimulated by one-year certificates of $2,500 or more, paying 4½ percent, time certificates of deposit almost doubled, increasing from $7,435,001 to $13,545,791.

The bank's growth brought changes in personnel both among officers and directors. At the January 1965 board meeting, Frederick Deane, Jr., was elevated from senior vice-president to executive vice-president and in March was elected to the board of directors. William T. Gordon, a senior vice-president, was designated chief executive officer in the simultaneous absence of the president and executive vice-president. In addition he was given responsibility for all branch operations. Dr. Carrington Williams, one of the earliest members of the board was elected a director emeritus.

Demand deposit growth was unusually strong, increasing by $11,956,120 during the year to a December 31 total of $106,329,-622. Total deposits were up 12.9 percent compared to an average of 12 percent for the other reporting Federal Reserve member banks in Virginia; 10.7 percent for similar banks in the Fifth Federal Reserve District, and 7.6 percent for all reporting banks in the United States. Conversion of these deposits into loans enabled the bank to show a 16.8 percent gain in total operating revenue for the year. Net operating earnings were $1,749,897, up 19.4 percent. Total assets at year's end stood at $251,328,977.

Despite steady salary increases and an increased staff to handle twenty-eight offices, salaries and wages continued to decline as a percent of gross income, while interest on time deposits steadily increased as this method of saving grew in popular favor.

Stimulating investment in mortgages was one way of increasing the bank's return on time deposits, which were demanding higher interest rates.

In still another contribution of bank personnel to the holding company, John S. McClure acted as senior vice-president and chief credit officer for Virginia Commonwealth Bankshares.

There still remained a space problem. In February the directors had authorized purchase of the Whittet & Shepperson property just north of the bank on Eighth Street in Richmond, but in return the bank was to organize an agent, Sulgrave Corporation, to buy land and erect a new building for the printing firm. The directors then authorized purchase of the Sutton property on Ninth Street, which backed on the Whittet & Shepperson building. Finally The Bank of Virginia would own a building running from Eighth to Ninth Street, less than half a block from Ninth and Main. The purchase was closed in 1966 for $325,050. These two purchases would enable the bank to provide drive-in facilities, parking and expanded office space adjacent to, and to be connected with, the main office at Eighth and Main. That office had been remodeled, with new wiring and air conditioning, and once more an open house was held, although it was a far cry from the Depression-clouded original event.

As the 1960s progressed prosperity began to outrun the supply of money and credit in financial pipelines, and interest rates moved upward. Again The Bank of Virginia was in the vanguard as far as interest paid to depositors was concerned. Beginning in May 1965 interest on regular passbook savings was increased from $3\frac{1}{2}$ to 4 percent, and from 4 to $4\frac{1}{4}$ percent on savings certificates up to six months in duration, and to $4\frac{1}{2}$ percent on those over six months. The new interest rates were extended to branches.

Now a big-time bank with many branches, The Bank of Virginia was also a target for the increasing rash of bank robberies that characterized the 1960s. The Petersburg Pike office, which had been robbed in August 1958, was robbed again in July 1965. In December the Norfolk branch suffered an eleven-thousand-dollar robbery.

Throughout the 1960s, the bank's top officers in Richmond and at the branches continued to take on more than their share of community service responsibility. Setting the tone for this continuing tradition, Herbert Moseley compiled a list of activities filling more than a full biographical page. These included service as treasurer of the United Givers Fund of Richmond; finance committee chairman for the Richmond Chamber of Commerce and the National Tobacco Festival; executive committee membership on the Consumer Bankers Association; board member, Richmond Baseball Advisory Board; member of the Richmond Redevelopment and Housing Authority, the State Commission on the Industry of Agriculture, and the State Revenue Resource and Economic Study Commission; state treasurer for Radio Free Europe; chairman of the Executive Committee of Fork Union Military Academy; trustee of Richmond Forward; chairman of the Virginia Industrial Development Corporation; member of the board of visitors of Richmond Professional Institute; director of Junior Achievement; trustee of Richmond Memorial Hospital and the Greater Richmond Community Foundation, among other contributions.

An active Baptist churchman and civic club member, Moseley also performed a number of tasks for Virginia Bankers Association and American Bankers Association. He has also been active in Bankers Political Action Committee, an organization set up by a group of bankers representing all sections of the United States. The first year, he served as state chairman for Virginia, followed by two years' service as a director of Bankers Political Action Committee as well as district chairman, covering Virginia and several other states.

Other Bank of Virginia officers kept the tradition alive. Among other assignments, Frederick Deane served in the 1960s as president of the Richmond Area Association for Retarded Children; president of Blue Cross of Virginia; one of twenty-eight businessmen members of the Council on Trends and Perspective of the United States Chamber of Commerce; member of the board of visitors of the College of William and Mary and the advisory council to its School of Business Administration, and, among other honors, was given the Meritorious Service Award by St. Paul's College in Lawrenceville. Deane was elected on December 1, 1966, to membership in the Young Presidents Organization, which is an honor for any young man who becomes president of his corporation under the age of forty. He later became chairman of the Rebel Chapter of the YPO in June 1971, covering six southern states.

In his turn William Gordon served on the boards of the Better Business Bureau of Richmond, the Central Richmond Association, Richmond Urban League, the Federated Arts of Richmond, and as a director and vice-president of the Richmond Chapter, American Red Cross, president of the Virginia College Fund, on the board of the Virginia League for Planned Parenthood, and as a director and treasurer of both the Virginia Thanksgiving Festival and Virginia State Advisory Board of the Salvation Army.

Other bank officers continued the tradition across the spectrum of community involvement in each of the bank's cities and for the state as a whole.

CHAPTER XIV

Refining the Philosophy

DESPITE A SHARP INCREASE in interest costs on time deposits and a much slower than normal loan growth due to more restrictive Federal Reserve Board limitations, the bank again established record net earnings for the year 1966. The inauguration of the municipal bond department took place on April 1. The purchase of revenue bonds was prohibited, and the new municipal bond department did not deal in the bonds of private corporations. In another updating of an early bank innovation, a profit-sharing plan was substituted for the year-end bonus, with Virginia Commonwealth Bankshares setting aside 10 percent of the consolidated after-tax profits of its affiliates that adopted the plan.

But the central theme of the bank was still expansion, as it had been since 1922. In October 1966 the new branch at 1415 Ridge Road was opened. Again the bank's annual report won *Financial World*'s first-place award for the fourth consecutive year. The proliferations of branches and holding company outlets presented all the major Virginia banking participants with an identity problem, similar to that experienced by the development of conglomerates in other lines of business. For banks the problem was how to inform the customers of small-town, formerly independent banks that they were now dealing with a major banking enterprise without destroying the local identity of the bank.

One after another the merged banks and holding companies adopted a logo, or symbol, to identify each bank as belonging to the system. Virginia Commonwealth Bankshares adopted three interlocking *V*s, which in 1966 appeared in all advertisements, literature, and publications and was worn as a lapel button by the eleven hundred staff members of the nine banks.

Beneath the growth and prosperity for Virginia banking, there continued through much of 1966 the money crunch, a growing scarcity of funds to lend. Many of the nation's major banks sold sizable portions of their market-depreciated municipal bonds at great loss to meet the loan demand of long-time customers and to pay off major liquidations of certificates of deposit. Many of these banks had sold six-month and one-year certificates and loaned the money out for two, three, or even five years.

The year 1967 began with a slower rate for the nation's economy, reflected in bank balance sheets, but The Bank of Virginia continued to display a healthy earnings picture although new loans continued to lag. Deposits increased by 20.9 percent over 1966 to a total of $283,104,665 and net operating income showed an 11.8 percent gain of $278,254 for a total of $2,629,188 for the year, making possible a return of 12.5 percent on stockholders' equity. Deposit growth necessitated another stock sale, this time of sixty-two thousand shares for a total of $2 million, to the holding company in order to increase capital funds.

Three new branches became Bank of Virginia outlets, making a total of thirty-three by the year's end. On March 1 the merger with the Bank of La Crosse and its South Hill branch was completed and on August 5 a new branch in the Lakeside area of Richmond expanded the bank's reach in the home city. Finally the facility at Bellwood Defense Supply Center was converted to a full-fledged branch office under the amended Virginia Banking Act of 1962. The board authorized a move of the Main Street branch in Norfolk to a new building at City Hall Avenue and Court Street, close to the refurbished downtown civic center planned by the city. At the same time, the plan to relocate the Charlotte and Boush Street office at the intersection of Military Highway and Virginia Beach Boulevard was approved, even though the lease at Charlotte and Boush would not expire until 1969. Another relocation was approved in Newport News, with the branch there to be moved to Thirty-first Street and Washington Avenue in a new office building to be erected.

The year 1967 saw the final retirement from active duty of its first president. In a move urged by Boushall, the bank's founder became honorary chairman of the board; Moseley became chairman and continued as chief executive officer; Deane was elected president and chief administrative officer, and Gordon moved up from senior vice-president to executive vice-president, signaling his succession.

And so after forty-five years, the first thirty-seven of them as chief executive officer, Thomas C. Boushall relinquished his last executive post with the bank. Even so his second floor office was still headquarters for many a national, state, and community betterment effort.

The new leaders—Moseley, Deane, and Gordon—began reorganization, staff promotions, and expansion programs. New departments were developed. The new retail division coordinated the efforts of the women's department, the direct consumer service, statewide sales finance, statewide charge plan, and the marketing department. These changes gave new zest to the whole staff in expanding the bank's growth and services.

Mergers and the continued growth of the holding company brought other changes among the bank officers. In March 1967 William L. Tiller resigned as vice-president and comptroller of the bank in order to devote full time to his other office as treasurer of Virginia Commonwealth Bankshares. Within the Bank of Virginia family, J. W. Buffington, vice-president and trust officer in Norfolk, resigned to become president of the newly organized First Colonial Bank of Virginia Beach, an affiliate of Virginia Commonwealth Bankshares.

Interest rates continued to climb in 1968 as the money crunch again began to make itself felt. Commercial and consumer loans were rising, but large sums were flowing abroad where interest rates were appreciably higher.

Through their foreign branches international banks were accepting deposits at high rates of interest and relending the money back to American banks in what were called Eurodollars at rates running from $8\frac{1}{2}$ to $9\frac{1}{2}$ and finally 11 percent. Anxious to serve long-time customers, large American banks were paying these rates for Eurodollars and in turn lending them to domestic customers at 8, 9, or 10 percent. In response the prime rate had risen to $8\frac{1}{2}$ percent. The only other recourse banks had was to sell tax-exempt bonds at a substantial loss. The situation was particularly acute in Virginia, where state law set a ceiling of 6 percent interest on mortgages and certain other types of loans. Finally, early in 1968, the banking fraternity joined hands to ask the General Assembly to increase the limit from 6 to 8 percent. The ensuing arguments before the legislature brought into the open the intense rivalry between banks, all of which were strictly regulated, and savings and loan associations, which were not as tightly controlled or as heavily taxed, and had been taking a larger and larger share of home loans.

As early as January 1964, William Gordon had told the bank's correspondent conference that commercial banks, which had 79.3 percent of total savings in 1945, had only about half that percentage in 1963, while savings and loan companies had doubled their percentage in the same period. In mortgage loans, banks had dropped from 22.2 percent of the market in 1945 to 13.2 percent in 1963, while savings and loan companies had increased their percentage from 27.7 to 43.5 percent. Here was a compelling, dollars-and-cents reason, Gordon argued, for banks to get out and sell. These figures and others used constantly by bank officers in both public speeches and private discussions of bank policy were the dividends from the emphasis on bank research begun years before with the retention of Dr. Pierce Lumpkin as consulting economist.

The Bank of Virginia responded in time-honored fashion with more emphasis on solicitation of new accounts and added deposits. The suggestion awards program for employees adopted a new concept of awarding S&H green stamps in lieu of cash, thus giving employees a larger choice of items. The first year, thirty-five thousand green stamps were distributed for suggestions, and year-end figures for 1969 showed the bank had gone against the national trend of lessened loan and deposit growth. Net operating income in 1969 climbed a healthy 9.4 percent over 1968, and resources topped $400 million.

With the help of mergers, but relying mostly on internal growth, the bank continued to rise among single banking units in the nation, from 229th in 1960 to 169th in 1968. In Richmond the bank retained third place after First and Merchants and State-Planters, although First National Exchange Bank in Roanoke and Virginia National in Norfolk, which had taken the merger rather than the holding company route, were larger.

Merger with the Peoples Bank of Whitestone and the Peoples Bank of Reedville, with a branch at Burgess, was completed on May 31, 1968, making The Bank of Virginia the first Richmond bank to enter the Northern Neck area. A new branch was opened in Henrico County at East Gate Mall shopping center, bringing the total to twenty-two branches in the Richmond area. More than compensating for the gain in these new assets was the spin-off of the Newport News branch office. As a branch of The Bank of Virginia, it was restricted as to the number of offices, viz., one; local banks, however, were permitted to establish additional branches. To overcome this limitation, the Newport News office became a branch of the Bank of Warwick, owned by the holding company and as a local bank could branch at will. This takeover was planned as of January 10, 1969, reducing the total resources of The Bank of Virginia.

Bank officers continued to contribute personally and generously to community betterment beyond membership on various boards and committees or organizations in this field, which is the lot of the concerned business executive. With bank approval, an officer, David Shepardson, accepted membership on the Richmond City Council in 1968 to fill out the unexpired term of James C. Wheat, who was resigning. In 1969 the bank contributed a substantial part of the capital for a $550,000 corporation called Better Richmond, organized to help black capitalists build low-rent apartments or homes for blacks. A retiring vice-president, John Orgain, later became Better Richmond's executive director. In the summer of 1968, the bank joined other businesses in employing underprivileged high school boys and girls through the Richmond Chamber of Commerce summer job program. Continuing a long association with the Consumer Bankers Association, Senior Vice-President Aubrey V. Kidd was elected its president in 1968. In a similar tradition Frederick Deane, the bank's president, was elected president of Virginia Blue Cross, which had become a large statewide organization.

In February 1969 Deane was elected a member of the Reserve City Bankers Association to serve as The Bank of Virginia's second member along with Mr. Moseley. The expanding operations of Virginia Commonwealth Bankshares were consuming great quantities of President Deane's time, and more of The Bank of Virginia's executive decision-making was falling on William T. Gordon. Accordingly, the board created a new position of vice-chairman of the board to be occupied by Deane and elected Gordon as the fourth president of The Bank of Virginia. The moves were effective November 1, 1969. By coincidence William Gordon's brother, Robert, was president and chief executive officer of First and Merchants National Bank, a competitor one block away.

As the number of banks owned by Virginia Commonwealth Bankshares increased, the need to service their accounts became acute, and the transfer of services and manpower from The Bank of Virginia continued. The bank's systems of personnel and staff services departments handling payroll and staff benefit programs for all holding company banks were transferred to the holding company.

Moseley received a compliment in 1970 from the Registered Bank Holding Company Associates when, though reducing the number of its board of directors from sixty (one representative for each member company) to only eighteen, it made Moseley a member. He was also elected a member of the six-man executive committee. In October of the same year, Moseley's picture appeared on the front of the *Southern Banker* as the banker of the month.

Toward the end of the 1960s, credit cards of all kinds had suddenly become the vogue, after years of trial and error and only gradual acceptance. Banks were attracted by the prospect of high interest rates—as high as $1\frac{1}{2}$ percent a month. The public came to like the convenience of charging its meals, gasoline, travel tickets, clothing, and accessories, and nearly every other kind of purchase. When both BankAmericard and Master Charge took the field, many of the larger banks distributed their cards to the public whether they had been requested or not. Advertising on a national basis encouraged their use. The results were rapid and drastic. Delinquent accounts and losses soared. Record-keeping expenses shot upward. A black market in stolen credit cards flourished, necessitating computer-equipped detecting organizations. After two years of steadily increasing problems, banks, government regulatory agencies, the Congress, banking authorities, and bank administrators began to take stock and initiate corrective measures, and by the end of 1970 a measure of stability had been restored and the number of cards in circulation appreciably reduced. Even though it was more experienced in the field than the newcomers, The Bank of Virginia had been caught up in the flood and had to absorb promotional costs and losses along with other business institutions. Even so in 1970 the bank's earnings showed a healthy increase from $3,076,000 in 1969 to $3,493,000.

By January 1971 The Bank of Virginia system had scored another first. The stock of Virginia Commonwealth Bankshares was registered for trading on the floor of the New York Stock Exchange, the first banking organization in Virginia to be so recognized. And growth continued. By June 1971 the entire new north Eighth Street building was fully occupied by bank and holding company personnel. To ease the growing load on Frederick Deane and Herbert Moseley, William Gordon as president and chief administrative officer now became the bank's chief executive officer.

For The Bank of Virginia the 1970s opened with two financial developments that had their effect on the balance sheet. Early in 1971 consultants were retained to study the concept of an overall identifying name for each of the several banks owned by Virginia Commonwealth Bankshares. The result was a recommendation first that *The* be dropped from the name and that each bank then change its name to Bank of Virginia plus a geographical suffix. Having determined to do so, the home office in Richmond on January 1, 1972 became Bank of Virginia-Central. The bank's Roanoke branch as of March 31, 1972, was spun off by being combined with the Salem and Vinton banks and their branches to become Bank of Virginia-Roanoke Valley, which could then branch in that area of the state. As of May 31, 1972, sixteen of the total eighteen banks had changed their names to Bank of Virginia, with appropriate suffixes. The Bank of Warren postponed its name change to October 2, 1972, in order that it might celebrate its one-hundredth anniversary under its original name. Thus after many readjustments over nearly half a century, the original idea of statewide banking under one banner was finally achieved. There was little fanfare. By this time the other banks in the state had taken their separate routes to the same end and were adopting a uniform designation and universal logo of their own.

However, as 1971 advanced, the nation's economy continued to decline. National unemployment rose from 4.9 to 5.9 percent. While Virginia felt the impact less than most other areas of the country—as had been the case in previous recessions—the unusual combination of inflation and rising unemployment had its psychological effect. Adding to the problem for banks was a spectacular drop in the prime interest rate charged the most prestigious customer accounts. At Bank of Virginia-Central the prime rate during the year fell from $6\frac{3}{4}$ percent at the beginning of the year to $4\frac{1}{2}$ percent by the year's end. The biggest factor in the earnings picture was the lack of opportunity to reduce interest paid on savings and time deposits to offset the decline in loan interest rate. The bank was able to reduce interest on regular savings from $4\frac{1}{2}$ to 4 percent in only half its cities and none of its smaller communities.

The bank showed an increase in assets from $447,852,000 at the end of 1970 to $507,497,000 by the end of 1971, carrying the total over the half billion mark forty-nine and a half years after the bank's beginning in 1922. The bank's trust investment division continued its outstanding performance, a national review group placing it among the top performers in the nation.

By now dozens of executives were serving on boards or special committees for well-established community service organizations. For the year 1970–71, Herbert Moseley headed the statewide fund-raising campaign for Radio Free Europe, adding one more activity to his long list. In 1970 Arthur J. Morris, the founder of the Morris Plan, who had served on The Bank of Virginia board from its first meeting in 1922, was elected its first and only Honorary Life Director and presented with a silver tray. In 1971 the bank took the internal step of formulating an Affirmative Action Program to increase the number of staff members of minority races, beginning with a new director of the program. The August 1972 board meeting was attended by the Governor of Virginia who saw a showing of a documentary television tape entitled *Tom Boushall—On Borrowed Time,* which had previously been televised locally.

Personnel changes continued to reflect bank growth and the passing of years. In 1970 Barry B. Anthony was elected executive vice-president in charge of branch administration. Aubrey V. Kidd resigned the same year as senior vice-president and secretary of the bank in order to serve full time as senior vice-president and corporate secretary of Virginia Commonwealth Bankshares. The year 1971 also recorded the death of Colonel Mills F. Neal, a board member since 1931, and of O. B. Wooldridge, a former director and chairman of the Portsmouth board, who had been vice-president at the Norfolk branch and later vice-president in charge of the Portsmouth branch for a number of years.

The competition for loans and the new avenues opened up for attracting lines of credit to consumers had by the beginning of the 1970s dispelled the concern of banking authorities over high-loan ratios, which had brought The Bank of Virginia under fire several times in the past. In 1966 the ratio of loans to deposits in New York City was between 75 and 80 percent. The Bank of Virginia's ratio had moved up during the 1960s and by 1970 was around 75 percent as a safe and permissible level. Supervisory authorities, who had once been critical of 60 percent took no particular notice of the 75 percent figure. The bank itself felt at ease, with 49 percent of its loan portfolio in consumer monthly payment paper bringing in a steady flow of cash.

There was further protection for depositors in investment portfolio liquidity in ninety-day government bills, short-term government bonds and a satisfactory proportion of early maturities in the tax-exempt, or municipal bond, portfolio. The Federal Reserve Board had taken one more constructive step by easing the process of the sharing of loans among holding company banks. A member company bank could more readily seek loan participation from its sister banks when customer loan demand grew too strong for any one bank. As the largest of the Virginia Commonwealth Bankshares group, The Bank of Virginia could also take the excess of any loan above the legal limit for smaller banks. This ability to balance off geographical loan demand against geographical deposit surpluses made for sounder and more profitable banking for each member bank as well as for the holding company.

In 1971 with 37 locations throughout the state, the Bank of Virginia represented almost a third of the 109 banking offices operated under the holding company banner. Although they had severed physical and spiritual ties with the Morris Plan and the implications that concept had for more conventional bankers, both The Bank of Virginia and Virginia Commonwealth Bankshares still believed the basic principle of consumer lending to be as sound in the 1970s as it had proved to be in the 1920s, if for slightly different reasons. Frederick Deane listed these in a speech in August 1970, reprinted as "Required Reading" by the *American Banker.*

A half century earlier, banks had been busy tooling up America. Industrial and business booms provided a ready market for commercial loans, and banks were virtually the only sources. Consumer buying power was in its infancy. As the nation entered the final third of the twentieth century, it was a different story. Big industry and business were turning to each other for short-term loans and to commercial paper or stock issues for long-term financing. Insurance companies with reserve funds to invest, savings and loan companies, mortgage companies, and other specialized financial institutions were in active competition. The resulting shrinkage in available commercial loan demand directed bankers to the consumer-type loan for utilization of available funds. The credit card field has been embraced as one facet of this development.

Deane's conclusion from these developments was that much of

the future of banking lay in small- and medium-sized business and in consumer lending, still expanding at a tremendous pace as the rising sun of the Consumer Age reached midmorning.

Practicing what it preached, Bank of Virginia-Central in 1972 extended the length of monthly payments on mobile homes from seven or eight years to ten years, as the popularity of this type of housing continued to advance. Matching the rise in the cost of new automobiles, the bank extended the repayment limit from thirty-six to forty-eight months on new cars. The 1960s had produced a steady rise in international trade, helped along by the development of containerized ocean freight handling. Southern ports had caught the fever of industrial resurgence for their region and were actively pushing their relatively low handling costs and ice-free conditions.

Foreign firms were establishing assembly plants or warehouses in the South, and American firms with southern connections were setting up their own facilities abroad or aggressively seeking new markets overseas. All this required financing. To VCB officials, alert to new opportunities, international banking seemed to offer the next big expansion move. State-Planters was already established with a foreign trade office in Tidewater. Virginia National was well connected through Allied Bank International, the nation's second-largest Edge Act bank, formed in 1968. Other major banks in the state were moving rapidly into the field, just as they had into mortgage companies, and to a lesser extent into factoring. To enter the foreign banking field, Virginia Commonwealth Bankshares had organized Virginia Commonwealth International and had acquired a bank in Nassau and one on Grand Cayman Island in the West Indies—Bank of Nassau and Bank of Virginia (Grand Cayman) Limited.

In order to complete the whole gamut of name change, the holding company's board authorized the officers to seek legislation at the 1972 Virginia General Assembly to permit, for the first time, the use of the word *Bank* in a corporate name that was not a bank operation in itself but was engaged in banking as a bank holding company. This legislation was passed and became effective on July 1, 1972. The subsequent stockholders' meeting necessary to authorize the corporate name change from Virginia Commonwealth Bankshares, Inc., to Bank of Virginia Company was held on the significant fiftieth anniversary date of the founding of Bank of Virginia-Central, July 17, 1972. The total name change of the holding company and its affiliated banks moved from a conglomerate group of names to one name with a distinguishing suffix. Thus was effected a statewide banking system under common identification.

Bank of Virginia-Central had previously spun off its Newport News branch to merge with the Bank of Warwick as it later spun off its Roanoke office as Bank of Virginia-Roanoke Valley on April 1, 1972. In mid-1972 it was likewise decided, as of early 1973, to spin off the three Norfolk branches and Portsmouth's one office as Bank of Virginia-Tidewater. As of July 17, 1972, however, Bank of Virginia-Central had recouped sufficient deposits to offset those departures from its balance sheet and even achieve a total greater than that prior to the spin-offs.

During its fifty-year history, The Bank of Virginia had been the ardent advocate of branch banking. Boushall had antagonized both the large and small banks by his constant effort to broaden the base of the large banks and thus enable them to serve the growing industry of the state. Hence there had never been a Bank of Virginia officer in the Virginia Bankers Association to rank higher than a board member or committee chairman, though there were many of these. Now that Moseley was among fellow branch bankers and fellow holding company officers, it became evident that he was entitled to become the Bank of Virginia's first elected officer. At the June 1972 annual meeting of the association, Moseley was unanimously elected second vice-president, and in 1973 he moved up to become first vice-president, to become president of the Virginia Bankers Association in 1974. The succession provided a fitting climax to his career in Virginia banking and recognition of The Bank of Virginia as a member of the Virginia banking fraternity.

Springing from The Bank of Virginia at Eighth and Main, the holding company had expanded in ten years from 5 banks with 35 locations to 17 banks with 114 branches and had established affiliates in mortgage banking, factoring, leasing, and international banking. The full story of holding company progress is told at some length in the pages of the appendix following this history of Bank of Virginia-Central. Suffice it to say here that as of July 17, 1972, the original assets of $375,000 on July 17, 1922, had, through the bank holding company route, achieved total assets of $1.06 billion over the last ten years, while the original mother bank represented, as part of that total, $504 million.

Epilogue

IF THE INSTITUTION that became Bank of Virginia-Central had a basic fault, perhaps it was that in its early years it was too far ahead of its time. It is one thing to ride the incoming tide of human events. It is far more difficult to precede that tide without capsizing. The opposition its early policies encountered was in part the natural reaction to one that consistently flouted tradition and consistently proved itself right in doing so. The fact remains that the bank charted the course Virginia banking would take years in advance. Demonstrating that the average man would use bank credit and repay his debts, it outlined the technique of making credit available to him, with the Virginia innovations of instalment loans, protection of the loan through borrower life insurance, automobiles as collateral, innovative popular checking accounts, credit services for merchants, and finally credit cards. Generating money to lend, it encouraged people to save with high interest payments, special-goal savings, savings stamps, and incentive plans for employees. With one vigorous promotion or advertisement after another, it proved that the use of credit could be promoted like any other product or service.

Opening branches in six cities, it clearly showed the advantages of the branching concept to the bank and to the state's economy, only to become circumscribed by laws advocated by competitors who finally saw the light only under the pressure of subsequent events. Toward the end of its first half century, still growing and branching, it provided the precedent, the manpower, and the spirit to launch a bank holding company, which in turn took the prestige of the bank's own name and continued its innovation with the first Virginia-owned banks on foreign soil.

Rounding out fifty years, it had the satisfaction of seeing all other major banks adopting its early philosophy and, one after another, most of its successful innovations. As a financial pioneer, as an interpreter and instigator of social and economic change, as an unrelenting foe of institutional inertia, Bank of Virginia has been a trail blazer, not only for the state of Virginia but for the nation as well.

Bank of Virginia Company: A History

As THE PRECEDING HISTORY of Bank of Virginia-Central details, plans for a bank holding company were vigorously investigated by the bank's management as early as 1961. Between the years 1948 and 1960, the General Assembly had failed to provide a legislative structure that would enable Virginia banks to compete more freely with each other in the state and thereby establish a system of strong banking units that could compete more effectively with out-of-state organizations, thus enhancing the economic growth potential within the state. As indicated, failure of the 1960 legislature to take any action on this important matter and the collapse in 1961 of the effort to establish a strong recommendation on the part of the Virginia Bankers Association led Herbert Moseley and Frederick Deane, the two top executives of what was then The Bank of Virginia, to take positive action for the establishment of a bank holding company. The officers of four other Virginia banks proved eager to join the movement with The Bank of Virginia, these four banks being The Bank of Salem in the western part of the state, the Bank of Warwick in Newport News, The Bank of Occoquan in northern Virginia, and The Bank of Henrico in the Richmond metropolitan area, which latter bank was already in friendly hands and available to us as a partner in this undertaking. These five banks joined hands, received the necessary Federal Reserve Board approval to become a registered bank holding company, and began operations as Virginia Commonwealth Corporation on December 21, 1962.

Herbert C. Moseley was president and chief executive officer and Frederick Deane, Jr., was executive vice-president and chief administrative officer. The board of directors consisted of Moseley and Deane and Thomas C. Boushall, chairman of the board of The Bank of Virginia; R. Colston Christian, general counsel for the corporation; Grover P. Manderfield, president of The Bank of Occoquan; Lewis A. McMurran, Jr., a director of the Bank of

NOTE: Prepared and edited by Dr. R. Pierce Lumpkin and Mr. Aubrey V. Kidd

Warwick; and D. Robley Wood, president of The Bank of Salem. S. Murray Rust, Jr., president of the Rust Engineering Company, joined the board in March 1963 to become the first representative of business and industry outside the company's banking group.

The Formative Years

When, in 1961, Moseley and Deane took the first steps to put Virginia Commonwealth Corporation together, they were well aware that the other larger and longer-established banks in the state would present formidable competition with programs of their own, but they hoped to realize a major advantage by being early in the field. With State-Planters Bank and Trust Company in Richmond applying for approval to organize a bank holding company only a few months after Virginia Commonwealth Corporation, and with First and Merchants and Virginia National battling for first place among Virginia banks, the Virginia Commonwealth Corporation management recognized the necessity for careful long-range planning within this increasingly competitive environment if it was to maintain its relative position by aggressively meeting the growth challenge that it now clearly faced. They recognized one major advantage over the two large banks that chose the unit bank approach through merger, namely, they could travel either the merger or the affiliation route. Affiliation was much more acceptable to small bank managers who refused to lose their identity and status by mergering into a unit bank. At the same time it was recognized that affiliation should not be offered to any bank willing to join the group but only to those with strategic locations, good branching potential, and quality management. While good geographic coverage of the state was sought at all times, the availability of a bank was generally the basis for opening negotiations.

Very shortly after the holding company began business, it was decided to merge The Bank of Henrico into The Bank of Virginia. The Buck-Holland Bill, which the General Assembly approved at its 1962 session, now permitted de novo branching to the extent of five miles outside the limits of the city in which the head office of a bank was located. It was felt that this five-mile margin for de novo branching would enable The Bank of Virginia

The branches (top to bottom). Left: Hallwood Office, Westhampton Office, Richmond, Portsmouth Office, Dinwiddie Office. Right: Petersburg Office, Boydton Office, Tidewater Regional Headquarters, Norfolk.

to meet the branching competition in the Richmond metropolitan area and, accordingly, the expense and duplication of overhead operations at a separate bank in Henrico County should be eliminated in the interest of overall consolidated earnings. On June 28, 1963, all legal work and approvals were completed and The Bank of Henrico was merged into The Bank of Virginia. Also, by midyear 1963 negotiations had been completed and supervisory approvals obtained for the merger into The Bank of Virginia of the Farmers Bank of Dinwiddie, located in the small village of Dinwiddie just a short distance south on U.S. Route 1 from Petersburg where The Bank of Virginia already had a banking office. This merger was also completed on June 28, 1963, and was the only acquisition bringing additional assets into the system ($3 million) in that year.

The first move of the holding company was into southwest Virginia where it had no banking outlets. All of the necessary negotiations and banking authority approvals were completed in 1963 so that on January 2, 1964, the Washington Trust and Savings Bank of Bristol and The Peoples National Bank of Pulaski became affiliates of the corporation. On that date, slightly over a year since the holding company began business, the banking group consisted of six separate banks operating a total of forty banking locations. These locations now extended from Bristol in the far southwest through Pulaski and Roanoke to Richmond in central Virginia and on to locations in the Hampton Roads area. In addition there were six banking locations in northern Virginia.

The year 1964, Virginia Commonwealth Corporation's second year in business, was one of significant growth for the holding company. As reported in the 1964 annual report, total assets increased $60.0 million from year-end 1963 to year-end 1964. Of this increase $23.7 million came from mergers and acquisitions, leaving an increase of $36.3 million from internal growth in the increasingly competitive Virginia financial arena.

As indicated above, the two new affiliations in 1964 (Washington Trust and Savings Bank, Bristol, and The Peoples National Bank of Pulaski) were negotiated and supervisory authority received in 1963, and the affiliations were completed on the first business day of 1964. The two mergers that occurred in 1964 were also negotiated in 1963, but supervisory approval did not come until January 1964. The Bank of Nokesville, located on

Virginia Route 28 just eight miles south of Manassas, agreed to merge into The Bank of Occoquan, and this merger was completed January 31, 1964, on which date The Bank of Occoquan changed its name to The Bank of Prince William. This represented a first step in the energetic drive of the management of this northern Virginia region, in conjunction with the Virginia Commonwealth Corporation management, in the spectacular rate of growth that occurred in the holding company's banking operation in this Washington metropolitan area, which took total assets of affiliated banks in this region from $9.2 million at the end of 1962 to $128.9 million at the end of June 1972.

The second of the two mergers completed on January 31, 1964, was the Hallwood National Bank, located on the Eastern Shore of Virginia and holding $5.6 million in total assets on the date of the merger. It merged into The Bank of Virginia, its office in Hallwood bringing to twenty-seven the bank's total locations, which extended from Roanoke through Petersburg and Dinwiddie to Norfolk and Portsmouth and as far as the Eastern Shore. This new banking office also provided a growth surprise. Coming into the group with $4.8 million in deposits, the Hallwood location supplied $16.5 million in deposits to The Bank of Virginia on June 30, 1972.

Nineteen sixty-four, the second year of operations, also witnessed the initial steps taken to establish centralized services for the banks at the parent company level. The auditing department of The Bank of Virginia was transferred to the corporation on April 1, 1964, and a broad program of audit coverage of the affiliated banks was instituted. Also in 1964 the corporation appointed a credit coordinator to assist the affiliated banks in appraising credit risks, particularly commercial borrowers, and to formulate uniform credit guidelines for all affiliated banks. A credit examiner was also appointed at the holding company level with the responsibility of establishing a continuing review of the banks' loan portfolios. In addition to these changes, the staff benefit programs of The Bank of Virginia were transferred to the holding company as of January 1, 1964, and these programs were offered to all the other affiliated banks. The programs included the retirement plan, the group life insurance program, and the hospitalization and major medical insurance coverages. Staff benefits have since been upgraded and expanded and made available to all affiliates.

The corporation also undertook its first major financing in 1964 with the private placement of $2.5 million of 4⅞ percent debentures on March 24. The proceeds of this financing went to supply additional capital to two of the affiliated banks. Thus Virginia Commonwealth Corporation embarked upon a financing program that was to prove of great significance in subsequent years, namely, obtaining long-term debt funds in the name of the holding company, thus using the credit strength of the consolidated group, and channeling these funds into the equity positions of the banks and subsequently into bank-related companies. Although the debt markets were thus used to raise the funds involved, the banks benefited from the addition to their equity accounts, including an increase in the maximum loan to a single interest and in other matters where supervisory regulations relate banking activities to its capital structure.

At the end of 1964, the group consisted of six commercial banks, with total assets and number of offices as follows:

	Total assets ($ thousand)	Number of offices
The Bank of Virginia	$ 217,030	27
Bank of Warwick	25,728	4
The Bank of Prince William	15,104	8
The Bank of Salem	14,896	2
Washington Trust and Savings Bank	11,067	2
The Peoples National Bank of Pulaski	6,679	1
Combined	$ 290,504	44

The next two years witnessed one additional acquisition, as an affiliated bank, and three acquisitions in the form of mergers into existing banks of the group. These four banks brought with them six banking offices and a little over $12.5 million in total assets. In addition, existing banks of the group opened seven de novo banking offices during the years 1965 and 1966, for a total of thirteen new offices, thus bringing the total to fifty-seven at year-end 1966.

The first of the acquisitions was Guardian National Bank of Fairfax County, which was merged into The Bank of Prince William as of May 15, 1965. The second was the Farmers Bank of Boydton located in southern Virginia, which was merged into The Bank of Virginia on August 31, 1965. The third acquisition in this period became a new affiliated bank under the name of

The Bank of Central Virginia. This bank resulted from the conversion of the State Industrial Loan Association of Lynchburg into a commercial bank effective April 1, 1966. The final acquisition during these two years was The National Bank of Rosslyn, which was merged into The Bank of Prince William as of September 15, 1966. At year-end 1966, the group consisted of the following banks:

	Total assets ($ thousand)	Number of offices
The Bank of Virginia	$ 263,106	30
Bank of Warwick	28,715	5
The Bank of Prince William	26,896	12
The Bank of Salem	17,358	4
Washington Trust Bank	15,576	4
The Peoples National Bank of Pulaski	8,666	1
The Bank of Central Virginia	3,092	1
Combined	$ 363,409	57

The first significant changes in the holding company's senior officers and directors took place in 1965. Three new directors were elected at the annual stockholders meeting in April, increasing the number to twelve and broadening the geographic and economic representation of the state. John P. Fishwick, at that time senior vice-president of Norfolk and Western Railway Company, subsequently to become its president, joined the board from the Roanoke area. Homer A. Jones, Jr., who was chairman of the executive committee of Washington Trust Bank, an affiliate of the group, represented the southwestern part of the state. Finally Floyd D. Gottwald, Jr., vice-chairman of the board of Ethyl Corporation and president of Albemarle Paper Manufacturing Company, with his business headquartered in Richmond, brought representation of a major nationwide industry to the board.

In 1965 Thomas C. Boushall, not being eligible, under board policy, for reelection as a director, was elected honorary chairman of the board. Herbert C. Moseley, president of the corporation as well as president of The Bank of Virginia, was named chairman of the board and continued as chief executive officer. Frederick Deane, Jr., executive vice-president of the corporation and executive vice-president of The Bank of Virginia, was named president of the holding company and continued as chief administrative officer.

Another significant development for the year 1965 was the adoption of a profit-sharing plan, which became effective January 1 of the following year. Under the plan as originally established, the holding company set aside 10 percent of the consolidated after-tax profits of the affiliates that had adopted the plan; the sum thus arrived at was to be allocated among the individual participants in the plan in proportion to their annual base compensation.

The corporation in 1965 went to the debt markets for the second time to raise funds to expand the capital base of some of the affiliated banks. As of July 15, 1965, an additional $2.5 million loan was negotiated with the General Electric Pension Trust under a term loan agreement identical to that negotiated in 1964. This brought the holding company's total long-term debt to $5.0 million. A change in the capital structure was completed earlier in the year with a two-for-one stock split effective March 29, 1965. After the split, there were 1,137,818 common shares outstanding in the hands of some four thousand stockholders.

It was recognized by 1966 that the name Virginia Commonwealth Corporation did not carry an adequate identification of the nature of the corporation's business. Since state law prohibited the use of the word *Bank* in the name of a corporation that was not a commercial bank, there was no way to capitalize, in the name of the holding company, on the very well-known name of its chief bank, The Bank of Virginia. In the meantime, the term "bankshares" was becoming more commonly used by bank holding companies, and it was decided to change the name of the corporation to Virginia Commonwealth Bankshares, Inc., to more closely identify it with the character of its business. This change became effective October 10, 1966. At the same time, the identifying symbol, or logo, consisting of three interlocking *V*s was adopted to provide a unifying signature for all of the banks affiliated with the group, one that would immediately identify each in its local community as being a part of the statewide group of banks operating under the Virginia Commonwealth Bankshares' banner. Over the years since, this symbol has become firmly established as the hallmark of the Virginia Commonwealth Bankshares' affiliates as well as the parent and is prominently displayed in all promotions and in other communications.

The year 1967 was one of consolidation. Three small banks became affiliated with the group, but the three together brought in total assets of only a little over $13 million. The one merger that year was that of the Bank of LaCrosse, in southern Virginia, into The Bank of Virginia.

The first of the three banks affiliated with the group in 1967 was The First Valley Bank, a newly chartered bank established in Weber City, just west of Bristol, which commenced business on March 20. The organization of this bank was assisted by several local businessmen, and it was agreed that local stockholders would retain a 20 percent minority interest. The new bank was put under the direction of the chief executive officer of the Washington Trust Bank in Bristol.

The second of the banks affiliated in 1967 was The National Bank of Commerce of Fairfax County, the name of which was changed to The American Bank, N.A., when it joined the group at close of business on August 31. This acquisition gave the group de novo branching privileges in Fairfax County, at that time the real growth area on the Virginia side of the D.C. metropolitan area. The third affiliation was American National Bank in Fredericksburg, which joined the group at close of business on October 31. For the first time, the corporation issued preferred stock in acquisitions, a total of 129,756 shares of convertible preferred being issued in exchange for the shares of these two banks.

These three affiliations brought the number of banks in the group to ten at the end of 1967, and these ten were operating seventy-one banking offices, fourteen more than were in operation at the end of 1966.

Deposit growth in 1967 was the most striking of any of the five years since the holding company began business. Total deposits increased by one-fourth over the year to top the $400 million mark at year-end. Excluding deposits, which came in through affiliations and the merger—a total of $16 million—there was still a 20 percent increase in internally generated deposit funds.

Significant changes in the governing board of the corporation took place at the stockholders meeting in April. John W. Riely, a partner in the legal firm of Hunton, Williams, Gay, Powell and Gibson, was named general counsel for the corporation and a member of the board of directors, replacing R. Colston Christian, who had previously served in both these capacities. John M. McGurn, then president of Virginia Electric and Power Company, was also named to the board.

In 1967 the company made its first public offering of debt with the sale of $4.5 million of 4¾ percent subordinated convertible debentures.

The vigor of the bank acquisition program was undiminished in 1968 when one new affiliation and five banks agreed to merge into existing banks of the group. As important as the bank acquisition program has been and continues to be in the life of the corporation, two things happened in 1968 of such significance that, although their outward signs were slight, they influenced the future reshaping of banking operations.

The first of these occurred late that year in the form of a charter acquired for an organization to be named Commonwealth Mortgage Company. One-bank holding companies that, prior to December 1970, were not under Federal bank holding company regulations had over the past decade accelerated a movement toward specialized financing firms enabling the concentration of expertise in a selected financial area in a clearly defined profit center, a separate corporation that could be kept directly under the watchful eye of top management. Not only did such separate specialized financing firms have a greater profit potential than if they were part of a bank but they also established a basis for a new source of funds, in addition to traditional deposits, in the form of the commercial paper market. At Virginia Commonwealth Bankshares this first small, barely noticed step initiated a process that was translated into an almost explosive growth so that, in just four years, these specialized financing affiliates were to contribute 22 percent of the total annual net income by 1972.

Also in 1968 a change was made in the official family of the holding company that was to have a significant bearing on the growth of these specialized affiliates. S. Wayne Bazzle was transferred from a senior credit position in The Bank of Virginia to the holding company with the title senior vice-president. Bazzle had come to The Bank of Virginia in 1957 as a management trainee, having just graduated from the University of Virginia. His rapid rise to senior officer status in the complex area of credit administration reflected not only his outstanding capabilities but also, and just as important from the point of view of the future potential of the organization, top management's speed in recognizing and rewarding outstanding performance. When Bazzle was named senior vice-president of the holding company, he was just thirty-one, the youngest of the senior officers in the group. Subsequently Bazzle was named acquisitions officer in the bank-related field and either initiated or was closely involved in each subsequent bank-related acquisition.

The second development that emerged in 1968 as a forerunner

of significant change in subsequent years was the spin-off of the branch office of The Bank of Virginia in Newport News into the Bank of Warwick. Bank of Warwick was one of the five original banks that set the holding company in motion, but its size in the Newport News area was an impediment to aggressive expansion both in widening its contacts with business firms and in establishing additional branch offices to compete more effectively with the other banks in the area. Because of the restrictive nature of Virginia banking laws with regard to de novo branching, the branch office of The Bank of Virginia in Newport News was limited in its ability to serve the area since that bank was not able to establish additional offices there. Accordingly, in the first step that was to develop into a regionalization program, The Bank of Virginia branch office in Newport News was spun off into Bank of Warwick on December 31, 1968. This made Bank of Warwick, with total assets of $56 million, the only affiliated bank serving the Peninsula area, including the city of Newport News, much of York County, and the city of Hampton. Subsequently, as mentioned later in this brief history, the state of Virginia was subdivided into five geographic regions, each with its own group of affiliated banks, to develop banking business exclusively in their own region under the general direction of a holding company officer with the title group vice-president.

An additional bank became affiliated with the group in 1968, this being a newly chartered one in the city of Virginia Beach called the First Colonial Bank. This gave the group a toehold in the fastest-growing city in Virginia at that time and the ability of de novo branching there as well as in the adjoining cities of Norfolk and Chesapeake.

Four banks joined the group in 1968 by merger. In the Northern Neck of Virginia, lying between the Potomac and Rappahannock rivers, The Peoples Bank of Reedville and Peoples Bank of White Stone agreed to merge into The Bank of Virginia. These two banks had total assets of just over $10 million and, between them, three banking offices in the lower end of the Northern Neck peninsula. These mergers were completed by May 31. Washington Trust Bank in Bristol looked north into Russell County for further expansion in the southwestern part of the state and, as of December 2, Russell County National Bank, with three offices and $8.7 million in assets, was merged into Washington Trust. In northern Virginia, Fidelity National Bank, which began in 1964 and had faced serious problems throughout its short existence, agreed to merge into The American Bank, and this merger was completed by December 31. Fidelity brought $25 million of total assets into the group. At the end of 1968 the holding company was operating with eleven banks in eighty-four banking locations as follows:

	Total assets ($ thousand)	Number of offices
The Bank of Virginia	$ 364,170	35
The American Bank	67,739	16
Bank of Warwick	56,336	7
Washington Trust Bank	32,681	7
The Bank of Salem	25,705	5
The American Bank, N.A.	11,664	4
The Peoples National Bank	11,640	2
The Bank of Central Virginia	7,508	3
American National Bank	5,498	2
The First Colonial Bank	3,128	2
The First Valley Bank	3,101	1
Combined	$ 589,170	84

New Directions

Following the exploratory discussions in 1968, the move into the diversification program based on separate specialized financial bank-related affiliates got under way decisively in 1969. Commonwealth Mortgage Company, whose charter was obtained in 1968, began business on February 3, 1969, with an initial capital of $110,000. Negotiations were initiated almost immediately for the acquisition of a small construction mortgage company located in Richmond and all approvals were received in time for this company to merge into Commonwealth Mortgage as of May 1. It had $2.2 million in total assets and thus provided a base for the beginning of the new mortgage operation. This company, which specialized in construction and land development loans, brought with it offices in Richmond, Arlington, Virginia Beach, and Fayetteville, North Carolina.

On July 31, 1969, Rusch Factors, Inc., of New York City joined the holding company group as a wholly owned affiliate. This company was founded in 1827 and specialized in old-line notification factoring, a process whereby the factor purchases outright the accounts receivable of its clients, thus creating a steady cash flow and eliminating all credit considerations for the client. Customers of the client are notified of the purchase and make payments on their accounts directly to the factor. Virginia Commonwealth Bankshares' move into the factoring industry put it in the company of a number of other banks and banking groups that were taking similar steps. It is estimated that just about one-third of total factoring volume in the United States in 1969 was handled by factoring subsidiaries of banks or bank holding companies. This was approximately double the bank-related factoring volume just two years earlier.

In addition to these two acquisitions in the bank-related field that were completed in 1969, the corporation announced, toward the end of the year, that agreement in principle had been reached with Affiliated Factors Corp. located in Montreal, Canada, for affiliation with the group. This was to be the first entry into the international field begun in 1969, with affiliation completed in 1970. In a joint statement by the chairman of the board and the president of Virginia Commonwealth Bankshares, Moseley and Deane, respectively, these moves were referred to as a real turning point for us. The statement added, "although our major efforts will continue in the field of commercial banking in the state of Virginia, we have now embarked on new endeavors that emphasize a high degree of specialization in their financial activities in contrast to the broad spectrum of finance found in commercial banking. Through this financial diversification we expect not only to be able to meet all of the varied needs of our customers and clients, but also to meet these needs more effectively and efficiently and, thereby, more profitably for the corporation."

The year 1969 saw two basic service affiliates created and put into operation in addition to State-Wide Insurance Agency, Inc., which had been acquired along with The Bank of Virginia in the organization of the holding company. Previously, data processing for the affiliated banks had been performed by the data processing department of The Bank of Virginia, the flagship bank. In 1969 this operation was incorporated as Virginia Commonwealth Services, Inc., a fully owned affiliate of Virginia Commonwealth Bankshares.

A second service affiliate established in 1969 was Virginia Commonwealth Credit, Inc., which quickly became the administrative unit for handling the credit card operations, including promotion and development, for several of the affiliated banks that supply funds for carrying the outstandings.

With the development of the bank-related diversification program, the corporation sought additional sources of funds in 1969 and, after considerable planning, entered the commercial paper market in September of that year. Arrangements were made with a New York commercial paper dealer to handle sales of Virginia Commonwealth Bankshares' paper but, at the same time, a program of sales of such paper through the investment department of the holding company was also initiated. The corporation ended 1969 with $13.2 million of commercial paper outstanding.

There was only one bank acquisition in 1969 and that was Security Bank and Trust Company in Danville, which became affiliated with the group on the final day of the year. This bank brought $25.7 million in assets into the group along with three banking locations in its southern Virginia community.

By 1969 it was becoming apparent that the overall bank acquisition and merger program in Virginia had reached certain limitations that would make it more and more difficult for such activities to continue except at a much slower pace. At the end of 1969, the ten largest banking groups in Virginia held 67.4 percent of total deposits in Virginia banks. At that time, six of these banking groups had total resources in excess of half a billion dollars. It was clear that the supervisory authorities and also the federal attorney general's office would look more and more critically at proposed acquisitions and mergers in the light of their effect on competition and concentration in banking in the state. It was generally believed by this time that approval of the acquisition of a large bank by any of the five largest banking groups in Virginia would no longer be probable. By now there were fewer banks left whose management would be interested in merger or affiliation.

The capital structure of the corporation was changed by two moves completed late in the year, namely, a three-for-two common stock split effective October 20 and completion of negotiations for a term loan in a total amount of $5 million from two lenders, the Ford Foundation and Northwestern Mutual Life Insurance Company. The Ford Foundation supplied $3 million of the funds on December 31, 1969, and Northwestern Mutual Life Insurance Company the remaining $2 million on a planned delayed takedown basis on September 1, 1970. The loan had a final maturity of fifteen years and incorporated warrants for the purchase of 100,000 shares of common stock. The completion of these loan negotiations put the corporation's total long-term debt at $12.5 million on December 31, 1969. Its total net worth at the end of 1969 was $37.8 million. The three-for-two stock split in October, plus other changes in outstanding shares primarily through acquisitions, put total shares outstanding at the end of 1969 at 2,541,473. This compared with 1,493,349 shares at the corporation's first year-end on December 31, 1962, restated for the two-for-one stock split in March 1965 and the three-for-two stock split in October 1969.

The corporation's board of directors was increased from twelve to fourteen at the stockholders meeting in April 1969 by the addition of Max H. Goodloe, president of General Medical Corporation, a rapidly expanding Richmond-based medical supply firm, and Blake T. Newton, Jr., president of the Institute of Life Insurance located in New York City. In 1969 S. Wayne Bazzle became more deeply involved in the emerging program of acquisitions of bank-related companies as well as in other management problems and policies, and in his second year with the parent company he was named executive vice-president.

In 1970 its eighth year as a registered bank holding company, the corporation pursued its diversification goals through establishing affiliates specializing in selected areas of finance but, in reflection of the changed status of the banking picture in Virginia, reported no bank acquisitions in that year. Agreement was reached with the directors and stockholders of The Merchants and Farmers Bank in Galax, in the western part of the state, for affiliation with the group, but supervisory approval was received so late in 1970 that this affiliation was not realized until January 2, 1971.

One other banking move of some significance for the future of the corporation was put under way in 1970—a move to establish a newly chartered bank in Roanoke County that would have de novo branching privileges throughout that county and in the contiguous cities of Salem and Roanoke. The Bank of Virginia had been operating a branch office in the city of Roanoke for many years, but it was stopped by existing Virginia law from establishing any additional offices in that area except through merger with some other bank. As pointed out earlier, the competitive structure of Virginia banking had now reached a stage where additional acquisitions and mergers were more difficult to effect, and there seemed no prospect of a merger into The Bank of Virginia of any of the banks in Roanoke. The corporation also had an affiliate, The Bank of Virginia of the Southwest (formerly The Bank of Salem) headquartered in the city of Salem, but this affiliate could only establish de novo branches in that city and five miles into adjoining Roanoke County and could not establish branches in the city of Roanoke, which was separated from Salem by a strip of Roanoke County. The purpose of the newly chartered bank would be to consolidate these banking operations in the Roanoke Valley area into a single bank headquartered in Roanoke County and to provide for de novo branching privileges that were needed to compete successfully in this market. All of the necessary banking authority approvals were not received until after year-end, so that the new bank, to be headquartered in the town of Vinton, was not established until March 31, 1971.

Although activities on the Virginia banking scene were less dramatic than in earlier years, the financial diversification program of the corporation was moving strongly in 1970. Existing affiliates were strengthened through additions to their capital base and three new affiliates were established. On July 7 negotiations were completed and the corporation purchased the assets of the equipment-leasing division of Cavanagh Leasing Corporation of New York for a total of $958,202. Established as a fully owned subsidiary of the holding company, Cavanagh Leasing Corporation (a newly organized Virginia corporation) provided the group with an equipment leasing service for the first time and also put the corporation for the first time in a really nationwide undertaking with offices or agencies in Richmond, New York, Chicago, Miami, Fort Lauderdale, Los Angeles, San Francisco, Pittsburgh, Fort Lee, New Jersey, Cleveland, and Atlanta.

During the early months of 1970, the holding company management completed negotiations with the directors and stockholders of Affiliated Factors Corp., a Quebec corporation engaged in the business of recourse factoring and commercial financing in Canada, for affiliation with the group. In order to acquire this foreign-based company, the corporation applied and received approval for the chartering of Virginia Commonwealth International, an international financial corporation that the Board of

Governors of the Federal Reserve System is authorized to charter under the Edge Act amendment to the Federal Reserve Act. Virginia Commonwealth International was chartered initially, and authorized on September 23, for the limited purpose of acquiring Affiliated Factors Corp., which affiliation was consummated on September 30, 1970.

With these 1970 acquisitions the holding company ended the year with a now fully activated mortgage company, Commonwealth Mortgage Company, a domestic factoring company, Rusch Factors, Inc., a nationwide equipment-leasing company, Cavanagh Leasing Corporation, a Canadian factoring and commercial financing company, Affiliated Factors Corp., and an international banking organization, Virginia Commonwealth International. In 1970 these bank-related affiliates contributed 8 percent to the net income of the company which contrasts with just 2 percent in 1969, the year in which the first step in this direction materialized.

The corporation went to the market place again to raise capital funds in 1970, but this time by a move that had been made by other banking organizations only a few times previously. The corporation registered with the Securities and Exchange Commission a public offering of $6 million in subordinated capital notes, but instead of handling this through the conventional underwriting arrangement with investment bankers, the notes were sold by officers of the company's affiliated banks and were sold almost entirely within the state of Virginia. To make the issue attractive, three maturities were offered, namely, five year, ten year, and fifteen year, with interest rates from 7½ to 8 percent and the purchasers were offered the option of receiving interest semiannually or by monthly check. The notes were sold in a short period of six weeks at a substantial savings to the corporation. Subsequently the Controller of the Currency and the Board of Governors of the Federal Reserve System have taken the position that bank officers should not sell securities issued by their parent holding company, and it thus appears that this technique can no longer be employed.

Within the parent company a marketing division was established in 1970 in response to the ever-increasing demand for a highly skilled and professional marketing service within the group. The marketing division is responsible for the advertising and public relations of the corporation, and its staff is available to assist each of the affiliates in marketing-related activities such as development of programs, promotion of existing services, market research projects, location studies, advertising, public relations, and sales-training programs.

The staff-relations and staff-services functions were also combined at the parent level in 1970 in a personnel division. Staff services had been moved to the parent company level earlier, but the recruitment, evaluation, and placement service had been left with The Bank of Virginia. Now the entire personnel service for all of the affiliates was centered in the holding company. At the end of 1970 the holding company organizational structure contained the general administrative offices consisting principally of the chairman of the board and chief executive officer, the president, the executive vice-president, and the corporate secretary, and in addition the following specialized divisions: audit, credit, credit examination, finance, investment, marketing, operations, and personnel.

Two new directors were added in 1970, one of these being S. Wayne Bazzle, executive vice-president, who was elected by the stockholders at the meeting in April. The other director named in 1970 was R. B. Bridgforth, Jr., president of Dibrell Brothers, Inc., tobacconists of Danville, Virginia. The board now consisted of sixteen prominent business and professional people, including the three top members of the Virginia Commonwealth Bankshares management team: Herbert C. Moseley, chairman of the board and chief executive officer; Frederick Deane, Jr., president and chief administrative officer; and S. Wayne Bazzle, executive vice-president.

In 1971 two additional directors were named to the board and one former member resigned, putting the number in that year at seventeen. The member to resign was John P. Fishwick, now president and chief executive officer of the Norfolk and Western Railway Company. His elevation to chief executive officer of the railway, increasing the demands on his time, caused Fishwick to request that his resignation from the board be accepted. The two new directors named in 1971 were Beirne B. Carter, president of Carter Machinery Company, Inc., with head office in Salem, Virginia, and Ralph S. Thomas who, shortly after his appointment to the board, was elected president of Robertshaw Controls Company, with headquarters in Richmond.

In 1971, the ninth year of the holding company's operations, the program of diversification into specialized financial areas was continued with the acquisition on October 1 of Canadian Factors Corporation, Limited. This was one of the oldest and largest full-notification factors in Canada, and as of December 31, 1971, it was combined with Affiliated Factors Corp. to form Canadian Affiliated Financial Corporation. This gave the holding company a financially strong factoring and commercial financing organization whose skilled and experienced management had established and maintained wide business contacts throughout Canada and abroad.

A second acquisition in the international field was the purchase of 75 percent of the shares of the Bank of Nassau, Limited, by the holding company's fully owned Edge Act corporation now named Bank of Virginia International (formerly Virginia Commonwealth International). This is a fully chartered banking institution, which has been operating in Nassau since 1964, and is capable of providing a wide range of commercial and personal banking services, Eurodollar financing, and trust and other international banking services.

On the Virginia banking front, as indicated earlier, the acquisition of The Merchants and Farmers Bank in Galax was completed on January 2, 1971, and The Bank of Virginia of Roanoke Valley began operations in September of that year. The Roanoke bank was the new bank established in Roanoke County, as previously described, and into which The Bank of Virginia of the Southwest in Salem and the branch office of The Bank of Virginia in Roanoke were merged as of March 31, 1972, to become Bank of Virginia-Roanoke Valley.

A new bank charter having been obtained in December 1971, Bank of Virginia-Loudoun was opened for business in Loudoun County at Dulles International Airport. This new bank in Loudoun County was put in the path of the rapid westward movement of population on the Virginia side of the D.C. metropolitan area.

In addition to these acquisitions completed in 1971, negotiations with the directors and stockholders of two additional banks for affiliation with the group were also successfully completed. These two banks were The Bank of Warren, located in Front Royal at the edge of the thriving Shenandoah Valley region, and the Bank of Whaleyville, located in Nansemond County, subsequently converted to the city of Nansemond, in the rapidly growing Hampton Roads area. Supervisory approval was received for these two bank affiliates late in 1971, and the affiliations were completed as of January 3, 1972. The name of The Bank of Warren was subsequently changed to Bank of Virginia-Warren following the celebration of its hundredth anniversary in the early fall of 1972. The Bank of Whaleyville became Bank of Virginia-Southeast at the time of its affiliation with the group. Each of these two new banks, of course, had de novo branching privileges in their respective areas, but the conversion of Nansemond County into the city of Nansemond in 1972 expanded the de novo branching capability of Bank of Virginia-Southeast to include the two counties contiguous to the new city along its western boundary in addition to de novo privileges in the contiguous cities of Portsmouth and Chesapeake.

Reference has just been made to two new names in the holding company group of affiliated banks, namely, Bank of Virginia-Warren and Bank of Virginia-Southeast, and reference was earlier made to Bank of Virginia-Roanoke Valley. These new names were part of an identification and communications program undertaken in late 1971 for the group as a whole. This program was designed to encourage the greatest possible recognition and public awareness of the holding company and the close interrelationships between its various affiliates and the services they render. Following detailed study by a highly qualified consulting firm, it was decided that the name of the lead bank—Bank of Virginia— not only identified the nature of the principal activities of the group and of their basic geographic operations area, but was also widely known outside the state of Virginia and in many countries outside the United States. Accordingly, it was decided to use the name Bank of Virginia for each of the banking affiliates with each being further identified by a suffix designating the city or area in which the bank operated. For example, The Bank of Virginia became Bank of Virginia-Central and its region of operations was the central Virginia region from just north of Richmond to the North Carolina border, and Washington Trust Bank in Bristol in the far southwestern part of the state was renamed Bank of Virginia-Southwest. The new names of all the banks are shown in the tabulation that follows, which also lists their total assets and the number of banking offices of each as of the fall of 1972.

Under state legislation existing in 1971, no corporation could use the word *bank* in its name unless it were a commercial bank as defined in the Virginia code. At its 1972 session, the state legislature changed this code section, permitting bank holding companies to employ the word *bank* in the name of the parent unit. With this enabling legislation in effect, and on the fiftieth anniversary of the flagship bank, Bank of Virginia-Central, the stockholders of Virginia Commonwealth Bankshares formally approved a change of name on July 17, 1972, to Bank of Virginia Company. The name of several of the affiliated service companies are to be changed to conform as nearly as legally permissible with that of the holding company.

On January 4, 1971, the first transaction for the new year on the New York Stock Exchange was for a hundred shares of Virginia Commonwealth Bankshares common stock. That was the date the corporation's stock was listed on the N.Y.S.E. Virginia Commonwealth Bankshares was the first bank or banking company in Virginia to be listed on the exchange and, at that time, was only the eleventh Virginia-headquartered company on the big board.

Additional capital funds were raised in the fall of 1971 through the sale of six hundred thousand shares of common stock under a public offering at a price of $21 1/4. The net amount realized from the sale was $12.1 million. Although per share earnings were adversely affected initially by the addition of these shares, the equity base of the corporation was considerably strengthened, greatly enhancing the firm's future growth potential. The commercial paper operation also continued in full progress throughout 1971 and, at the end of the year, the amount of paper outstanding was $44.1 million. As was the case since the inception of the commercial paper program, proceeds from the sale of this paper went entirely to provide operating funds to the corporation's bank-related affiliates.

In 1972 the diversification program continued with the same vigor as in the preceding three years and further acquisitions put the corporation into all the major financing areas that management had decided was appropriate for the firm at this time. On October 5, 1972, Hanover Mortgage Corporation and Richmond Finance Corporation, both headquartered in Richmond, were added to the bank-related list. These two firms supplied consumer financing, Hanover through second mortgage loans and Richmond Finance through conventional consumer loans. In addition, agreement was reached in 1972 with the directors and stockholders of General Finance Service Corporation, a consumer financing company in Pennsylvania, for affiliation with the group. At this writing, supervisory approval is required before the affiliation can be completed. These latter three affiliations put the corporation into the consumer financing field on a separate affiliate basis, as contrasted with consumer banking that had been undertaken in the group's commercial banks for many years. The corporation was now operating successfully in consumer financing, equipment leasing, mortgage, construction, and other real estate financing, factoring, and commercial financing. With the pattern now filled in, management's policy was centered on developing each of these areas to their full potential within the availability of resources to the group. Growth in the bank related area was to continue not only on an internal competitive basis but also through selected acquisitions that would contribute to the aims of the corporation.

Another Canadian acquisition was completed in 1972 with Continental Discount Corporation's being fully affiliated on June 15—as of June 1 for accounting purposes. This is a commercial and consumer financing company operating in several areas in the Province of Quebec.

Nineteen seventy-two was also a year for reorganizing the corporation to provide for the enlarged and diversified activities of the holding company and its affiliates. In 1971, to provide greater flexibility in top management decision-making and a basis for smooth management succession, an office of the chairman had been established, consisting of the chairman of the board and chief executive officer, the president and chief administrative officer and the executive vice-president. R. Norris Hatch, formerly an officer of Bank of Virginia-Central, which he joined in 1940 and served primarily in its Norfolk, Portsmouth, and Eastern Shore offices until becoming chairman of the board and chief executive officer of Bank of Warwick in Newport News on January 1, 1969, was added to the office of the chairman with the title of vice-chairman of the board as of June 1, 1972, having been elected a director of the company on April 19.

Another significant development in 1972 was the regionalization of the commercial banking operations in the state of Virginia. The state was divided into five geographic regions with the banks of each under the general direction of a group vice-president, a new holding company official designation established for this purpose. Each bank of the various regions, together with the total resources and number of offices of each in the fall of 1972 were as follows:

	Total assets ($ thousands)	Number of offices
Central		
Bank of Virginia-Central	$ 508,082	36
Northern		
Bank of Virginia-Potomac	109,960	19
Bank of Virginia-Warren	17,547	2
Bank of Virginia-Fairfax	18,087	5
Bank of Virginia-Fredericksburg, N.A.	13,343	4
Bank of Virginia-Loudoun	908	1
Southwest		
Bank of Virginia-Southwest	50,488	8
Bank of Virginia-Galax	23,307	3
Bank of Virginia-Pulaski	16,121	3
Bank of Virginia-Scott	6,190	2
Near Southwest		
Bank of Virginia-Roanoke Valley	69,852	8
Bank of Virginia-Danville	33,705	3
Bank of Virginia-Lynchburg	12,224	4
Tidewater		
Bank of Virginia-Peninsula	81,401	8
Bank of Virginia-Tidewater	10,222	4
Bank of Virginia-Southeast	4,418	1
Combined	$ 975,855	111

In addition to the sixteen banks in Virginia, Bank of Virginia Company was operating the following bank-related affiliates:

	Total assets ($ thousands)
International banking	
Bank of Virginia International	$ 3,288
The Bank of Nassau, Ltd.	15,306
Bank of Virginia (Grand Cayman), Ltd.	3,591
Canadian	
Canadian Affiliated Financial Corp.	26,888
Continental Discount Corp.*	23,829
Commercial financing	
Rusch Factors, Inc.	54,104
Cavanagh Leasing Corp.	16,999
Real estate financing	
Commonwealth Mortgage Co.	44,754

Consumer financing
    Hanover Mortgage Corp.†   1,966
    Richmond Finance Corp.†   439

* Acquired June 15, 1972
† Acquired October 5, 1972

Bank of Virginia Company was also operating the following service affiliates: State-Wide Insurance Agency, Inc., BankVirginia Credit Card Company, BankVirginia Properties Company, and BankVirginia Service Company.

The finance industry is pivotal in the economic growth of the nation and the southeastern region of the United States is now spotlighted as having the greatest growth potential for the next decade or more of any section in the nation. Bank of Virginia Company has its base in commercial banking in Virginia, which is a leader in economic growth in the southeastern region. With management teams that have demonstrated outstanding performance capabilities, the expectation of continued growth and profitability is well based.

Index

Index